The Trials of Henry Flipper,
First Black Graduate
of West Point

The Trials of Henry Flipper, First Black Graduate of West Point

DON CUSIC

McFarland & Company, Inc., Publishers

Jefferson, North Carolina, and London

LIBRARY OF CONGRESS CATALOGUING-IN-PUBLICATION DATA

Cusic, Don.
    The trials of Henry Flipper, first Black graduate
of West Point / Don Cusic.
        p.   cm.
    Includes bibliographical references and index.

    ISBN 978-0-7864-3969-0
    softcover : 50# alkaline paper ∞

    1. Flipper, Henry Ossian, 1856–1940.   2. United States.
Army — Officers — Biography.   3. United States Military
Academy — Alumni and alumnae — Biography.   4. African
American military cadets — New York (State) — West Point —
Biography.   5. Soldiers — United States — Biography.
6. African American soldiers — Biography.   I. Title.
U53.F55C87   2009
355.0092 — dc22   2008041419
[B]

British Library cataloguing data are available

On the cover: Henry Flipper; Fort Davis Historic Site, 1887;
photograph of West Point academy insignia ©2008 Fotosearch

Manufactured in the United States of America

McFarland & Company, Inc., Publishers
    Box 611, Jefferson, North Carolina 28640
    www.mcfarlandpub.com

Table of Contents

Preface

Henry Flipper is not a household name; outside of western historians and West Point students and faculty, he's barely known. However, Henry Flipper is an intriguing figure in American history. He was born a slave, lived in Atlanta through the Civil War, was dismissed from the army in a controversial court-martial, worked for a cabinet secretary during the Harding administration and died after World War II had started in Europe. Flipper lived during the terms of 14 presidents, from Franklin Pierce to Franklin D. Roosevelt.

I first discovered his story in 1992 while doing research on an encyclopedia of cowboys (*Cowboys and the Wild West: An A to Z Guide from the Chisholm Trail to the Silver Screen*, Facts on File, 1994). His story seemed intriguing, so I began putting things about Flipper I ran across into a file box. I found his autobiography and a few other things, read them and increasingly felt compelled to pursue the Flipper story. In the summer of 1998 I went to Atlanta to do research at the Atlanta University Library, the Atlanta Public Library and Atlanta Historical Center as well as to find where Flipper last lived. While in Atlanta, I realized I was doing research on August 13 — the date he was thrown in jail at Fort Davis in 1881.

When I first discovered the remarkable story of Henry Flipper, I was surprised more people had not written about him. With the interest in civil rights and the history of African Americans such a popular topic, I thought surely someone would have delved into Flipper's story. I soon discovered why he had remained virtually untouched; Henry Flipper was, in contemporary terms, the Clarence Thomas of his day. The story of his life — and particularly the very conservative beliefs he held — simply did not fit with the stories and struggles that resonated with the civil rights advocates of the 20th century.

By the end of 1998, I had written a draft of this biography but I wasn't satisfied; I knew much more needed to be done. Other projects took precedence, but I kept adding information when I ran across something related to Henry Flipper. The Flipper material sat untouched in a file box for years, but it was never off my mind. A number of times I decided to forget the whole project — this was way out of my field of writing about country music! — but I could never get the Flipper story out of my mind. Finally, in the spring of 2007, I traveled to Fort Davis, Texas, where there is a wealth of information on Flipper at the Fort Davis Historic Site, and completed my research.

By the end of the book I found I had come to respect Henry Flipper, although I certainly did not agree with many of his points of view. He was an African American who managed to maintain his dignity in an era when most African Americans were denied respect and dignity. It takes someone who is incredibly strong and self-confident to endure what Henry Flipper endured during his time at West Point and even afterwards. Yet Flipper stood his ground.

The title for this book begins *The Trials of Henry Flipper* because Flipper's life was a series of trials. The court-martial at Fort Davis was the biggest and most literal "trial" in his life, but Flipper endured trials at West Point as an undergraduate and then, after his termination from the army, endured further trials for the rest of his life. The verdict cannot be "not guilty" in all of those trials; still, Henry Flipper was a man of his time, the latter part of the 19th and first half of the 20th century. His story is remarkable and it is a story worth preserving.

During my time working on this book I've been helped by several remarkable people. When I decided to go to Fort Davis, Texas, for research on Flipper I contacted the staff and became acquainted with Mary Williams, a truly remarkable woman who serves at the Fort Davis Historic Site and is an expert on Henry Flipper. She opened up the files there to me and helped me in countless ways. She is a researcher's dream and I treasure her help as well as her friendship. It's people like Mary Williams who make working on a book like this a true joy.

When Mary found out I was interested in doing a book on Henry Flipper, she contacted Tom Phillips, another expert on Flipper, who lives in Mississippi. Tom was so excited to hear about my Flipper interest that he immediately called me. I was due to teach a class when I received his phone call but was able to call him that night and we remained on the phone for several hours discussing Henry Flipper. Tom is a passionate researcher and historian and is consumed with the story (particularly the court-martial) of Henry Flipper. He and William Dobak wrote a book, *The Black Regulars: 1866–1898*, that was informative and helpful; but his greatest contribution came from phone calls and e-mails in which he poured out his great knowledge of Henry Flipper.

When I finished a draft, I sent it off to Mary and Tom, who read it and offered suggestions and corrections. Without Mary Williams and Tom Phillips, this book would have been riddled with errors. I cannot thank them enough for the help they gave me.

I owe a great deal of gratitude to Mike Curb and the Curb Family Foundation; the professorship they endowed for me at Belmont University allows me to pursue projects like this biography of Henry Flipper. Mike is a treasured friend who never fails to support my efforts and ideas.

I thank my assistant, Allecia Morrone, who helped on a number of other projects while I completed the final corrections to the Henry Flipper story.

I thank my wife for her continued love and support, even though she was rather vague about who Henry Flipper was and exactly why I felt compelled to write a book about him. Still, she always encouraged me to pursue this topic. My sons Jesse, Eli and Alex and my daughter, Delaney, along with her husband, Scott, always remind me that there are things more important than writing books, even when I'm lost in the midst of a project that absorbs my time and interest.

1

The Early Years

Thomasville sits amongst rolling hills in the southernmost part of Georgia, just north of the Florida state line. At 324 North Dawson Street sits the Ponder house, a two story white wooden house built by Ephraim Ponder, a slave trader originally from Virginia who was born around 1810. Ephraim moved from Virginia to Thomasville around 1855 and established a group of manufacturing companies, with his slaves working as mechanics. The population of the town at that time was about 1,500.

Festus Flipper was a slave, the property of Ephraim Ponder. Born in 1832 in Guinea Station, Virginia, north of Richmond, Festus called himself "Flippo" after his first owners; however, he was called "Flipper" by the Ponders and those around him. Festus was first sold to James Ponder and then, in June 1855, James sold Flipper to his nephew, Ephraim, for $1,180.

Isabella Buckhalter was the property of the Reverend Reuben H. Lucky, a Methodist minister in Thomasville. Isabella married Festus Flipper and was pregnant with their first child when Festus was sent back to Virginia, where he apprenticed with a carriage-trimmer, learning to work with leather to provide the comfortable seats and "trim" on a carriage. Festus also learned to make shoes of leather. This is why Festus was in Virginia when their first child, Henry Ossian Flipper, was born in Thomasville on March 21, 1856.

In November 1857 Ephraim Ponder purchased a lot in Atlanta for $1,460. The 25-acre property sat beside Marietta Road. The former estate is now bordered by Ponder Avenue, Third Street NW, Oxford Street and Guyton Street NW. Ponder built a large, imposing home of stone covered with white plaster, two stories tall. The front porch, which covered the entire front of the house, faced southwest and the grounds were filled with boxwood and fruit trees. This was one of the finest estates in Atlanta when it was built.

Along Marietta Road, Ponder built frame buildings to house his slaves and three large buildings for manufacturing. The Ponders owned 65 slaves and most of the men were mechanics. Outside of the household servants, a gardener and coachman, all the slaves were permitted to hire out their services. Ponder protected them, but left them alone; the public dealt directly

The Ephraim Ponder house in Thomasville, Georgia (photograph courtesy Jack Hadley Black History Memorabilia, Inc., Thomasville).

with slave workmen for their services and paid them directly. Most of the slaves thus acquired a small savings.

The move to Atlanta caused a problem for the Flipper family because it meant Festus was separated from his wife and two children, Henry and Joseph Simeon, who was born on February 22, 1859. Flipper appealed to Ponder to purchase his wife and sons, but Ponder stated he was financially unable to do so. The Reverend Lucky was unable to purchase Festus Flipper because of the large price for such a talented and highly trained slave. In the end, Festus Flipper provided the money to purchase his wife and children, with the agreement that Ponder would some day repay Flipper.[1]

The Ponder home in Atlanta was not peaceful and harmonious; in 1852 Ephraim married Ellen B. Gregory, a beautiful, wealthy lady fourteen years younger than he. The couple was unable to live together so Ephraim Ponder moved back to Thomasville in 1859. In a divorce petition filed in 1861, Ponder alleged that his wife had committed adultery as far back as 1854 with several men, that she was a drunkard who had threatened him with a pistol and, in general, did not treat him with respect. The divorce papers showed the house to be valued at $10,000, while the slaves were valued at $45,000.

In 1858 Ponder had indentured his slaves to Ellen so she was, in effect, co-owner of them. Living without her husband present, Ponder's wife virtually ignored the slaves, leaving them to do as they wished while she carried on her affairs. The entire estate had to remain as it was because neither the husband nor wife could liquidate the property and sell the slaves without the consent of the other — and they could not get along well enough to agree on this. And so the Flipper family was allowed to operate an independent business under the protection of their owner and acquire some wealth. The only thing required of Flipper was that he pay a portion of what he received to Mrs. Ponder. Neither Mrs. Ponder nor the guardian, a wealthy railroad stockholder appointed by Ephraim Ponder who resided in another city and made only periodic visits to the estate, bothered the Flippers or other slaves on the estate.[2]

There was a class distinction among slaves, and Henry Flipper was fortunate to be born amongst the upper class of slaves. This "class" structure ranged from field hands engaged in manual labor on the bottom rung to household slaves and skilled laborers on the top rung. Additionally, a slave benefited if the owner was a prominent man. The Reverend Lucky, the initial owner of Flipper's mother, was not only a Methodist minister but also president and secretary of the board of education in Thomas County and principal of the Fletcher Institute, a school operated by the Methodists. Ephraim Ponder was a prominent financier, while his brother, William, owned a large plantation. Although the Flippers were slaves, they were among a privileged group who had access to upper-class living in the South through their prominent, wealthy owners and their own positions in these households.

Henry Flipper was a mulatto. Mulattos were "more socially acceptable than blacks" and "often refused to associate or identify with their darker brethren," according to Lowell and Sara Black in their book, *An Officer and a Gentleman: The Military Career of Lieutenant Henry O. Flipper*.[3] The Blacks note the "mulatto aristocracy was complete with its aversion to full-blooded blacks" and list examples of African Americans of lighter complexion discriminating against those who were darker.[4] Mulattos generally felt superior and often received preferential treatment from white society. "The educated mulattoes became the elite of non-white society and formed the nucleus of the Negro middle class." This group of upper and middle classes included "military and civilian professionals, successful businessmen, large scale farmers, carpenters, skilled mechanics, barbers, high-placed waiters, servants, and coachmen," while the lower class, "which constituted the vast majority of Negroes, was comprised of day laborers, low-paid domestics and sanitation workers." In 1860, mulattoes comprised 11.2 percent of the Negro population; in 1890 they were 15.2 percent of the Negro population.[5]

The issue of slavery dominated the national news when Henry Flipper was born in 1856. Two years earlier, in 1854, a new political party, the Republicans, had been formed from a coalition of Whigs, Free-Soil Democrats and Liberty Party men, which held as a central tenant the abolition of slavery. About a month and a half after Flipper was born, five pro-slavery settlers in the town of Lawrence, Kansas, were killed by abolitionist John Brown and his family. In August, Brown was attacked in his own town of Osawatomie, Kansas, by about 300 pro-slavery raiders but he managed to escape.

In the halls of Congress, Senator Charles Sumner, the abolitionist senator from Massachusetts, was beaten bloody and unconscious by Representative Preston Brooks of South Carolina two months after Flipper was born. A few days earlier, Senator Sumner had denounced South Carolina's Senator Andrew Butler, the uncle of Brooks, and accused him of leading South Carolina towards secession. The debate in Congress at that time was whether Kansas would be a slave state or a free state.

In November 1856, the pro-slavery candidate James Buchanan was elected president over former President Millard Fillmore and explorer John C. Frémont. On March 4, 1857, Buchanan took the oath of office for president, succeeding Franklin Pierce. In his inauguration speech, Buchanan urged Americans to tolerate slavery in order to "save the union." Five days later the Supreme Court ruled that Dred Scott, a slave who had been taken by his owner from Missouri to Illinois, a free state, was not "free." The Court ruled that no Negro born a slave had citizenship. The ruling struck a strong blow against the abolitionist movement and fortified the pro-slavery forces.

The next year, 1858, two opponents for the United States Senate from Illinois, Abraham Lincoln and Stephen A. Douglas, gave a series of seven debates over two months that argued the issue of slavery, with Lincoln stating, "A house divided against itself cannot stand.... I believe this government cannot endure, permanently half slave and half free."[6] Douglas argued that the fate of democratic government — the United States remaining as a single union — was more important than the fate of the Negro. Lincoln argued that slavery was morally wrong and should be abolished.

Meanwhile, storm clouds continued to build in other parts of the country. At the end of 1859, the year the Flippers moved to Atlanta, John Brown was hanged in Charleston, near Harpers Ferry, where he had seized the U.S. military arsenal in order to provide arms and ammunition for a slave revolt. He was captured by a group of marines headed by Captain Robert E. Lee. The 59-year-old Brown received praise from northern abolitionists.

In 1860 the population of the United States stood at 31.4 million people, with 58 percent of them working on farms. There were four million slaves in the United States. In November, Abraham Lincoln won the presidency on an abolitionist plank. A little over a month later, on December 20, South Carolina voted to secede from the Union after debating the issue for just twenty-two minutes.

Throughout the spring of 1861, states seceded from the Union one by one. After South Carolina came Mississippi, Florida, Alabama, Georgia, and Louisiana — all in January — then Texas, Virginia, Arkansas, North Carolina and, finally on June 8, Tennessee. This made a Confederacy of eleven states; in March they elected Jefferson Davis as president. Davis, a West Point graduate and former secretary of war, took his oath and established his office in Montgomery, Alabama.

On March 3 Abraham Lincoln took the oath of office of president of the United States, declaring in his inaugural address that the Unites States was one nation. On April 14 he was faced with the bombardment of Fort Sumter, a 73-member United States garrison, in the Charleston, South Carolina, harbor. The next day, Lincoln called the bombardment an "insurrection" and asked for 75,000 volunteers for military service. Although Lincoln would not use the word "war," a war had begun; on May 6 the Federal troops at Fort Sumter surrendered and were sent to New York, while Confederate forces moved into the Fort.

Lincoln ordered Southern ports blocked so the Confederacy could not export cotton or receive goods from foreign nations. In July the first real battle of the war, the battle of Bull Run, was fought, with the Southern army winning the day.

And so the Civil War began on a summer day in 1861; no one knew then that it would continue for four more bloody years before it ended. By the end of 1861 both armies had been organized under two West Point graduates; 35-year-old General George McClellan headed the Union forces, while 52-year-old General Robert E. Lee headed the Southern forces.

In October of that year, Ephraim Ponder filed for divorce from his wife, a divorce proceeding that continued for ten years before it was resolved. Meanwhile, the slaves had no worry about being sold because both Ponders had to agree to a sale, and the Ponders were disagreeable to each other.

During 1862 the Civil War saw major battles at Hampton Roads, Virginia, where the two iron-clad ships *Monitor* and *Merrimac* fought to a standstill: at Fort Donelson, just north of Nashville, Tennessee, where the Federal forces routed the Rebels and occupied that city for the rest of the war; at Shiloh, on the Tennessee-Mississippi border where the first major battle of the war occurred. There, the Union army lost approximately 13,000 men and the Confederates lost about 10,000, including renowned General Albert Sidney Johnson.

The Northern forces at Shiloh, under General Ulysses Grant, emerged victorious, but outside Richmond the Confederate forces defeated General George McClellan, who had attempted to take the Confederate capital. In New Orleans the federal forces under Admiral David Farragut captured that port, but in the second battle of Bull Run in Manassas, Virginia, the South won again. At the battle of Antietam in Sharpsburg, Maryland, the "landscape turned red" when the Union forces under McClellan, with vastly superior numbers, could not defeat General Lee's troops. At Fredericksburg, Virginia, the Union army soldiers were cut to pieces when they tried to attack the entrenched Rebel army fortified at the top of a hill.

In Atlanta, Georgia, life went on without direct involvement in the Civil War's fighting. On January 1, 1863, President Lincoln issued his Emancipation Proclamation, which freed all the slaves in the Confederacy; but it did not change the day-to-day lives of slaves in Georgia. Meanwhile, the war raged in Chancellorsville, Virginia, where Confederate forces defeated the Union army but lost Stonewall Jackson, one of their leading generals. Then, in Gettysburg, Pennsylvania, during a three day period beginning July 1, the Federal army won a decisive victory over General Lee's troops, routing the Confederate army. At the same time the South lost at Gettysburg, it also lost Vicksburg, Mississippi, a key port that was taken by General Grant on July 4. In September the Southern forces won at Chickamauga, but lost Chattanooga in November. Also in November, President Lincoln traveled to Gettysburg to deliver a dedication for the cemetery established for Union soldiers who had fallen during the battle. The echo of this Gettysburg Address, delivered on November 19, 1863, still resounds years later.

In 1864 the two armies fought at the Wilderness, in Spotsylvania, and at Cold Harbor, Virginia, while General William Tecumseh Sherman led the Union army towards Georgia in an attempt to cut the Confederacy in two and end the war. However, on June 27, the Union army was stopped at Kennesaw Mountain, outside Atlanta, when Confederate forces under General Joseph E. Johnston dug in at the top of the mountain and repulsed the Union attack.

In Atlanta, Henry Flipper turned eight years old in the spring of 1864 and began his formal schooling. Earlier, one of the slave mechanics on the Ponder estate, John F. Quarles, who knew how to read and write, had requested permission to teach the slave children. Mrs. Ponder agreed, even though Georgia had passed a law in 1861 forbidding the teaching of reading and writing to any Negro. Quarles' "school" occupied the woodshop during the evening hours where slave children began their education. It was here that eight-year-old Henry Flipper first learned the "three R's." The first book he studied from was *Webster's Blueback Speller,* reprinted by a Confederate printer. After the war, Quarles graduated from Westminster College in Pennsylvania (in 1870) with a degree in law and became the first black admitted to the Georgia state bar. He served as United States consul to Málaga, Spain, 1877–78.[7]

After his defeat at Kennesaw Mountain, Sherman regrouped and headed for Atlanta. On July 20 Sherman and his Union forces fought against Confederate forces led by General John Bell Hood at Peachtree Creek, north of the city. Confederate soldiers dug breastworks on the Ponder estate; Union forces, under Major General John W. Geary, captured the estate and destroyed the manufacturing buildings and slave quarters. The two-story mansion remained standing, although it was saturated with shot and shell. By the time the Union army left, the mansion was uninhabitable.

Flipper's mother had to sew clothing for Southern soldiers; Festus avoided military service, through Ponder's influence, although he was conscripted twice. On September 2 Sherman took over the city after routing Hood's forces and ordered residents to evacuate. Then, on November 15, 1864, Atlanta became engulfed in flames as Sherman and his troops torched the city before heading east towards Savannah. Sherman was determined that Atlanta, an industrial and railroad center for the Confederacy, would not help the Southern cause any longer.

Just before Sherman entered Atlanta, Mrs. Ponder and her slaves fled by train to Macon, Georgia, 103 miles southeast of Atlanta. Here the Flipper family stayed in the basement of a hotel owned by Governor Joseph Brown, where they hid Mrs. Ponder's dishes and furniture. Mrs. Ponder prepared to leave Macon for Fort Valley as the Union army came towards Macon; however, the

The Ponder House after the Civil War Battle of Atlanta (photograph courtesy Atlanta Historical Society).

Union forces withdrew from Macon, then headed East as they marched to Savannah and the sea, leaving a charred and ruined path 60 miles wide.

The Flippers stayed in Macon for nine months. During this time, young Henry saw captured Union soldiers march through town on their way to the dreaded Confederate prison camp in Andersonville. Henry also saw Union troops under General James Harrison Wilson marching on a road outside Macon; the Flippers knew the huge contingent of Union soldiers meant the end of slavery. One of the soldiers even gave Festus some molasses, which provided some tasty meals.

In the spring of 1865, Festus Flipper and two of his sons, Henry and Joseph, returned to Atlanta in a wagon after traveling from Macon to Jonesboro by train. The train tracks from Jonesboro to Atlanta had been destroyed by the Union army; in Jonesboro the Flipper boys saw thirteen Confederate soldiers hanging from trees and the ground covered with shallow graves. In Atlanta, a city in ruins, the Union army occupied city hall and humiliated or tortured any Confederates they could find. Festus set up a shoe shop in his home, where he repaired the boots of Union soldiers (who paid in Federal greenbacks), while Isabella cooked for Union officers. Young Henry worked in the shoe shop, making children's shoes.

In April 1865 the Civil War finally ended when Grant's troops cornered Lee's army and forced their surrender at Appomattox, Virginia, on April 9. Less than a week later, President Abraham Lincoln was assassinated by actor John Wilkes Booth while watching a play in Ford's Theater in Washington, D.C.

In Atlanta, the Flipper family moved to Decatur Street, where Festus set up another boot and shoe shop in a brick building located in front of their house. Isabella continued to cook, establishing a sort of restaurant in their home. Both Flippers received food as well as money for their work. Business improved while Atlanta was being rebuilt, its population doubling to around 20,000 during the six years after the Civil War. Festus Flipper managed to purchase a house on the corner of Houston and Bell streets a few blocks from Auburn Avenue, where the family lived until 1874.

By the end of the Civil War, the Flippers had a good reputation in the community and were fairly well off. Although Festus was illiterate (Isabella could read and write), the Flipper family stressed the value of education to their children. For a short while, they hired the wife of an ex–Confederate captain to teach the children; then the American Missionary Association opened a school, which the Flipper boys entered in March 1866. Teachers at the school were the Reverend and Mrs. Frederick Ayers from Cincinnati, home of the American Missionary Association, and two ex-slaves, James Tate and Grandison B. Daniels. Soon Rosa and Lucy C. Kinney from the association came to Atlanta to teach at the school, located on Armstrong Street in an old church building. The school grew and purchased a railroad car, where additional classes were held.

The Flipper children attended this school until they entered the Storrs School in 1867, which was also under the control of the American Missionary Association. This two-story structure was formerly the Confederate commissary and was relocated to Houston Street; it provided education for fifty-seven years. Named after Storrs Congregational Church in Cincinnati, the school emphasized the Bible and religious studies in addition to the "three R's." From Storrs, Henry, with thirty-three other students, was promoted to the Atlanta Normal School where, in addition to attending school for one dollar a month, he helped in the construction of the men's dormitory.

In 1869 Henry Flipper entered Atlanta University, which had been chartered in 1867 and was also operated by the American Missionary Association.

Although the term "university" is connected to this school, in reality it was more like a junior high and high school because blacks did not have the educational background to attend a full-fledged university at that time. The Reverend Ayers, who led the founding of the university, was joined by the Reverend Edmund Asa Ware, who had a degree from Yale. The American Missionary Association was part of a large movement of Northerners who came to the South after the Civil War to help educate former slaves. Henry Flipper was the perfect age to receive the benefits of this educational movement, having turned nine three weeks before the end of the Civil War.

The Flipper family continued to do well because of the talents and expertise of Festus Flipper, who had a popular shoe shop on Decatur Street. The family had grown to include five sons; after Henry and Joseph came Festus Jr., Carl and Emory. In the fall of 1872, 16-year-old Henry was sitting in the doorway of his father's shoe shop when he overheard a conversation about a West Point cadet from Georgia scheduled to graduate in June 1873. Since congressmen could recommend a cadet for West Point whenever there was an opening for someone from their state, this meant there would be a vacancy for a cadet from Georgia in the fall of 1873.

The Flippers were staunchly Republican — the party of Lincoln — and after the Republican nominee for Congress, J.C. Freeman, was elected in the fall of 1872, Flipper sent a letter in January 1873 requesting the appointment to West Point. Freeman replied two days later, on January 23, and requested that Flipper obtain the endorsements of his teachers and some prominent Republicans.

On March 19 Flipper sent these endorsements and on March 22 Freeman replied: "I have received an invitation from the War Department to appoint, or nominate, a legally qualified cadet to the United States Military Academy from my district. As you were the first applicant, I am disposed to give you the first chance; but the requirements are rigid and strict, and I think you had best come down and see them. If after reading them you think you can undergo the examination without doubt, I will nominate you. But I do not want my nominee to fail to get in."[8]

Flipper replied in a letter dated March 24, sending his education qualifications. Freeman then requested a physical examination, which Flipper passed. On April 5 Freeman sent a letter notifying Flipper that he was accepted at West Point and was required to be there on or before May 25, 1873.

In the 1872 elections, President Ulysses S. Grant was reelected to a second term. During the seven and a half years since the end of the Civil War, there had been a great deal of changes for Negroes and the South. In December 1865 the Thirteenth Amendment to the Constitution, which outlawed slavery, was ratified; that same month the Ku Klux Klan was organized in Pulaski, Tennessee. In April 1866 the Civil Rights Act was passed by Congress, giving Negroes United States citizenship. The next month there were riots by whites in Memphis that left 46 dead and a number of Negro schools and churches burned.

In the spring of 1867 two Negro colleges were founded: Morehouse College in Atlanta and Howard University in Washington, D.C. In July 1867 Congress passed the Reconstruction Act, which imposed major social and political reforms on the former Confederate States of America and established a military government in the region. This act, signed by President Andrew Johnson, guaranteed Negroes the right to vote. The act was fairly lenient, pardoning a number of senior officials who returned to offices and legislatures, but the Southern states refused to adopt the Fourteenth Amendment, which protected the civil rights of Negroes. It was a time when Southern blacks feared for their lives; on September 9, 1867, Festus Flipper and some other blacks were severely beaten in Shermantown, just outside Atlanta. At the end of that year, Congress began impeachment proceedings against President Andrew Johnson after he attempted to fire his secretary of war, Edwin Stanton. (Congress believed they had to approve the firing since they had approved the appointment of Stanton as secretary of war.)

In 1868 General Grant was elected president, but in September all 28 Negro members of the Georgia legislature were expelled on the grounds that, although Negroes had the right to vote, they did not have the right to hold public office. This came less than two months after Georgia was readmitted to the Union. At this point, Tennessee, Arkansas, North Carolina, South Carolina, Florida, Alabama and Louisiana were all back in the Union, although Mississippi, Texas and Virginia were still holdouts.

In February 1869, Negroes were assured the right to vote when the Fifteenth Amendment passed. The month before, the National Convention of Colored Men was established, with noted Negro author, journalist and orator Frederick Douglass elected as its first president. During 1870 two Negroes took seats in Congress: the Reverend Hiram R. Revels became a member of the Senate from Mississippi in February, while Joseph H. Rainey of South Carolina became the first Negro member of the House of Representatives, in December. Revels completed the term of Jefferson Davis; by this point, all the Southern states had rejoined the Union.

A number of Southerners complied reluctantly with their new rules; in April 1871 a "Force Act" was passed by Congress to halt the activities of Ku Klux Klan members to stop voter registration, voting and jury service by Negroes. In March the delegation from Georgia rejoined Congress after agreeing to ratify the Fifteenth Amendment, reratify the Fourteenth Amendment, and allow elected Negroes to serve in the legislature. These actions came after the federal military came down in defense of Governor Rufus Bullock, who supported Reconstruction efforts.

In June 1872, the law that created the Freedmen's Bureau lapsed. This law helped Negroes gain rights and protected their lives, giving them a recourse against injustice. It also helped with the founding of schools and dispersion of food and medical aid.

After the appointment of Henry Flipper to West Point, a local newspaper editor contacted him. Flipper did not want an article about himself in the newspaper. In his autobiography, Flipper states, "I feared some evil might befall me while passing through Georgia en route for West Point, if too great a knowledge of me should precede me." Flipper did submit to an interview where others were present and one "advised me to abandon altogether the idea of going to West Point, for, said he, 'Them northern boys won't treat you right'.... My Southern friend might as well have advised an angel to rebel as to have counseled me to resign and not go."[9]

The next day the newspaper noted Flipper had been appointed to West Point. A short while after this, while Flipper was at the Post Office, he reported that "a gentleman beckoned to me, and we withdrew from the crowd ... after relating — indeed, repeating, to my amusement, the many hardships to which I should be subjected, and after telling me he had a very promising son ... whom he desired to have educated at West Point, offered me for my appointment the rather large sum of five thousand dollars." Flipper "refused instantly" because "I had so set my mind on West Point that, having the appointment, neither threats nor excessive bribes could induce me to relinquish it, even if I had not possessed sufficient strength of character to resist them otherwise."[10]

The requirements for a cadet at West Point were that a young man must be between the ages of 17 and 22, at least five feet tall and in good physical health. Mentally, the cadets had to pass tests in reading and writing, English grammar, descriptive geography of the United States, and the history of the United States. In the subject of arithmetic, the cadet had to be proficient in addition, subtraction, multiplication, division, reduction, simple and compound proportion, and vulgar and decimal fractions. At the time of Flipper's entry into West Point, no one was allowed to be a cadet at the military academy if they had served in the army or navy of the Confederacy during the Civil War.

The pay for cadets was $500 a year, of which around $5 a week had to be paid for board, washing, lights, etc. The cadet was also required to purchase a uniform for $88.79. As part of the agreement, the cadet received a free education if he served in the army for four years after graduation.

Flipper first saw West Point and the hills surrounding it from the deck of a ferryboat on the afternoon of May 20, 1873. After the ferry docked, Flipper asked for directions from a soldier and, receiving them, went into the adjutant's office, where he was required to show his certificate of appointment and write in a book basic background information: his full name, age, state, county, and place of birth, his occupation when at home, the name and occupation of his father, and the state, congressional district, county and city of residence.

Flipper walked into the office at the barracks, hat in hand, "when three cadets, who were seated in the room, simultaneously sprang to their feet, and

West Point in 1877 (photograph courtesy Special Collections and Archives Division, United States Military Academy Library).

welcomed me somewhat after this fashion: 'Well, sir, what do you mean by coming into this office in that manner, sir? Get out of here, sir.'"

Flipper walked out and was ordered by a cadet who followed him to button his coat and stand at attention. Then the cadet barked to Flipper, "Now sir, when you are ready to come in, knock at that door." Flipper knocked, although the door was wide open, and a cadet replied, "Come in." Flipper went and stood at attention; one of the cadets made some corrections to Flipper's stance, then asked "in a much milder tone" what he wanted. Flipper replied that the adjutant had sent him there. Then the cadet "arose, and directing me to follow him, conducted me to the bath-rooms." After this, Flipper was led to the hospital where he underwent a rigid physical examination, which he passed.[11]

Flipper's initiation into West Point was rather mild by comparison to some other cadets, although the military style was certainly established: a "plebe" had to ask permission, defer to upperclassmen, follow orders unquestioningly, and stand at attention when in the presence of his military superiors. Meanwhile, the superiors (particularly upperclassmen) shouted orders at the plebe.

A view down the Hudson River from West Point in 1877 (photograph courtesy Special Collections and Archives Division, United States Military Academy Library).

After his first West Point dinner in the mess hall, Flipper went to his barracks, collected his baggage and was told to have his room arranged in a particular order in 30 minutes. Flipper put his room in order in the allotted time and a cadet corporal came to inspect it. According to Flipper, "He walked deliberately to the clothes-press, and, informing me that everything was arranged wrong, threw every article upon the floor, repeated his order, and withdrew." This scenario was repeated three times within the next two hours. Finally, Flipper's room passed inspection by the cadet colonel and the plebe went to bed. Flipper had to obtain permission from a cadet officer to go anywhere or do anything and "to get such permission I must enter their office cleanly and neatly dressed, and, taking my place in the center of the room, must salute, report my entrance, make known my wants, salute again, and report my departure."[12]

The plebe's day began at five in the morning when reveille was sounded and a booming voice was heard saying, "Candidates, turn out promptly." The plebes were expected to jump out of bed, get dressed, and line up in forma-

A typical cadet's room at West Point circa 1877 (photograph courtesy Special Collections and Archives Division, United States Military Academy Library).

tion. They stood at attention until the drummers and fifers had marched to the barracks; the company rolls were called, and then they were dismissed.

The plebes then ran to their quarters and put things in order for an inspection, which occurred a half hour after roll call. On the first inspection a cadet corporal went to Flipper's room and "upset my bedding, kicked my shoes into the middle of the room, and ordered me to arrange them again and in better order." This scene occurred in every single plebe's room.

After breakfast, another room inspection was held and this time the cadet corporal said, "Very well, Mr. Flipper, very well, sir." Later, during his first morning as a cadet plebe, a different cadet colonel inspected Flipper's room "and declared everything out of order, although I had not touched a single thing after once satisfying the first corporal." Flipper then had to rearrange his room to satisfy this second cadet corporal.[13]

The mail was delivered at eleven that morning and Flipper was surprised to receive a letter from James Webster Smith, the only other black cadet at West Point. According to Flipper, the letter "reassured me very much, telling me not to fear either blows or insults, and advising me to avoid any forward conduct if I wished also to avoid certain consequences." Flipper noted that it was "a sad letter" and "I don't think any thing has so affected me or so influenced my conduct at West Point as its melancholy tone. That 'sad experience' gave me a world of warning."[14]

2

West Point

Henry Flipper was the seventh "colored" cadet to be appointed to West Point and the fifth to enter. Charles Summer Wilson from Massachusetts was the first to be nominated: The second was Henry Alonzo Napier from Tennessee; the third was Michael Howard from Mississippi; and the fourth was James Webster Smith from South Carolina. All four were nominated in 1870 but only Smith and Napier were admitted. Napier left in 1872 because of a deficiency in math and French.

In 1872 there were two African Americans nominated for the United States Military Academy. James Elias Rector from Arkansas was nominated but failed to enter, while Thomas Van Rensselaer Gibbs from Florida entered but left in 1873 because of a deficiency in math.

Flipper knew of these cadets and, while he was still in Atlanta, had heard Smith was no longer at the academy. However, after reading the letter Smith sent on his first day at West Point, Flipper learned that Smith had not been dismissed. At four that first afternoon, Flipper paid his first visit to Smith but, since the meeting was brief because of drill, the two arranged to meet the next day.

At this first drill, the plebes watched the upperclassmen march in lock-step formation and perform a brief military drill using rifles. Flipper and another plebe "had quite a lengthy conversation about the fine appearance of the cadets, their forms, so straight and manly, evoking our greatest admiration." But after this initial conversation, the other plebes confronted the white plebe and "the gentleman discovered ere long that he too was prejudiced" and he and Flipper never had another conversation.[1] What emerged was a practice whereby the other cadets "cut" Flipper, or isolated him. No other cadet would speak with him or associate with him. Also, it was made known to Flipper that he was not welcome at social functions such as dances.

On May 26 another Negro cadet, John Washington Williams of Virginia, entered West Point.

On May 28 all the plebes were marched to the Drawing Academy and given examinations in grammar, history and geography; exams in orthography

21

and reading were given the following day. On May 30 the Academic Board orally examined the plebes in mathematics. A few days later, Flipper learned he had passed.

Flipper's plebe days began at five in the morning with reveille, then a drill at five-thirty, breakfast and classes, then another drill at four in the afternoon. Flipper admitted that "plebe drill" or "squad drill" was "a horror" to plebes. There were "torturous twistings and twirlings, stretching every nerve, straining every sinew, almost twisting the joints out of place and making life one long agonizing effort." He admitted he "formed an opinion, a morbid dislike of it then, and have not changed it," but he also noted the advantage of these exercises "can not be overestimated. It makes the most crooked, distorted creature an erect, noble, and manly being." Flipper also observed that "squad drill and hazing" were effective because they "successfully mould the coarser characters who come to West Point into officers and gentlemen [because] they teach him how to govern and be governed." Flipper continued that these exercises in drills and hazing were more effective in "polishing" a cadet's "asperities of disposition and forming his character than any amount of regulations could be. They tame him, so to speak."[2]

On the morning of June 22, Henry Flipper and the rest of the plebes at West Point marched out to their first camp, where they set up a small city of tents and began military drills. It was a summer of living in a camp, with the plebes at the beck and call of upperclassmen — fetching them water, cleaning their equipment, doing them favors. This hazing was not against regulations and it was widespread. Flipper noted the "contemptuous look and imperious bearing" from upperclassmen "lowers a plebe, I sometimes think, in his own estimation. He is in a manner cowed and made to feel that he must obey, and not disobey; to feel that he is a plebe, and must expect a plebe's portion. He is taught by it to stay in his place."[3] Flipper admitted that he was rarely hazed at this first camp and, compared to his white classmates, had an easier time.

Camp consisted of rising at five in the morning for roll call, then policing the camp (cleaning it up and making sure it was in top order), then squad drill for an hour, followed by straightening up their own tent before breakfast at seven. At eight there was a troop parade, then guard duty or "free time" before artillery drill at nine, which involved firing and cleaning either cannons or rifles. After a rest period in the afternoon, there was more drilling. During the night, "guard duty" was assigned and upperclassmen generally tried to confuse the plebes with pranks in the dead of night. Some of these pranks included the upperclassmen pretending to be unwarranted visitors. This continued until August 28. The next day the plebes moved back into barracks and the camp was broken down. After this camp, the plebes were considered "cadets and gentlemen."

The cadets attended classes at West Point from September 1 until the end of June. During the first year ("Fourth Class"), cadets studied mathematics, French, Spanish, use of small arms (fencing and bayonet) and tactics of artillery and infantry. In January and June, examinations were held to ascertain the progress of each cadet to determine their class standing. After these examinations, cadets could be dismissed from West Point if they failed. During that plebe year, John Washington Williams was deficient after the January exams, and Flipper was ordered to tutor him. But in June, Williams was dismissed from West Point.

At the end of his plebe year, Henry Flipper was in a class with 83 others; in both mathematics and French he was ranked 48th, in Spanish 37th and in drawing 40th.

The "Negro press" first surfaced in the early 1800s as a way for abolitionist thinkers to express their views. In the period after the Civil War, there were a number of publications, often carried for distribution by Pullman porters on trains by, for and about Negroes. After Flipper and Williams of Virginia were admitted to West Point, an article ran in the *New National Era and Citizen*, which was published in Washington, D.C., and advertised itself as "the national organ of the colored people." The article was headlined "Colored Cadets at West Point" and stated that if black cadets "in their honorable school-boy careers cannot meet social as well as intellectual recognition while at West Point, let them study on and acquit themselves like men, for they will meet, out in the world, a worthy reception among men of worth, who have put by the prejudices of race and the shackles of ignorance.... If our young men of ability have the stuff in them to make men out of, they need not fear 'to be let alone' for a while; they will ultimately come to the surface and attain worthy recognition."[4]

Another Negro paper quoted the *Era and Citizen* article, then stated:

Never has any bond people emerged from slavery into a condition full of such grand opportunities and splendid possibilities as those which are within the reach of the colored people of the United States; but if those opportunities are to be made available, if those possibilities are to be realized, the colored people must move into the fore-front of action and study and work in their own behalf. The colored cadets at West Point, the colored students in the public schools, the colored men in the professions, the trades, and on the plantations, can not be idlers if they are to compete with the white race in the acquisition of knowledge and property. But they have examples of notable achievements in their own ranks which should convince them that they have not the slightest reason to despair of success. The doors stand wide open, from the plantation to the National Capitol, and every American citizen can, if he will, attain worthy recognition.[5]

Flipper himself noted that, for him and the two other black cadets at West Point during his first year (Smith and Williams of Virginia), "'To be left alone' was what we wished. To be left to our own resources for study and improvement, for enjoyment in whatever way we chose to seek it, was what we desired. We cared not for social recognition. We did not expect it, nor were we disappointed in not getting it. We would not seek it. We would not obtrude ourselves upon them. We would not accept recognition unless it was made willingly. We would be of them at least independent. We would mark out for ourselves a uniform course of conduct and follow it rigidly. These were our resolutions. So long as we were in the right we knew we should be recognized by those whose views were not limited or bound by such narrow confines as prejudice and caste, whether they were at West Point or elsewhere."[6]

In June 1874, Henry Flipper passed his exams and was promoted to "Third Class," or the second year at West Point. In July and August, he and the rest of his class entered camp for practical training and ranked above the new plebes who had just entered West Point. Flipper noted that it was those who had just completed their plebe year who did the most hazing.

During the second year ("Third Class") cadets studied "Mathematics," "French," "Spanish," "Drawing" (topography) and "Tactics of Infantry, Artillery and Cavalry."

On July 1, 1876, Henry Flipper became a first classman, with only one more year to go in order to graduate from West Point. "To me it was to be not only an end of study, of discipline, of obedience to the regulations of the Academy," said Flipper, "but even an end to isolation, to tacit persecution, to melancholy, to suspense. It was to be the grand realization of my hopes, the utter, the inevitable defeat of the minions of pride, prejudice, caste." He added, "My friends, my enemies, center their hopes on me. I treat them, one with earnest endeavor for realization, the other with supremest indifference."[7] At this point, he stood forty-sixth in a class of eighty-five.

Although Flipper was a senior, he still had to endure indignities, but he held firm to the privileges of his rank. First classmen had rank over the other classes and "To be subject to me, to my orders, was to them an unbearable torture. As they looked forward to the time when I should exercise command over them, they could not help feeling the mortification which would be upon them."[8]

One day in the summer of 1876, Flipper and a white third classman both inspected the troops. "Not wishing to subject him to more mortification than was possible, I gave him all the latitude I could," said Flipper, "telling him to use his own discretion, and that he need not ask my permission for any thing unless he chose." Flipper noted: "This simple act, forgotten almost as soon as it was done, was in an exceedingly short time known to every cadet throughout the camp, and I had the indescribable pleasure, some days after, of knowing that by it I had been raised many degrees in the estimation of the corps."

The next time Flipper was on guard he was the junior and another officer the senior. According to Flipper, "He came to me voluntarily, and in almost my own words gave me exactly the same privileges I had given my junior." Flipper concluded that when he "did a more Christian act, did to others as I would have them do to me, and not as they had sometimes done, I gave cause for a similar act of good-will, which was in a degree beyond all expectation accorded me."[9]

Flipper noted that when he inspected the guard, some of whom "were from the South, and educated to consider themselves far superior to those of whom they once claimed the right of possession.... I know it was to them most galling, and although I fully felt the responsibility and honor of commanding the guard, I frankly and candidly confess that I found no pleasure in their apparent humiliation."[10]

On June 17, 1876, Flipper went to camp at West Point for ten days, then he went to Philadelphia to visit the Centennial Exhibition with other cadets. During that spring and summer, the United States celebrated its one hundredth birthday with a big centennial in Philadelphia. The Centennial was opened on May 10 by President Grant. The 284-acre park had a number of exhibition halls that demonstrated developments in electricity, the internal combustion engine and steam power; the largest steam engine ever created was on display in Machinery Hall. On June 25 Alexander Graham Bell demonstrated his new invention, the telephone. Bell was trying to raise money to establish a telephone system, but bankers were cautious, believing the telephone might be merely a curiosity.

On that same June 25, General George Armstrong Custer and 265 of his troops of the Seventh Cavalry were killed on the Little Big Horn River in Dakota Territory by Sioux and Cheyenne warriors. The approximately 2,500 Indians were under Chiefs Sitting Bull and Crazy Horse. Custer had graduated from West Point in 1861; he was 37 years old. The deaths of Custer and his troops aroused a huge outcry in the United States against Indians in the West and the army vowed to solve "the Indian problem." Although the Indians won the battle with Custer, they lost the war of survival. After the battle of the Little Big Horn the fate of the Indians was sealed: they were doomed to a war of attrition.

After ten days in Philadelphia, Flipper and his classmates returned to camp at West Point. "First class camp" was for those entering their final year at West Point and it was much more enjoyable. Duties of first class camp included training in artillery, ordnance and engineering; also, telegraphy and night signaling with torches were taught. Most lessons were of a practical, military nature—firing guns, building batteries and bridges, and setting up telegraph communications.

During Flipper's time at first-class camp, a plebe came to his tent to borrow some ink. Flipper noted that he "readily complied with his request, feeling proud of what I thought was the beginning of a new era in my cadet life. I felt he would surely prove himself manly enough, after thus recognizing me, to keep it up, and thus bring others under his influence to the same cause." After several more visits, the plebe asked Flipper if he could borrow his algebra book and Flipper complied. The cadet returned the borrowed India ink at night, raising a tent corner and leaving the ink on the floor. Flipper saw the ink when he returned and wrote, "I was utterly disgusted with the man. The low, unmanly way in which he acted was wholly without my approval. If he was disposed to be friendly, why be cowardly about it? If he must recognize me secretly, why, I would rather not have such recognition. Acting a lie to his fellow-cadets by appearing to be inimical to me and my interests, while he pretended the reverse to me, proved him to have a baseness of character with which I didn't care to identify myself."

In September, the plebe returned the borrowed algebra book. Flipper had his name on the cover and back of the book and his initial "F" in two places on the cover. But "when the book was returned he had cut the calf-skin from the cover, so as to remove my name. The result was a horrible disfiguration of the book, and a serious impairment of its durability." Flipper said, "The mere sight of the book angered me, and I found it difficult to refrain from manifesting as much. He undoubtedly did it to conceal the fact that the book was borrowed from me." Flipper's view was that "Such unmanliness, such cowardice, such baseness, even, was most disgusting."[11]

During the fourth and final year ("First Class"), cadets studied "Military and Civil Engineering and Science of War," "Mineralogy and Geology," "Ethics and Law," "Tactics of Artillery, Cavalry, and Infantry," "Ordnance and Gunnery" and "Practical Military Engineering" (Civil Engineering).

Flipper was proud of his achievements to date. "I was the first person of color that had ever commanded a guard at the Military Academy of the United States.... Is my authority recognized? Indeed it is," he said. "During my first year I many times overheard myself spoken to as 'the nigger,' 'the moke,' or 'the thing.' Now openly, and when my presence was not known, I always hear myself mentioned as Mr. Flipper."[12]

At the end of 1876, New York governor Samuel Tilden won more popular and electoral votes than Ohio governor Rutherford B. Hayes, but Tilden was one vote short of the required number of votes in the electoral college. There was a special electoral commission established which awarded the contested electoral votes to Hayes in an outcome questioned for vote rigging. Ulysses S. Grant ended his presidency when Rutherford B. Hayes was sworn in as the 19th president of the United States on March 3, 1877. On May 1, Hayes kept his promise to withdraw all federal troops from the South, thus ending Reconstruction.

As time moved forward, Flipper observed, "I find myself near graduation, with every prospect of success. And from the beginning to the close my life has been one not of trouble, persecution, or punishment, but one of isolation only. True, to an unaccustomed nature such a life must have had many anxieties and trials and displeasures, and, although it was so with me, I have nothing more than that of which to complain. And if such a life has had its unpleasant features, it has also had its pleasant ones, of which not the least, I think, was the constantly growing prospect of ultimate triumph."[13]

During his time at West Point, Henry Flipper kept notes of events, thoughts and feelings that he experienced there. In his autobiography, written soon after he graduated from West Point, he made it clear that he separated himself from the other black cadets at West Point. Speaking of the treatment of black cadets at West Point, Flipper stated color was not the problem, although "It may be color in some cases, [however] in the great majority of instances it is mental and moral condition. Little or no education, little moral refinement, and all their repulsive consequences will never be accepted as equals of education, intellectual or moral. Color is absolutely nothing in the consideration of the question, unless we mean by it not color of skin, but color of character, and I fancy we can find considerable color there."

The key, according to Flipper, was to provide an example for others to emulate because, he reasoned, others will act towards us as we act towards them. He stated, "We must force others to treat us as we wish, by giving them such an example of meekness and of good conduct as will at least shame them into a like treatment of us. This is the safer and surer method of revenge. 'Therefore if thine enemy hunger, feed him; if he thirst, give him drink; for in so doing thou shalt heap coals of fire on his head.'"[14]

Flipper believed strongly in self-determination and the strength of individual character. In determining the future treatment blacks would receive at West Point, he stated, "The remedy lies solely in our case with us. We can make our life at West Point what we will. We shall be treated by the cadets as we treat them. Of course some of the cadets are low — they belong to the younger classes — and good treatment cannot be expected of them at West Point nor away from there. The others, presumably gentlemen, will treat everybody else as becomes gentlemen, or at any rate as they themselves are treated."[15]

During his first year at West Point, Flipper roomed with James Webster Smith; along with John Washington Williams, they were the three black cadets at the academy. In his second and third years at West Point, Flipper lived alone and was the only black cadet. During his last year, he roomed with Johnson Whittaker, an African American cadet who entered in 1876. Only Flipper graduated.

Of their dismissals, Flipper was content that all were justified. On Williams, he said, "I do express the belief that his treatment was impartial and just. He was regularly and rightly found deficient and duly dismissed." Of the other two he said, "Smith had trouble under my own eyes on more than one occasion, and Whittaker has already received blows in the face, but I have not had so much as an angry word to utter."[16]

The most controversial dismissal was that of Johnson Whittaker, who entered the academy in September 1876, in Smith's vacancy after several appointed white candidates had failed. Flipper and Whittaker roomed together during Flipper's last and Whittaker's first year at West Point. Whittaker was dismissed three years after Flipper graduated. In his book, *Assault at West Point*, author John F. Marszalek described Whittaker as "unbelligerent" and religious, a man who "turned the other cheek, yet stood on his rights just as Flipper had done," but was labeled a "coward" by other cadets. On the morning of April 6, 1880, Whittaker did not show up for drill. He was found lying in his room, his hands and feet tied to his bed, unconscious as blood came from his head. In the court-martial conducted, Whittaker was accused of faking this crime in order to get sympathetic attention from the public and media and of lying to the court of inquiry that followed the incident. On June 10, 1881, he was found guilty of both charges, dishonorably discharged from the military academy, and ordered to spend a year of hard labor in the penitentiary. He was later acquitted but still ordered dismissed from the military academy.

The problem with Whittaker, contrasted with the success of Flipper, was noted after Flipper graduated, in the *New York World*: "[Whittaker, a] poor young mulatto, [was] completely ostracized not only by West Point Society, but most thoroughly by the corps of cadets itself. Flipper though got it right, and, strange to say, the cadets seem to have a certain kind of respect for him.... Flipper had remarkable pluck and nerve, and was accorded his parchment.... He is made of sterner stuff than poor Whittaker."[17]

Flipper believed the role of the academy was "to transform young men into a like ilk.... The country entrusts them with this great responsibility. To prove faithless to such a charge would be to risk position, and even those dearer attributes of the soldier, honor and reputation. They would not dare ill-treat a colored cadet or a white one."[18] Flipper was upset at being accused of "manifesting a lack of dignity in that I allowed myself to be insulted, imposed upon, and otherwise ill-treated." He answered that "true dignity ... consists in being above the rabble and their insults, and particularly in remaining there. To stoop to retaliation is not compatible with true dignity, nor is vindictiveness manly."[19]

James Webster Smith was court-martialed at West Point for lying when he insisted he was trying to keep another cadet from stepping on his toes as an explanation for "inattention in ranks" while marching. The other cadet denied this and Smith was dismissed from the academy. Smith was not a popular cadet at West Point and author John Marszalek noted the cadet's "belligerent attitude, his loud and constant demands for his rights both at the Academy and in the outside press, and his apparent political influence made him intensely hated." One of his professors described Smith as "malicious, vindictive, and untruthful."[20] The same author noted that, "Rather than appeal to newspapers or politicians or belligerently fight for his rights, Flipper apparently fought his ostracism and the surrounding hostility with quiet strength and determination. He stood up for his official rights but did not

Cadets at West Point in 1877 (Special Collections and Archives Division, United States Military Academy Library).

try to intrude in other matters. He had the amazing internal fortitude to be able to withstand four years of isolation and insults."[21]

Flipper's "strategy" of getting through West Point worked; he graduated, while other black cadets who entered before him did not. The goal of graduating from West Point was the most important thing in Henry Flipper's life up to that point. To those who question his acceptance of racism or tolerance of racist practices at West Point, Flipper would certainly reply that he emerged the victor and not the victim. Proof of that victory was on the diploma he carried from West Point and his commission in the United States Army as the only black officer at that time.

The final steps toward graduation began on June 1, 1877, when final examinations began. The first examinations were in mineralogy and geology, and Flipper "maxed it" and knew [he] would graduate." He also wanted to graduate "as high up as possible."

The next examination was in law and Flipper again "maxed it." It was one of "the proudest moments of my life," Flipper observed. "All that loneliness, dreariness, and melancholy of the four years gone was forgotten. I lived only in the time being and was happy. I was succeeding, and was meeting with that success which humble effort never fails to attain."[22]

The examination that followed was in "civil and military engineering" and Flipper did well here; but in the examination of "ordnance and gunnery" he was "less successful." Flipper noted that "A good recitation in ordnance and gunnery would have brought me out forty-five or six instead of fifty." This last examination, held on June 11, concluded three days before graduation on June 14.

An article in the *New York Tribune*, reporting the examinations, stated that Flipper "has a good command of plain and precise English, and his voice is full and pleasant." The article added, "Mr. Flipper will be graduated next week with the respect of his instructors, and not the less of his fellows, who have carefully avoided intercourse with him. The quiet dignity which he has shown during this long isolation of four years has been really remarkable."[23]

Articles about Flipper and his impending graduation appeared in a number of newspapers. A correspondent from the *New York Times* stated, "While all concede Flipper's progress, yet it is not believed that he will be allowed to graduate. No negro has passed out of the institution a graduate, and it is believed that Flipper will be eventually slaughtered in one way or another. The rule among the regulars is: No darkeys need apply."[24]

A rumor had begun, after Smith's dismissal from West Point in the spring of 1877, that Flipper had also resigned. Hearing the rumor, an officer at the academy invited Flipper to his quarters, where, Flipper said, he "assured me that prejudice, if it did exist among my instructors, would not prevent them from treating me justly and impartially.... He further assured me that the officers of the Academy and of the army, and especially the older ones, desired to have me graduate, and that they would do all within the legitimate exercise of their authority to promote that end."[25]

The graduation ceremonies on the morning of June 14, 1877, were held outside, under maple trees in front of the academy building. Prior to the awarding of diplomas, a number of speakers addressed the cadets.

As Major-General W.S. Hancock noted, "great leaders are born." Hancock continued: "Great responsibilities in time of danger are not given to the ignorant, the slothful, or to those who have impaired their powers of mind or body by the indulgences of life. In times of danger, favorites are discarded. When work is to be done, deeds to be performed, men of action have their opportunities and fail not to seize them."[26]

G.W. McCrary, secretary of war in the Rutherford Hayes administration, stated, "The profession does not ennoble the man, but the man ennobles the profession." He added, "Character, young men, is everything; without it, your education is nothing; without it, your country will be disappointed in you. Go forth into life, then, firmly resolved to be true, not only to the flag of your country, not only to the institutions of the land, not only to the Union which our fathers established, and which the blood of our countrymen has cemented, but to be true to yourselves and the principles of honor, of rectitude, of temperance, of virtue, which have always characterized the great and successful soldier, and must always characterize such a soldier in the future."[27]

Major-General John M. Schofield, superintendent, U.S. Military Academy, awarded the diplomas. When Henry Flipper received his diploma, the crowd stood and applauded; he was the only cadet to receive such an honor. A newspaper reporter who attended the graduation wrote: "He deserves it. Any one who knows how quietly and bravely this young man — the first of his despised race to graduate at West Point — has borne the difficulties of his position; how for four years he has had to stand apart from his classmates as one with them but not of them; and to all the severe work of academic official life has had added the yet more severe mental strain which bearing up against a cruel social ostracism puts on any man; and knowing that he has done this without getting soured, or losing courage for a day — anyone, I say, who knows all this would be inclined to say that the young man deserved to be well taken care of by the government he is bound to serve. Everybody here who has watched his course speaks in terms of admiration of the unflinching courage he has shown. No cadet will go away with heartier wishes for his future welfare."[28]

Flipper received a number of letters congratulating him on his graduation, including some from high ranking political officials. An article in *The New York Herald* quoted a cadet saying about Flipper, "We have no feeling against him at all, but we could not associate with him. You see we are so crowded together here that we are just like one family, possessing everything in common and borrowing everything, even to a pair of white trousers, and we could not hold such intimate fellowship with him. It may be prejudice, but we could not do it; so we simply let him alone, and he has lived to himself, except when we drill with him. The boys were rather afraid that when he should come to hold the position as officer of the guard that he would swagger over them, but he showed good sense and taste, merely assuming the rank formally and leaving his junior to carry out the duty."[29]

"I was the happiest man in the institution, except when I'd get brooding over my loneliness.... I learned to hate holidays," revealed Henry Flipper.

"At those times the other cadets would go off skating, rowing, or visiting. I had nowhere to go except to walk around the grounds, which I sometimes did. I more often remained in my quarters. At these times barracks would be deserted and I would get so lonely and melancholy I wouldn't know what to do."[30]

About a year after he graduated from the academy, Henry Flipper wrote of his years at West Point: "I hardly know how I endured it all so long. If I were asked to go over it all again, even with the experience I now have, I fear I should fail. I mean of course the strain on my mind and sensitiveness would be so great I'd be unable to endure it."[31]

Henry Flipper as a West Point graduate, 1877 (Special Collections and Archives Division, United States Military Academy Library).

Flipper did, indeed, have to endure a lot at West Point, although his stoic nature, his dogged determination to graduate, and his practice of overlooking insults and slights while casting a positive light on his ordeal allowed him to keep himself focused on the successful completion of his West Point education. It was a monumental achievement, but Flipper's sense of destiny gave him a towering inner strength.

Flipper tried to be philosophical and forgiving about the prejudice he faced at West Point and noted that "it is natural" that "the prejudice of race is not yet overcome entirely."[32] Flipper believed the education of blacks would "cure" prejudice because "a bad temper, precipitation, stubbornness, and like qualities, all due to non-education, are too often attributes of colored men and women. These characteristics lower the race in the estimation of the whites, and produce, I think, what we call prejudice. In fact I believe prejudice is due solely to non-education and its effects in one or perhaps both races." However, he continued, "There is, of course, a very large class of ignorant and partially cultured whites whose conceptions can find no other reason for prejudice than that of color.... This is the class we in the South are accustomed to call the 'poor white trash.'"[33]

In answer to the suggestion that Congress could somehow "solve" the injustice blacks faced at the United States Military Academy, Flipper responded, "If my manhood cannot stand without a governmental prop, then let it fall.... Congress has no control over personal whims or prejudices."[34] Flipper felt that social equality must be earned, and that it "would be earned through the process of education."[35] "I have this right to social equality," he stated, "for I and those to whom I claim to be equal are similarly educated. We have much in common, and this fact alone creates my right to social and equal recognition."[36]

Discussing "rights," Flipper further stated, "I don't want equal rights, but identical rights. The whites and blacks may have equal rights, and yet be entirely independent, or estranged from each other. The two races cannot live in the same country, under the same laws as they now do, and yet be absolutely independent of each other.... On the other hand, whatever brings them into closer relationship, whatever increases their knowledge and appreciation of fellowship and its positive importance, must necessarily tend to remove all prejudices, and all ill-feelings, and bring the two races, and indeed the world, nearer that degree of perfection to which all things show us it is approaching. Therefore I want identical rights, for equal rights may not be sufficient."[37]

3

In the Buffalo Soldiers

After graduation, Flipper was given a "graduating leave" until he began active service in the army. There were rumors that he might be assigned to Howard University, in Washington, D.C., to continue his education, but Flipper preferred active duty, preferably in the Ninth or Tenth ("colored") Cavalry, known as the "Buffalo Soldiers."

On June 30, a little over two weeks after his graduation, a reception was given in his honor in New York City, hosted by Mr. James W. Moore at the Lincoln Literary Musical Association located at 132 West Twenty-Seventh Street. A newspaper article noted that, at 9:45 P.M., "Lieutenant Flipper entered the room in full uniform. A heavy yellow horse-hair plume fell down over his cavalry helmet. His coat was new and bright, and glittered with its gold buttons and tasseled aigulets. By his side hung a long cavalry sabre in a gilt scabbard. His appearance was the signal for a buzz of admiration."[1] Among the guests was Charles Remond Douglass, son of Frederick Douglass.

On July 1, he went to Atlanta. On the way, he stopped in Chattanooga, where he "paid his respects to the commandant and was introduced and shown through the barracks." In Atlanta, he read a story in the *Atlanta Constitution* about his New York reception. The article began with "Flipper has flopped up again" before stating, "Common people are generally embarrassed at receptions given to themselves, but not so with Flipper. The reception was exceedingly high-toned, as well as highly colored." That same newspaper covered his return to Atlanta, beginning the article with "Flip's done come home!" The article continued: "His coming has created quite a sensation in colored circles.... 'Dat's him!!' said a dozen of the curious darkeys.... 'He's one ob de United States Gazettes!' shouted a young darkey.... Among his colored friends he was a lion, and they could not speak their praises in language strong enough. A darkey would approach the young man, cautiously, feel of his buttons and clothes, and enthusiastically remark: 'Bad man wid de gub-ment strops on!'"[2]

In an article about his reception in Atlanta, that same newspaper had the headline "Flipper as a Fraud. Freeman's protégé on southern civilization —

He Talks At The Reception and Makes of Himself an Ass — the Anomalous Creature on Exhibition — He Shows The Cloven Foot." The article read as follows: "The relations between the races in this city have for years been such as to make remarks like those in which Flipper indulged not only uncalled for, but really distasteful. They are not to be blamed for his conduct.[3]

"Flipper was dressed lavishly in regimentals and gold cord, and sat upon the stage with his immense and ponderous cavalry sabre tightly buckled around him. He had the attitude of Wellington or Grant at a council of war. He was introduced to the audience by J.O. Wimbish, a high-toned negro politician ... who bespattered the young warrior with an eulogy ... [that] was real slushy in its copiousness and iffusiveness." Flipper was quoted: "The gentlemen of the army are generally better educated than the people of the South."[4]

The article was countered by one in the *Atlanta Republican*, which directed itself against the *Constitution's* long article. The *Republican* article stated: "In regard to the ostentatious manner in which the lieutenant conducted himself on that evening, nothing could be further from the truth.... It is not strange, however, that the *Constitution*, whose judgment and sense of right and justice have been perverted through years of persistent sinning, should see things in a different light. The 'uncalled for and distasteful' remarks were doubtless those made in regard to the fact that Northern people coming into contact with Southern prejudice are tainted by it, and that West Pointers are generally better educated than the Southern people.... Of course this would stir up the wrath of the *Constitution*; for what could be more hateful in its sight than truth?"[5]

While in Atlanta, Flipper became engaged to Miss Anna White. However, Henry's brother, Joseph Simeon, warned White that Henry "wasn't the marrying kind." After objections from her family, who thought that being the wife of an army officer in the desolate, dangerous West would not be suitable for her, the engagement was broken off.[6] From Atlanta, Flipper went to Macon, Georgia.

Rumors seemed to run rampant around Flipper. One such rumor circulating at the time was that he would join the "Liberia Movement" headquartered in Charleston, South Carolina. African Methodist Episcopal church minister B.F. Porter attempted to organize blacks to leave the United States and emigrate to Liberia to escape American racism. Porter wanted Flipper to become commander-in-chief of this group and help recruit men for an army and navy. Flipper answered this offer with a letter to the *Charleston News and*

Courier, published October 19: "I have no sympathy whatever for the 'Liberian Exodus' movement, that I give it neither countenance nor support, but will oppose it whenever I feel that the occasion requires it."[7]

After he was honored at a reception in Charleston, South Carolina, Flipper then spent time with his parents in Thomasville, where his father had a shoe making shop.

During the five months Flipper spent on graduation leave, he noted:

> I was treated with the utmost respect and courtesy except in Atlanta. The white people, with one exception, didn't notice me at all.... One young man, whom I knew many years, who has sold me many an article, and awaited my convenience for his pay, and who met me in New York and walked and talked with me, hung his head and turned away from me, just as I was about to address him on a street in Atlanta. Again and again have I passed and repassed acquaintances on the streets without any sign of recognition, even when I have addressed them. Whenever I have entered any of their stores for any purpose, they have almost invariably 'gotten off' some stuff about attempts on the part of the authorities at West Point to 'freeze me out,' or about better treatment from Southern boys than from those of the North.... In Thomasville, Southwest Ga., where I was born, and which I had not seen for eighteen years, I was received and treated by the whites almost as one of themselves.

He commented further:

> Whenever I have traveled in the South it has been thrown into my face that the Southern people had, would, and did treat me better than the Northern people. This is wholly untrue. It is true that the men generally speak kindly and treat me with due courtesy, but never in a single instance has a Southern man introduced me to his wife or even invited me to his house. It was done North in every place I stopped. In many cases, when invited to visit gentlemen's residences, they have told me they wanted their wives to meet me.[8]

Nor was the Southern press particularly hospitable to Flipper. An article in a New Orleans paper stated:

> Flipper is described as a little bow-legged grif of the most darkly coppery hue, and of a general pattern that even the most enthusiastic would find it hard to adopt. Flipper is not destined to uphold the virtues and graces of his color in the salons of Boston and New York.... Just what Flipper is to do with himself does not seem altogether clear.... His prospects don't appear to be very brilliant as regards social delights or domestic enjoyments.... Personally we are not interested in Flipper.[9]

"What is of importance, and great importance too, is how they will treat me in the army, when we have all assumed the responsibilities of manhood, coupled with those of a public servant, an army officer," said Flipper after his graduation. "Of course the question cannot be answered. I feel nevertheless assured that the older officers at least will not stoop to prejudice or caste, but will accord me proper treatment and respect."[10]

Flipper joined the United States Army when it was in decline. At the end of the Civil War, there were over a million troops in the Union army; less than a year later there were under 80,000. During the next three years, the army was reduced to about 57,000 troops. During the 1869–1870 period it was reduced again to 37,000 troops, and then dropped to 24,000 troops by 1890. The primary role of the army from the end of the Civil War to 1890 was to protect settlements in the West and specifically to fight Indians.

Congress first established a regular army in September 1789 with 840 men authorized; however, there were only 672 men in the service. The United States Military Academy at West Point, New York, was founded in 1802 under Thomas Jefferson to provide a corps of officers. This led to new rules for the army; it built roads, led explorations and conducted scientific surveys. The Corps of Topographical Engineers, created in 1838, played a major role in the exploration and mapping of the West before the Civil War. The army also established forts in the West that were usually the first settlements and served as markets as well as protection for settlers. The Bureau of Indian Affairs was created in 1832, two years after the Indian Removal Act was passed by Congress, to help "manage" Native Americans. The army was charged with carrying out these policies.

By the 1840s the army was known as a place where immigrants could find work and learn English; at this point, about 47 percent of recruits were immigrants. By the beginning of the Mexican War (1846), there were a little over 8,500 troops; at the end of the war in 1849 there were over 10,700 troops.

After the Civil War, a new system was established: there would be a Division of the Missouri, a Division of the Pacific, and a Division of the East. The Division of the Missouri included the departments of Arkansas (Arkansas and Indian Territory), Missouri (Missouri, Kansas, and Colorado and New Mexico territories), the Platte (Iowa and Nebraska, Utah and some of the Dakota territories along with some of Montana) and Dakota (Dakota and Montana territories and Minnesota).

In 1868 there were about 2,600 army men in the West and around 200,000 Indians. Some posts had less than 50 men in isolated areas. Still, the army was charged with defeating the Indians and managed to do so over a 25-year period because of organization, weapons and the simple fact that white settlement made it impossible for nomadic Indians to survive. During a significant part of this period (1869–1883), the army was led by its commanding general, William Tecumseh Sherman. Being a soldier was tough work. During the Civil War, soldiers received $16 per month; but Congress, in a budget-cutting mood, reduced the soldiers' pay to $13 in 1871.

Lieutenant Henry O. Flipper was assigned to the Tenth Cavalry. These were the "Buffalo Soldiers," African American soldiers in the United States Army who served in the regular peacetime army after the Civil War. They were given the name "Buffalo Soldiers" by the Indians, who thought their hair was like the buffalo's.

During the Civil War, almost 180,000 blacks served in the Union army; 33,380 were killed. This proved to the government and the army that African Americans could be good soldiers, so when the post–Civil War army was organized, it was agreed there would be some regiments of Negro troops. The authorized strength of the post–Civil War army was 54,641 officers and men (the actual number was much smaller), and on July 28, 1866, Congress passed an act that authorized six regiments of "colored" troops. Two regiments would be cavalry (the 9th and 10th) and four would be infantry.

In 1869 the four infantry troops were combined into two, the 24th and 25th, at the same time other white regiments were combined. Congress required white officers to lead the black troops (the reasoning being that there were no experienced Negro officers); further, a certain percentage of officers must have had active field service during the Civil War. The leaders of the cavalry units were Edward Hatch of Iowa, who headed the 9th Cavalry, and Benjamin Grierson of Illinois, who headed the 10th Cavalry. (George Armstrong Custer refused an assignment with the 9th and managed to obtain a spot with the white 7th.) The 24th Infantry was organized in 1869 from two regiments stationed in Louisiana, Texas and New Mexico. Their first commanding officer was Colonel Ranald McKenzie, and William R. Shafter served as lieutenant colonel. The 25th Infantry was organized in New Orleans in 1869 from remnants of the 39th from North Carolina and the 40th stationed in Louisiana. The troops signed up for an enlistment of five years. Most were illiterate, and the army set about teaching them to read and write by assigning a chaplain to the task.

According to some historians, the Buffalo Soldiers were not treated equally with the white soldiers by the government.[11] However, in *The Black Regulars, 1860–1898*, authors William Dobak and Thomas Phillips state that the Negro troops were "Armed and equipped, clothed, fed, housed, and paid the same as whites"; and that "The army furnished all its soldiers alike with the same food, clothing, housing, and equipment and expected them to accomplish the same tasks."[12]

Dobak and Phillips assert that, "Given the army's small size and its vast responsibilities, the War Department did not dare to reduce the effectiveness of one-tenth of its force by discriminating against the black regiments in the distribution of weapons and equipment," and that "The army did not cripple one-fifth of the mounted troops by deliberately assigning poor horses to the 9th and 10th Cavalry."[13] The authors note that "Army records show that black troopers were sometimes poorly mounted. It is clear, though, that these shortages were common throughout the cavalry and that the white regiments were often no better off."[14] Dobak and Phillips conclude: "The black regulars faced racial prejudice from individuals both inside the army and out. In the army, though, they found an organization that needed their services and that could not afford to discriminate against them in the matters of food, housing, clothing and equipment."[15]

By August 1867, nine companies of the 10th Cavalry had been organized. Three were assigned to Indian Territory, and the others were sent to posts and camps in central Kansas where the Kansas Pacific Railroad was being constructed. The spring and summer of 1867 meant the 9th and 10th cavalries moved west. They were on the Great Plains or in the southwest of west Texas, Arizona and New Mexico for the next 20 years to patrol the Mexican border, fight Indians and protect citizens on the frontier, although most citizens (especially in west Texas) hated Negro soldiers. The Buffalo Soldiers had a thankless task.

Flipper was originally ordered to report to Fort Concho, in west Texas, but at Houston he was informed that his company was en route to Fort Sill, Indian Territory (now Oklahoma), so his orders were changed to go to Fort Sill. Flipper reported for duty at Fort Sill and "From the moment I reached Sill I haven't experienced anything but happiness. I am not isolated. I am not ostracized by a single officer." While at Fort Sill, Flipper wrote, "My mind shudders, shrinks from the sweet and yet sad anticipations of the years I have not seen and may perhaps never see. But there is a sweetness, a fondness that makes me linger longingly upon the thought of those unborn days."[16]

When Lieutenant Henry Flipper arrived at Fort Sill, he was assigned to be post signal officer and taught the troops military signals. The captain of Flipper's company, Nicholas Nolan, was a widower with a son and a daughter. After the company had settled at Fort Sill, Nolan returned to San Antonio where the captain, who was over fifty, married Annie Dwyer, who was twenty-one. Nolan brought Annie and her sister, Mollie Dwyer, back to Fort Sill, and Annie insisted Flipper share meals with them. Flipper began going horseback riding with Mollie Dwyer and notes that "On Sundays we and other officers and their ladies used to chase coyotes and jackrabbits on the plains."[17]

Flipper had some interesting experiences at Fort Sill. Once, an infantry officer, Lt. S.R. Whitall, had been sent to arrest an Indian. Flipper described the officer as "a mean, brutal, overbearing fellow" and said "the Indians fired on him and he failed to get his man." So Flipper was sent to arrest the Indian. Flipper took ten men in a covered wagon with him but approached the Indian camp alone and talked to them in Indian sign language. They consented to hand over the Indian suspect if two friends could go with him. Flipper agreed and arrived at the adjutant's office with his prisoner the next morning, while Whitall was "dumfounded [*sic*], surly and discourteous." "He did not like me anyway," remarked Flipper.[18]

Lieutenant Colonel J.W. Davidson had given orders that no one was allowed to walk on the grass when crossing the parade ground. Flipper was officer of the day when he was summoned to the parade ground around 11:00 one morning because the sentinel had arrested Davidson's son (who was 18 or 19 years old) and put him in the guardhouse. Flipper, who refused to release the boy because his orders were to arrest anyone violating this order, was summoned to the general's quarters. There, Flipper found himself in the midst of a family argument, with Mrs. Davidson yelling, "I want you to let my boy out of that guardhouse at once"; the general countered with "You keep him there till I order his release. I'll teach him a lesson." Mrs. Davidson continued arguing until the general said, "Madam, I'll have you to know I'm the commanding officer of this post," whereupon she promptly replied, "And I'll have you to understand I'm your commanding officer."[19] Davidson's son was eventually released.

At Fort Sill there were a number of shallow ponds in the 40-mile stretch between the fort and the Red River that collected water during the rainy season. These ponds held stagnant water most of the year, which caused a number of cases of malaria at the fort and led to the deaths of a number of soldiers. Flipper was assigned by Davidson to supervise digging a ditch that would drain these ponds. Flipper had the services of a company of cavalry to help him carry out this duty. After the ditch was finished, the commanding officer and some other officers came and inspected it. Davidson got down in the ditch and told Flipper the grade was wrong — the water would have to run uphill to get out. Although to the eye it appeared that Davidson was right, Flipper stood his ground and insisted the ditch would drain the water. When the rains came, the ditch carried the water away so there were no more ponds and the cases of malaria went down. This became known as "Flipper's Ditch."

In November 1879, Flipper led a group of twenty soldiers and a guide with two wagons to the Staked Plains of Texas, in the western part of the state, to investigate a large lake which had reportedly been discovered there. Since this was a dry, arid area, a source of water could open up the area for settlement. On the way the group stopped to camp at "Tepee City," whose inhabitants included one family living in a dugout house carved out of the side of a hill. Before dinner the man of the house came to the soldiers and asked who was in charge. After Flipper was pointed out to him, the man asked Flipper to administer the oath of office of postmistress to his wife. Flipper protested that he had no authority to do this. But the man insisted his wife was unable to ride over one hundred miles to Fort Worth for the oath to be administered, and government papers stated that any army officer could administer this oath. Flipper had dinner with the family — fried venison with bacon, some fruit, coffee with cream, milk, butter — and then administered the office.

The dinner was a nice break from the usual fare of fried bacon and soldier bread that Flipper lived on in the army. Flipper described "Soldier bread," a staple in the cavalry's diet, as "Flour ... mixed with salt and water into a rather stiff dough. It is then put into a Dutch oven till about an inch thick. Water is then poured in till about an inch deep. The lid is put on and a hot fire is maintained under and over the oven till the water is all converted into steam and the bread completely serrated [sic]. When hot and freshly made it is good and very palatable, but when it gets cold, it falls and becomes hard and soggy and a mule can't eat it."[20]

Flipper's life at Fort Sill included dealing with Indians, who were often fed by the government. For about four or five months Flipper served as commander of "G" Troop because Captain Phil L. Lee was under arrest and another first lieutenant was on sick leave. Lee was the cousin of General Robert E. Lee but had served in the Union army during the Civil War; he and Flipper became close friends while they were stationed at Fort Sill. While at Fort Sill, Flipper oversaw the building of a road from that fort to Gainesville, Texas.

During his time at Fort Sill, Henry Flipper wrote his autobiography, *The Colored Cadet at West Point*. It was published by Homer Lee & Co. in New York in 1878. This was one of the first autobiographies by a black man.

Frederick Douglass did not publish his autobiography, *The Life and Times of Frederick Douglass*, until 1881 and Booker T. Washington's autobiography, *Up From Slavery*, was not published until 1900. Other books by blacks followed, but Flipper was the first of a number of prominent African Americans to write his life story for the American public.

Flipper and his company were ordered to go to Fort Elliott, Texas, in November 1879. The company left ahead of Flipper, who remained behind and started about an hour later. As Flipper traveled on the road out of Fort Sill, he looked back at the Fort from the top of a hill, where he stopped and "wept like a child." It was "the last time in my life I have ever found it possible to weep," said Flipper. "I hated to leave Fort Sill." Flipper saw Fort Sill only one more time, a year later, when he and his troop marched through on the way to the Rio Grande.[21]

At Fort Elliott, located in the panhandle of Texas, Flipper was made post adjutant, serving as the executive officer of the fort, the ranking officer on the commanding officer's staff, in charge of transacting all the fort's business. The senior officer was Captain Nolan. During his time there, Flipper was sent to investigate the case of a large amount of ammunition which had been stolen from the ordnance room. Flipper went to Atascosa, a little town on the New Mexico border inhabited mostly by Mexicans. Flipper arrived on a Sunday morning with a dozen men and searched every house, looking for the ammunition. Finally, he went to a store owned by a Mr. McMasters and there, in the back room, he found the paper packages the ammunition came packed in — but not a single cartridge. McMasters could not explain how the wrappings got there, so Flipper took a number of the papers and reported back to Fort Elliott.

The U.S. marshall at Fort Worth went to Atascosa and returned with the mail rider and another man. It turned out the quartermaster sergeant in charge of the ammunition had been stealing it and sending it through the country by mail rider to sell to the cowboys. The soldier was sent to Leavenworth for three years. A friend of the guilty soldier had burned down the office of the commanding officer in order to destroy the court-martial records, but the papers were saved because Flipper had taken them to his quarters to read.

At Fort Elliott, the two prisoners were kept overnight in the guardhouse, which led to Nolan and Flipper being charged by a grand jury for violating the law that stated the army could not be used for arresting or holding civilians. Eventually, Captain Nolan went to Fort Worth, stood before the court and pleaded guilty, whereupon he was fined one dollar. Nolan asked that the same plea, and same fine, be levied against Flipper and it was done. Nolan paid the two dollars and then left.

A Negro officer in the army created an awkward situation for the officer corps. In the field and in day-to-day work at the fort, there were generally no problems. Each man did the job assigned to him, and if he was competent and worked well with others, there were no difficulties. There was the uncomfortable situation of a black officer commanding white men — even a white private often considered himself superior to a black officer — but this was solved in Flipper's case because he was in the 10th Cavalry, an all black regiment. Also, he was a second lieutenant, the most junior officer.

The awkwardness occurred after hours, when officers and their families held picnics, outings and dinner parties. Henry Flipper was single, and having a single black man in a social setting around white women was a social taboo. Black men were often viewed as sexual creatures who were a threat to white women because (1) they could not control themselves or (2) the women, weak because of their sex, could not control themselves. And there was nothing more taboo than the thought of sexual relations between a black man and a white woman.

There was also the idea of "place," where each member of society knew their "place" and remained there. The rich were superior to poor, educated were superior to uneducated, those who came from aristocratic families were superior to those from lower class families, and whites were superior to blacks. In the 21st century these ideas seem ridiculous and hard to grasp; however, they were a common assumption of 19th century society, and one of the keys to getting along in this world was knowing your place.

Flipper was certainly aware of knowing his "place" when he received an invitation from Mrs. J.A. Maney, wife of Lt. J.A. Maney of the 23rd Infantry (white) for a birthday party at their quarters one day at Fort Elliott. He "did not go because [he] thought it was only a courtesy invitation." Flipper went to bed early but was roused by Lt. and Mrs. Maney, who insisted he come to their party, which he did. When he arrived, people were dancing. "She wanted me to get right into it with her," said Flipper, "but I could not. It was beyond me." A square dance followed, and she insisted he dance with her "against my protest" and they danced. After that, "I had to dance every square dance ... with her or some other lady till the dancing ended."[22]

4

At Fort Davis

Flipper and several troops were ordered to go into the field in the spring of 1880 to engage in the campaign against the Mescalaro Apache leader Victorio, who led his war party through New Mexico, southwest Texas and northern Mexico. The trip involved a 1200 mile march, and when they reached the Red River the group could not cross because it was flooded. For the next several days, they waited but the rain continued to fall. Finally, Flipper devised a plan where the wagons were unloaded and a tent fly was wrapped around the body of one wagon, making it a boat. Then a man swam across the river with a rope that was tied to the wagon; he secured the rope to a tree. This resulted in the wagon becoming a ferry that carried their supplies, the women and children across the river. After this the men swam the horses and mules across.

Lieutenant Flipper took part in the Indian Wars, a set of battles the army conducted against Native Americans in the West. The primary job of the U.S. Army after the Civil War was to make the West safe for settlers. This meant the elimination of the threat of Indians in the West, so the army established reservations, coerced Native Americans to settle on these reservations and, if they would not, waged war against them. It also involved the destruction of the buffalo, because the Indian culture depended so heavily on these animals, as well as the establishment of Indian treaties, which provided land and peace for Indians but were inevitably broken and thus led to more bloodshed.

The period from 1866 to 1891 is the era of the Indian Wars in the West, although the history of warfare against the Indians certainly goes back to the 17th century, when English settlers first came to the United States. From 1789 to 1865 there were fights with Indians in the Old Northwest (Indiana and Ohio); the battle of Fallen Timbers (1794) saw "Mad" Anthony Wayne lead troops (including Meriwether Lewis and William Clark) in a victory against Indians. In November 1811 William Henry Harrison defeated Tecumseh's village of Tippecanoe. In 1813 Tecumseh was killed at the battle of the Thames, and Andrew Jackson defeated the Creek Indians at Horseshoe Bend in 1814. During the 1820s and 1830s, there was a great deal of Indian removal from eastern lands but it was generally peaceful. There was the Black Hawk War of 1832 and the second Seminole War (1835–1842) in the East, while in Oregon Territory there was the Rogue River War, Yakima War and the Campaign of 1858 to defeat Indians there. During the Civil War, there was the Minnesota Uprising (1862), and the army moved against the Sioux in Dakota Territory. There was also the Sand Creek Massacre (1864) in Colorado, wars in the Southwest and fighting in California. But it was not until after the Civil War that the army turned its full attention to the West and the Native Americans living there. By this time, Indians had been virtually removed from all lands east of the Mississippi, and the Great Plains between the Mississippi River and the Rocky Mountains were home to most American Indians.

The Indian Wars were not "wars" in the traditional sense; certainly the methods and reasons for the army fighting contrasted sharply with the methods and reasons for the Indians fighting. Therein lies the essential problem in this "war." First, the army was structured for full-scale warfare in which large armies organized and attacked one another; the Indians, on the other hand, did not engage in this type of warfare. Instead, they used the element of surprise, avoided large-scale confrontations and preferred to hit quickly and then retreat and isolate settlers or soldiers in order to win. For the army, it was a war that was conducted as a series of small skirmishes; for the Indians, it was an attempt at self-preservation as they engaged in battles for their homes and lives.

The army had to clear roads into the West so settlers and freighters could pass; the Indians were in the way. Further, the army had to ensure that settlers in the West were safe from Indian attacks. Thus the first "war" was Red Cloud's War (1866–1868), which the army lost. This war involved the Bozeman Trail, which went right through Sioux and Cheyenne territory on the way to the Montana goldfields. This war led to the Fetterman Massacre and Wagon Box Fight and concluded with the Treaty of Fort Laramie when the army agreed to abandon its forts along the Bozeman Trail and the Indians burned them to the ground. But the Indian victory was short-lived and, in the long run, almost irrelevant.

During the period from 1865 to 1868, there were fights against the Snake and Paiute Indians in California, culminating in the battle of Infernal Caverns (1867). From 1867 to 1869 there were a number of fights on the Texas plains against the Comanche, Kiowa, Arapaho and Cheyenne Indians. After the Treaty of Medicine Lodge (1867), in which Indians agreed to settle on permanent reservations in Indian Territory, Major General Philip Sheridan planned a winter campaign to punish all renegade Indians. This led to the battle of the Washita (1868), in which General George Armstrong Custer destroyed an Indian village.

On the West Coast, the Modoc War (1872–1873) began after the Modoc Indians, under Captain Jack, left the Klamath Reservation and holed up in the Lava Beds in northern California, where 50 Indians held off about 400 soldiers before their leaders were captured and hung in October 1873. Meanwhile, in the Southwest, General George Crook, head of the Department of Arizona, used Buffalo Soldiers against the Apache. In Texas there was the Red River War, which ended in June 1875 when Quanah Parker surrendered.

During 1876–1877, the army organized a campaign against the northern Cheyenne and Sioux to clear the Montana-Wyoming and Black Hills regions. An ultimatum was given in November 1875 for all Indians to move to reservations, but few complied. This led to a series of military engagements, beginning with a war on the Powder River in March 1876. In May and June, a huge concentration of Indian warriors, led by Sitting Bull and Crazy Horse, gathered in the Bighorn-Yellowstone region. This led to the battle of the Rosebud (June 17, 1876) and the battle of the Little Bighorn (June 25, 1876), in which Custer and the Seventh Cavalry were slaughtered. Although this was a major victory for the Indians — and a major defeat for the army — this latter battle mobilized public opinion against the Indians and inspired the army, the public and Congress to wipe out the troublesome Indians once and for all. This resolve led to the final stage of the Indian Wars.

In 1877 the Nez Perce War occurred because Chief Joseph and his people were ordered off their homelands after gold was discovered there. Chief Joseph led his people 1,700 miles but was captured about 30 miles from the Canadian border after winning a series of skirmishes against the army. Sitting Bull and Crazy Horse had gone to Canada but came back in May 1877 to the Red Cloud Agency and surrendered. There was the Bannock War in 1878 in the Oregon-Idaho-Wyoming area; wars against the Ute in Colorado and Utah that led to the Meeker Massacre; and during 1866–1886, wars against the Apache in Arizona and New Mexico that ended with the capture of Geronimo. The war in the Southwest was the last major campaign waged by the army against the Indians.

Victorio was a successor to the Apache leader Mangas Colorado. On September 2, 1877, Victorio led a group of Apaches away from the San Carlos Reservation on the upper Gila River in Arizona. For two years — from 1877 to 1879 — Victorio led his group around New Mexico, looking for a home that satisfied both his people and the American government. Victorio and his band of Apaches were harassed by soldiers and Indian police until they surrendered at Fort Wingate, New Mexico. The army held them at Ojo Caliente, their old home, for almost a year before they decided to return the Apache to San Carlos. The women, children and old men traveled back to the Arizona reservation but Victorio refused to return and, with about 80 men, took to the mountains. Victorio wanted to settle at Ojo Caliente and stayed there until September 4, 1879, when he was convinced he was about to be arrested and tried. On September 6, an eight-man herd guard to Company E, Ninth Cavalry, was killed by Victorio and about 60 Apaches.

In September and October, Victorio and his band of Apaches killed several settlers while the Ninth Cavalry pursued them. Then Victorio headed for Mexico, chased by Major A.P. Morrow, who had to return to the American side of the Rio Grande. The Apaches stayed in the Candelaria Mountains of Chihuahua, where they were joined by 70–90 more men. The Indians wiped out two parties of Mexicans — killing 26 men — so General Trevino organized an expedition against them in late December 1879. In January, they came back across the border into the United States and clashed several times with Major Morrow's troops.

Flipper and the other soldiers took the field against Victorio. The Apaches had been driven into Mexico by the 9th Cavalry (colored). The Apaches then returned to Texas. Here they were met by two troops from the 10th Cavalry (colored) and some of 9th Cavalry (colored) and 8th Cavalry (white), along with a company of Texas Rangers. The troops set up in Fort Quitman, an abandoned fort on the Texas side of the Rio Grande, where Flipper was made post quartermaster and acting commissary of substance.

Flipper and two other men were sent to Eagle Springs, about 100 miles away, after two survivors from an Indian raid against soldiers some forty miles away arrived in only their underclothing at the camp and reported the attack. Flipper rode hard, for twenty-two hours straight and mostly at night, through hostile Indian country, and arrived at the tent of General Grierson to give his report. "I felt no bad effects from the hard ride till I reached the General's tent," reported Flipper. "When I attempted to dismount, I found I was stiff and sore and fell from my horse to the ground." This woke up the general, who asked Flipper what was the matter. The sentinel had to answer for Flipper while another man unsaddled his horse and laid the saddle blanket on the ground. Flipper "rolled over on it and with the saddle for a pillow, slept till the sun shining in my face woke me next morning."[1] Flipper then rode back to Fort Quitman.

The morning after Flipper left, Colonel Grierson was traveling by ambulance with an escort of six troops when he was attacked by Indians. The army group took refuge behind some rocks and sent a courier to the troops with Flipper at Fort Quitman. Flipper and his troops rode hard for 15–20 miles to join the fight. They found "G" Troop already there with heavy fighting underway. "We got right into it and soon had the Indians on the run," said Flipper. The soldiers lost several men and 19 horses, and some soldiers were wounded, including an officer. They killed 19 Indians. The soldiers were buried where they fell and Flipper was "detailed to read the Episcopal service over them." Then "a volley was fired and the buglers sounded taps." Flipper stated that "This was the first and only time I was under fire, but escaped without a scratch."[2]

Several days later, the troops received word the Indians had returned from Mexico and a trap was laid for them at Fresno Spring. From one in the afternoon until midnight, the soldiers rode without resting, set up a cold camp (no lights or fires), and kept their horses saddled. Around 11:00 the next morning the Indians entered the canyon. A wagon train headed to Eagle Springs from Fort Davis had been diverted to Fresno Spring and the Indians saw it and attacked, forcing the soldiers to come out of their hiding places and open fire. "The Indians turned and fled and we never saw them again," remembered Flipper, "although we took up the trail and followed them."[3]

The Tenth Calvary, commanded by Colonel Benjamin Grierson, chased Victorio, who on August 4 moved northwest. On August 7, Captain Thomas C. Lebo and his troops came upon Victorio's supply camp in the Sierra Diablo Mountains and destroyed it. Since he could not reach water and had no fresh beef, Victorio returned to the Tres Castillas in Mexico on August 11. On October 1, American troops under Colonel Eugene Carr and Colonel George Buell and Mexican troops under Colonel Joaquin Terrazas were hit by the Apaches at Tres Castillas in the Candelaria Mountains. Terrazas ordered the Americans to return across the border, then, with his Mexican troops, he attacked Victorio, killing him, 60 warriors and eighteen women and children.[4]

On September 18, 1880, the *Indianapolis Leader* printed a letter from Lieutenant Flipper extolling the new paper for the Negro community. In the letter, Flipper wrote, "We are, to too great an extent, a local people. Hardly a man of any prominence in any community is known outside that community. This is a source of great weakness to us, and is not as it should be. Our prominent men should be known to each other and to their people. Otherwise we are 'unknown and unknowing' and the 'status quo' of any people is its death."

Flipper continues:

> I read the "news" and "jottings" from the various sources with great care and pleasure and profit. Many persons of both sexes are brought to my notice, of whom I desire to know more and with whom I hope to have personal acquaintance when opportunity offers.
>
> The interchange of ideas and opinions so judiciously fostered by the *Leader* is most beneficial to the race in every way. It is educating them, draining out of them what the Creator has put in them and elevating and ennobling them in every respect. It is a great educator. I read and study it as carefully and assiduously as I do my "Theory and Practice of Courts-martial," or any other of my professional books. I could not and would not do without it now that it has become a part of my being.[5]

In a plea for subscriptions, the *Leader* often ran under a headline "Subscribe for the Leader," "Let every colored man who favors the elevation of his race subscribe for the *Leader*; and let every white man who believes that slavery was a crime against humanity and that it is the duty of the ruling race to aid the Negro in his struggle for moral, social and intellectual elevation do likewise."[6]

Colonel Grierson, regional commander of the 10th Cavalry (Fort Davis Historic Site).

In December at Fort Davis, two officers went on leave, which led Major N.B. McLaughlen, who was in command of the fort, to appoint Lieutenant Flipper as acting assistant quartermaster and post quartermaster and acting commissary of subsistence and post commissary. These were jobs generally assigned to a junior officer of Flipper's rank. The

Fort Davis in 1871 (Fort Davis Historic Site).

quartermaster was responsible for all the property and vehicles on the fort, the care and feeding of the animals at the fort and the hiring of civilian employees. The commissary was, essentially, a grocery store. Soldiers received a ration from the army but could purchase other items of food at the commissary. Flipper and his company were out of the field until May 1881. During May, June and July, Flipper's company was in the field, while Flipper remained at the post.

Sitting at dinner in his quarters one evening in February 1881, Flipper looked out his window and saw the haystacks on fire. There was eight to ten inches of snow on the ground at the time. All afternoon and night, Flipper and the troops worked to put out the fire, which consumed one stack; but the others were saved. Flipper was covered with ice from throwing buckets of water on the fire; the water that missed or splashed back was frozen on his high cavalry boots.

Flipper believed the fire had been started by a white clerk whom he had discharged, although this was never proved. Several days later, Flipper took to his bed with a severe case of typhoid malarial fever, which he had probably contracted at Fort Sill. There was no medicine on the post. The post surgeon and commanding officer, Major McLaughlin, stayed with Flipper, sitting up all night with him. One night, the post surgeon sent for McLaughlin and told him that Flipper would probably not live the next hour. However, Flipper gradually recovered, although the first time he tried to ride his horse after this illness, he "couldn't hold him. I had to call a soldier to help me down and take me home and the horse to the stable."[7]

Captain Nolan was also assigned to Fort Davis, and his wife and his sister-in-law, Molly, joined him, which allowed Flipper to continue riding with Mollie Dwyer. Lieutenant Pratt was replaced by 1st Lieutenant Charles Cooper, who was soon promoted and replaced by 1st Lieutenant Charles E. Nordstrom. Flipper and Nordstrom shared a set of double quarters that had a common entrance and common hall. According to Flipper, Nordstrom "came from the civil war Army, was a Swede from Maine, had no education and was a brute." He reported that Nordstrom "hated me and gradually won Miss Dwyer from her horseback rides with me and himself took her riding in a buggy he had."[8]

Major McLaughlin was replaced by Colonel W.R. Shafter of the 1st Infantry (white) as commanding officer of Fort Davis on March 12, 1881. In *Pecos Bill: A Military Biography of William R. Shafter*, biographer Paul Carlson states that Shafter "drank heartily, gambled earnestly, ate plentifully and cursed incessantly.... People often pictured him as a fat, incompetent buffoon of a field commander." However, Carlson noted that Shafter was "energetic, ambitious, and determined.... He epitomized the American frontier type" because "once he understood what had to be done, he wasted little time in formalities but assumed responsibility, gave orders, and took action. His drive was intense."[9]

William Rufus Shafter was born October 16, 1835, near Galesburg, Michigan, the son of an abolitionist whose cabin may have been used as a station on the underground railroad by runaway slaves on their way to Canada. Shafter taught school, then enlisted in the army in June 1861, shortly after the start of the Civil War. During the Peninsula Campaign, Shafter fought in the battle of Fair Oaks Station, about seven miles east of Richmond, and was commended for his bravery. Thirty-two years after that battle, he was awarded the Congressional Medal of Honor.

While serving as an officer in Tennessee during the Civil War, according to Carlson, "Only a few of the enlisted men and fellow officers liked Shafter. Some believed his attention to detail and discipline too severe; others, cowed by his harassment, were bitter and resentful." He was described by a fellow officer as "a gambler and a mean skunk so the officers and men say ... a man without principles."[10]

During the Civil War, Shafter recruited and organized a command of black troops during a time when most army officers refused to serve with black troops. In the battle of Nashville, December 15 and 16, 1864, Shafter and his colored troops were heavily engaged in the action; 85 of his officers and enlisted men were killed during that battle. Shafter left the army in October 1866, spent a short time teaching school, then applied for a commission in the army. In late January 1867, Shafter accepted the rank of lieutenant colonel of the Forty-First United States Infantry, one of the new black regiments. He received his commission because white officers did not want to work with colored troops.

Photo. by Van Sickle, Kalamazoo

Colonel William "Pecos Bill" Shafter, Flipper's commanding officer at Fort Davis (Fort Davis Historic Site).

In June 1867, Shafter moved to Texas with the 41st Infantry, where he served under Colonel Ranald S. Mackenzie. The 41st was consolidated with the 36th and became the 24th Infantry in 1869. Shafter spent most of the next fifteen years in Texas, commanding black troops and fighting Indians. He was not loved by his men, who filed misconduct changes twice against him. In March 1868, Shafter "swore at and publicly upbraided several of the men.... The angry men did not forget the humiliation and a year later filed several serious misconduct charges" against him, including harassment and unlawful behavior. The second incident, where he granted the illegal use of an ambulance and hospital "for his troops to hold a fandango," occurred in late 1868. Four general charges were filed against him: "conduct to the prejudice of good order and military discipline; conduct unbecoming an officer and a gentleman; disobedience of orders; and violation of the law."[11] In both cases there was no action taken against Shafter by the army.

Biographer Carlson describes Shafter as "a responsible, if coarse and abrasive, officer.... The flaws did not seriously disturb Shafter or his happiness and peace of mind. He was a bulky, lumbering, disheveled man, with distinctive features and blue eyes that peered out from shaggy brows. He talked quickly and cockily, his language concise, pungent, and often sarcastically profane."[12] Carlson adds that Shafter "got into fights with his men and looked down disdainfully from his huge frame upon the Spanish-speaking people among whom he lived and with whom he dealt. Some people believed that he regularly took licentious liberties with young women while on military leave in San Antonio."[13] Carlson notes that, "although he had difficulty getting along with subordinates and enlisted men, his superiors believed that he was a reliable officer who got results." In his 1875 campaign to reach the Pecos River, he drove his men hard, an act which earned him the nickname "Pecos Bill."[14]

In 1875, when Shafter turned 40, he stood five feet eleven inches and weighed "almost 230 pounds." He was described as "corpulent, but nevertheless considered the most energetic man of his rank in the department ... enjoying the respect but rarely the affection of his men, who viewed him as coarse, abusive, and gruff.... To many men he was a volatile martinet."[15] During the fall and winter of 1874 and 1875, Shafter was involved in the Red River War, which sought to stop Indians from cattle rustling, thieving and harassing ranchers and settlements. This war was initiated by General Philip Sheridan in response to pressure from congressmen in western territories and states to provide safety for ranchers and settlers in their districts. The settlers pressured congressmen to support legislation favoring the white pioneers and, since the seats of these congressmen depended upon the votes of these settlers, Congress demanded action against the Indians by the army.

Shafter was sent to West Texas to an area known as the Staked Plains (Llano Estacado), which is a flat area with "an almost limitless ocean of waving grass, sunshine, and space nearly unbroken by rolling hills or gully-washed river valleys ... void of timber [and which] had only scattered water holes, and lacked adequate landmarks."[16] During this campaign, Shafter and his black troops covered 2,500 miles, mapped the area and cleared it of Indians.

In 1880, upon assuming command of Fort Davis, Shafter assigned Major McLaughlen the duty of ordnance officer and appointed his regimental adjutant, First Lieutenant Louis Wilhelmi, as post adjutant to replace Lieutenant Nordstrom. Shafter and Wilhelmi had served together and became friends in 1879 when both served with the First Infantry at Fort Randall in the Dakota Territory. Lieutenant Flipper was relieved of his job as quartermaster; but, since Shafter had no acting commissary of substance, Flipper remained in that position.

The commissary was an adobe building at the south end of Fort Davis consisting of an office and a storehouse. The commissary sergeant, who was Carl Ross during Flipper's tenure, handled the day to day work of the commissary, keeping the books, recording the sales and preparing reports. As commissary officer, Flipper's job involved making major decisions, relaying instructions and holding overall responsibility for the commissary.

Lieutenant Flipper had two bosses as commissary officer. As commander of Fort Davis, Colonel Shafter was one boss, and the other was the chief commissary of subsistence for the Department of Texas, located in San Antonio. During most of Flipper's tenure, that was Major Michael P. Small. From Fort Davis to San Antonio was almost 500 miles; there was a telegraph line connecting the two places and mail was delivered twice weekly by stagecoach.

Each day, commissary money was received from the sales of foodstuff to individuals. Officers received credit and usually paid by check, while enlisted men were required to pay in cash. Sergeant Ross recorded the money received in a ledger and kept it in the office safe until the total funds for the week were turned over to Lieutenant Flipper on Saturday. These funds were comprised of Mexican as well as American money and checks from officers. Since the area where Fort Davis was located was continually threatened by Indians and outlaws — both American and Mexican — the funds, which were sent from other forts as soon as possible after the end of each month, were not sent regularly to San Antonio. Instead, the commissary officer sent a "Statement of Funds" each week to San Antonio, and in this way the chief commissary was informed of the commissary funds at the Fort.

Each week, Lieutenant Flipper filled out a standard issue form reporting the amount of commissary funds at the fort on Saturday, and Sergeant Ross prepared a statement for Flipper's signature reporting these funds. There were two copies of this report submitted to the commanding officer along with the funds on hand. The commanding officer was required to count the funds, confirm that the amount on hand was the same as what was reported on the forms, and then sign the form where it said "Examined and found correct." One copy was sent to the chief commissary of subsistence in San Antonio, and the other was sent directly to the commissary general at the War Department in Washington.

Colonel Shafter had a routine of inspecting and signing this report on Sunday morning, unless he was off the post, and then Captain Kinzie Bates, his second in command, signed the forms. In addition to the commissary report, Colonel Shafter inspected the soldiers and buildings each Sunday morning and allowed the men at the fort to attend chapel or spend time with their family or in recreation after the garrison passed inspection.

The inspection of commissary funds and signing the report was a routine affair. After the forms were signed, the commissary officer was in charge of the funds; however, unlike other commissary officers, Flipper kept the funds in a trunk in his private quarters instead of in a safe in the commissary or quartermaster offices. The commissary office had a small safe where Sergeant Ross kept the books and sales receipts, while the quartermaster's office had two large safes. Flipper said he kept the funds in his private quarters because "I felt more secure to have them in my own personal custody."[17] Shafter was apparently unaware the funds were kept in Flipper's quarters.

The officers' quarters at Fort Davis were built to house one officer; however, since there were not enough quarters at Fort Davis for all the officers, they shared quarters. Lieutenant Flipper's quarters at Fort Davis consisted of two rooms; the front room was a sitting room facing the parade ground, and the back room was a bedroom. The quarters at Fort Davis were built like a duplex, with a common hall between the two sections and a front porch extending in front of the building. Lieutenant Nordstrom lived in the quarters adjoining Flipper's.

Lieutenant Flipper had two servants at Fort Davis. Walter D. Cox, a soldier in Company A of the 10th Cavalry, took care of his horse, while Lucy E. Smith took care of his home, doing cooking, cleaning and washing. Lucy Smith was possibly Henry Flipper's mistress at Fort Davis and, if so, this no doubt caused much gossip amongst the officers and their wives, especially if she had a husband living at Fort Stockton, about a day's ride away. Lucy was known as "Mrs. Smith," and speculation that her husband lived at Fort Stockton comes because she visited that fort in the spring or early summer, about four months after she started working for Flipper. After this brief interlude, she returned to Flipper.[18]

Lucy Smith kept some of her clothes in Henry Flipper's personal trunk, which sat in Flipper's sitting room. This was the same trunk where Flipper kept the funds from the commissary. Flipper supposedly kept his trunk locked and each time Lucy needed to get into the trunk, she asked him for the key.

As a second lieutenant of cavalry, Henry Flipper earned $125 a month, but his commissary bill showed that he purchased a large amount of groceries on credit. In addition to buying food for his own household, Flipper probably gave credit to enlisted men and others — who were not entitled to credit — and these amounts were put on his commissary bill. This practice has been ascribed to Flipper's generous and open-hearted nature.[19]

On April 16, 1882, Flipper sent the commissary funds to San Antonio; however, in mid–May Flipper realized that the cash he had was less than what he should have. He tried to cover this up by changing the amounts written in ink by Sergeant Ross and recording a different amount. The cash kept disappearing from his trunk and by the end of that month there was a deficiency of $800.66. During this period, Colonel Shafter signed off on the commissary fund report once and Captain Bates signed off twice because the amount recorded was the same as the funds they counted. However, the amounts originally recorded by Sergeant Ross — and unchanged — were sent to the commissary general in Washington.

One conclusion is that someone was stealing money from Flipper's trunk. But who? Lucy Smith is a logical person because she had access to the key to Flipper's trunk and probably kept the key for periods of time. Flipper trusted Lucy, so if she was stealing money from him — or if she allowed others access to the trunk to take money — he was apparently unaware of it.

On May 9, Flipper received a telegram from Major Michael Small, the chief commissary in San Antonio, stating he would be away from his headquarters during that month and requesting that no funds be invoiced until June. During May and June, there was no contact between Major Small and Lieutenant Flipper while Small was on an inspection tour of Forts. (Fort Davis was not on his itinerary.)

During June, Sergeant Ross prepared commissary statements which were signed by Flipper but not by Shafter (who was at the Fort on three Sundays) or Bates (who was in command on one Sunday). Flipper kept these statements in his private quarters. Later, Flipper stated that as the chief commissary was absent from his headquarters, this meant that all activities connected to the funds were suspended until he returned. However, Colonel Shafter and Captain Bates — who would probably not remember an individual instance of an activity as routine as this — believed they had signed the forms. But it is also possible that Colonel Shafter was lax and did not fulfill one of his duties as commanding officer.

The fiscal year ran July 1 to June 30, and on the last day of June for the 1880–1881 fiscal year, Lieutenant Flipper notified the commissary general at the War Department that he had on hand $3,791.77, which was the amount recorded by Sergeant Ross. The problem was that he actually had much less.

On Saturday afternoon, July 2, news arrived at Fort Davis that President

James Garfield had been shot in the railway station in Washington; Flipper heard the news from Lieutenant Wilhelmi, who came to Flipper's quarters with the news. At this point, the name of the assailant was unknown. Upon hearing the news, Colonel Shafter cancelled all nonessential activities on the post and ordered the flag to fly at half mast. The news on Sunday was encouraging; it looked like the president would recover, so Flipper announced that the burro races, originally scheduled for July 4, would be held the following Sunday, July 10. On July 6, activities on all forts resumed their regular activities. For the rest of the summer, everyone was attuned to the condition of the president, lying in a hospital in Washington. It was especially a distraction for the military because the president is their commander in chief.

On June 29, Major Small sent a notification to all commissary officers that all funds from fiscal 1880–1881 must be sent to him in San Antonio to forward to the commissary general in Washington. Flipper received this notice from Major Small on July 8 and knew he had to find some way to come up with $3,791.77 to send to San Antonio. However, Flipper put this notice in his desk in his quarters; he did not reply to the request. That same day, department headquarters ordered Colonel Shafter to inspect the funds and books of the quartermaster and commissary departments. At this point, there was a difference of $1,440.43 between the amount Flipper had reported to have on hand and what was actually on hand.

Henry Flipper had not received any royalties from Homer Lee and Company, which had published his autobiography, *The Colored Cadet*. Flipper believed they had sold 5,000 copies at $2 apiece and this meant $10,000 in gross income, which translated to $2,500 in author royalties. Flipper had notified Homer Lee and Company to deposit his royalties in a bank in San Antonio. Believing that money had been sent from Homer Lee — but that he had not been notified of it — Flipper wrote a personal check for $1,440.43 and placed it in the commissary funds. The problem was that Flipper had no account at that bank and Homer Lee and Company had not sent a royalty check of any amount. That meant that Henry Flipper submitted a fraudulent check.

When Colonel Shafter sat in the commissary office with Sergeant Ross and Lieutenant Flipper to verify the accounts, he held the check Flipper had written and said to the Lieutenant, "This is a very large check, Mr. Flipper." Flipper's reply, according to the Colonel, when asked later, was "Yes, but I have been troubled getting exchange and have put it in San Antonio at my own risk in small amounts, and have drawn my own check for the amount."[20] That was the first lie that Flipper told his commanding officer about the commissary funds.

Since the amount on hand (which included the fraudulent check) and the amount recorded as being on hand in the commissary books was the same, Colonel Shafter signed off on this report and ordered Lieutenant Flipper to send the funds to San Antonio immediately. Flipper then ordered Sergeant Ross to prepare the required invoices and receipts for this transfer. However, after Shafter left the office, Flipper told Ross to date the invoices July 9 because "he had had difficulty in getting checks and that he had some more yet to get ... that he had to see the merchants to get the checks if possible." Further, he said that troopers were "expected from the field and he supposed he would get checks then."[21]

The 10th Cavalry, Company A (Flipper's company), had been in the field since the end of May and was expected to return to Fort Davis on July 10. The commissary office had extended credit to officers and enlisted men (the latter were apparently credited to Flipper's account) and Flipper thought that he would receive those checks and money when the troops returned to the fort. On July 9, Lieutenant Flipper returned to the commissary office with the funds he had taken with him and received the invoices and receipts prepared by Sergeant Ross. Flipper told Ross to record "To amount transferred to Major M.P. Small, C.S., U.S.A.— being balance from fiscal year ended June 30th, 1881—$3,791.77" in the cash book. However, Flipper did not send this report or money on to Major Small in San Antonio; instead, he kept it with him in his living quarters.

Shafter inspected the funds on Sunday morning and saw the statement which said that $3,791.77 was in transit to San Antonio. This was the second time Flipper lied to his commanding officer. The other part of the report noted that there was $150.17 in Flipper's "personal possession, in office safe." This was Flipper's third lie to his commanding officer, because the funds were actually stored in Flipper's personal trunk in his quarters.[22]

During the rest of July, the statements that Flipper presented to Shafter showed the amount of $3791.77 "in transit," while the amounts in Flipper's possession increased until the end of July when the reports showed $726.13 in Flipper's possession. Colonel Shafter signed off on each of these statements. On August 5, Major Small — who had returned to San Antonio — sent Lieutenant Flipper a letter stating that he had not received a response from his letter of June 29 requesting that all reports and funds for the 1880–1881 fiscal year be sent to him and requesting the funds be transferred. Small added that "no weekly statement of funds pertaining to the present fiscal year has been received at this office from your post."

The letter from Major Small arrived at Fort Davis on August 12; however, Lieutenant Flipper was already facing problems regarding the funds at Fort Davis before this letter arrived. On Saturday, August 6, the statement prepared by Sergeant Ross showed that Flipper had $2,166.07 in his possession and he would be required to present this amount to Shafter the next day. Flipper informed Ross that he did not have enough funds to present because there were unpaid bills from officers who were currently in the field. Sergeant Ross, who earned $39 a month, loaned Flipper $131 to help square the account.[23]

Flipper was still short of funds when he presented his statement to Colonel Shafter on Sunday, August 7, and told the colonel that officers in the field were behind in their accounts. Flipper estimated the shortfall to be $150–200, and Shafter told Flipper to telegraph one of the officers (Lieutenant Woodward) to pay his bill. Shafter told Flipper he would not count the funds until the amount on hand was correct.

On Tuesday, August 9, Shafter and Flipper met again, but Shafter did not count the funds. The previous day, Monday, August 8, Major Small had received a statement dated July 30 that showed his request for a statement of funds for fiscal year 1880–1881 had been received but the funds labeled "in transit" had not arrived. Major Small sent a telegram to Lieutenant Flipper notifying him of this but Flipper did not reply to the telegram; instead, he put the telegram in his desk in his living quarters.

Since Major Small did not receive a response about the missing funds from Lieutenant Flipper, he sent a telegram to Colonel Shafter on Wednesday, August 10, informing him that he had not received the funds listed "in transit" and requested Shafter to reply by telegraph when and how the funds were sent. Colonel Shafter went to the commissary office and told Sergeant Ross to find Lieutenant Flipper and tell him to report immediately to headquarters.

Shafter confronted Flipper with the telegram from Major Small. Flipper replied "the funds had all been sent" on July 9 and he "had made the receipts and invoices, written a letter of transmittal, made a description of the checks and included them all with the checks in an envelope," and after he prepared them at his quarters, "had taken the package addressed to the Chief Commissary of the Department ... to the post office and deposited it in the post office." Shafter then asked Flipper if he had a copy of the letter or a description of the checks (so payment could be stopped), but Flipper replied that he had not kept either a copy of the letter or a description of the checks. (Flipper told the colonel that a description of the checks, along with the checks, had been enclosed in the report sent to the chief commissary.) When Shafter asked Flipper why he had not kept a copy, Flipper replied that "it did not occur" to him and "it was a mistake" because "it was done in the evening after office hours and in order to get it off ... [he] had neglected to keep a list of the checks and had failed to have that letter of transmittal entered in the Letter Book." As soon as this interview ended, Shafter sent a telegram to Major Small, informing him of the substance of the conversation.

Reconstructing the events of that Wednesday, August 10, 1881, at Fort Davis, it seems that Flipper left the meeting with Colonel Shafter and went to his quarters, took out a number of checks from his trunk and went to the commissary building, arriving at about 11:00 A.M., and placed 32 checks— including his own fraudulent check of $1,440.43 — on Sergeant Ross's desk and told Ross to prepare an undated letter of transmittal to Major Small in San Antonio, listing the checks and stating the total amount was $3,791.77, which pertained to the previous fiscal year. Sergeant Ross wrote the letter and learned, at this time, that the funds which he thought had been sent on July 9 were still in Flipper's possession — over a month later. There was a further problem, pointed out by Ross: the checks Flipper submitted totaled $2,853.52, while the report stated the amount was $3,791.77. Flipper replied that he would finish the letter himself, and then he took the letter and checks back to his living quarters.

By this point, Colonel Shafter had become suspicious of Flipper and questioned his trust in the young lieutenant. Shafter was also concerned about himself; as post commander, he was responsible for all the soldiers at the fort and all that went on at that garrison. He knew there was money missing with no clear explanation. If something was wrong, it could damage his career. So when Shafter saw Lieutenant Flipper's horse in front of Sender & Siebenborn's store, across the road from the fort in the town of Fort Davis, that evening— with the saddlebags on — he reacted quickly. First, his mind jumped to the possibility that Flipper — who had over $2,000 — might head to the Mexican border, about 60 miles away. Shafter was upset and felt he had to play it safe.

Shafter rode back to Fort Davis, ordered Lieutenant Wilhelmi's horse to be saddled and brought to the adjutant's office, then rode to the adjutant's office and told Wilhelmi to ride out to the store and bring Flipper back to the fort, inform him he was relieved of his duty as commissary of substance and order him to immediately turn over the Commissary Department funds. Shafter also told Wilhelmi to inform First Lieutenant Frank Edmunds that he was now commissary of substance and should obtain the funds and receipts from Lieutenant Flipper.

Around sundown on August 10, Wilhelmi rode to the store and saw Flipper inside, apparently reading while dressed in his uniform. Wilhelmi stayed on his horse as he asked Flipper — who was seated just inside the door — if he was busy. Flipper replied that he wasn't, so Wilhelmi requested that he ride back to the fort with him. Flipper complied and on the way back to the Fort Wilhelmi informed Flipper that he had been relieved of his duties as commissary and was to turn over all the commissary funds to Lieutenant Edmunds. Flipper dismounted at his quarters, while Lieutenant Wilhelmi rode to Major Bates' quarters, where Edmunds was waiting. Lieutenant Edmunds then walked down to Flipper's quarters.

When Lieutenant Edmunds walked into Flipper's quarters, he saw "a large sum of money ... piled indiscriminately on his desk, currency and silver.... The funds had the appearance of having been dumped out of something.... They were all mixed up together." Edmunds said to Flipper, "Good gracious, you don't keep all this money in your quarters, do you?" Flipper said that he did and then transferred the funds to Edmunds, who carried about $2,166 — which included $700–800 in silver — out in a bag. By this time, it was around 7:30 in the evening.

Around 8:30 that evening, a second telegram from Major Small arrived at Fort Davis saying he had not received a reply from Flipper to the telegram sent two days previously. By this time, Flipper had returned to town, where he spent the evening with Fort Davis businessmen W.S. Chamberlain, Joseph Sender and others at a Mexican circus. The following morning (although it could have been a little later), Shafter again confronted Flipper and asked if he had received the telegram from Small; Flipper replied he had. Shafter then asked why he wasn't informed about this. Flipper replied, according to Shafter, "in effect that he thought it was only some temporary delay in the mail, that it would reach San Antonio soon and that it was not worthwhile to trouble me about it." Shafter supposedly replied, "I preferred to be troubled about such matters." Shafter then sent a circular letter to all officers at Fort Davis requesting documentation for all checks given to Flipper between April 17 and July 9 and sent Lieutenant Wilhelmi to Sender & Siebenborn's to ascertain what checks had been sent from their store to Flipper. Shafter also sent a telegram to Major Small about the matter, concluding "Lieut. Flipper has been a very good and attentive officer but his carelessness in this transaction is inexcusable."

During that day — Friday, August 12 — Flipper completed the transfer of all the goods in the commissary to Lieutenant Edmunds. No longer required to do staff duties, Lieutenant Flipper was now briefly back with the 10th Calvary, Company A. Meanwhile, Colonel Shafter was convinced that Flipper had not been honest with him regarding the commissary funds. A stage robbery would have explained the loss of funds in the mail, but there had been no stage robbery. When Flipper received the circular letter that Shafter sent to all officers requesting a record of the checks sent to the commissary, Flipper listed four checks but left out the one for $1,440.43. There was money missing and records amiss and Colonel Shafter was convinced he had a major problem on his hands with Lieutenant Henry Flipper.

5

Missing Funds

On Saturday morning, August 13, Colonel Shafter sent for Lieutenant Flipper and, sometime around 9:00 A.M., questioned him again about the missing commissary funds with Wilhelmi and Edmunds present. According to Shafter, the Colonel said, "Mr. Flipper, you presented to me a very large check for commissary funds," and Flipper replied, "Yes, one for $1,440." Shafter then asked, "Why was not that in the list of checks a day or two ago when I sent around for it?" and Flipper replied, "I forgot it, sir."[1]

"Fourteen hundred and forty dollars is a very large check for a man to forget under the circumstances," said Shafter. "And now I will say that I don't think you have ever sent those checks. I may be doing you an injustice. If I am, I shall be very sorry for it and will apologize and make all amends that I can to you after I am through, but I am going to treat you just as though I knew you had stolen those checks." Flipper replied, "Colonel, you are doing me a very great injustice as I did mail those checks, just as I have told you." "Very well," replied Shafter. "I hope you did and I shall be found to be in the wrong in the matter." Shafter then told Wilhelmi and Edumunds to thoroughly search Lieutenant Flipper's quarters and "if anything suspicious was found" that Flipper was to be placed under arrest.

When Lieutenants Wilhelmi and Edmunds entered Flipper's sitting room, they searched his desk while Flipper stood in the doorway of the back room and conversed in Spanish with three people in his bedroom — a woman and two men — who were there at the time the officers arrived. In the top drawer of the desk, Wilhelmi found "a lot of silver" and then found private letters in the pigeonholes of the desk. Flipper was asked if he had any objection to Wilhelmi viewing the letters and Flipper replied he had none. In the envelopes Wilhelmi found a check for $16 and three weekly statements each for May and July; he asked why these had not been sent to San Antonio. Flipper replied he felt it was unnecessary since Major Small had not been at his headquarters during that time.

Lieutenant Edmunds discovered "considerable money in the desk scattered around in different places," as well as a number of private papers. In another corner of the room, where Flipper's trunk sat, the lid of the trunk was closed but unlocked. He opened the trunk and found a woman's clothing; tucked in the midst of the clothing was the commissary statement for August 6. When Flipper was asked why that had not been sent, he replied, "I sent a duplicate of that." However, duplicates were not retained at Fort Davis and should have been sent to Washington. Edmund pointed this out.

The trunk had a tray inside and there Edmunds found about $80 in currency and a $20 gold piece. There was also a watch and some jewelry in the trunk. After he searched the trunk, Edmunds remembered that Flipper's manner indicated "that something was wrong." Flipper sat in a rocking chair while Edmunds examined books on a table in the middle of the room. Tucked in the books, Edmunds found $85 in currency.

After Edmunds checked behind some pictures on the wall and Wilhelmi finished searching the desk, the two went into the bedroom, which caused the three Mexicans to move into the sitting room; two of the Mexicans left the quarters and one sat down in the rocking chair that Flipper had left. Neither Wilhelmi nor Edmunds knew the Mexican remaining in the house, who watched while the bed, sewing machine and wardrobe were searched. Flipper's clothes — "mixed up with those of his servant" — were searched but no money was found.

Back in the sitting room, Wilhelmi ordered the Mexican to leave and then looked at the table in the middle of the room, which held some books. There he found a letter of transmittal prepared by Sergeant Ross on August 10. When asked why the letter was there, Flipper replied, "That letter had been written sometime early in July and that he had not the number of checks to make up the $3,700." Flipper was requested to turn his pockets out. When he opened his coat and pulled out a handkerchief, a check tumbled out. It was Wilhelmi's own check for $56 for commissary stores given to Flipper a few days before. After showing currency in his other pockets, the money and check were returned to him. Lieutenant Wilhelmi then informed Flipper that he would have to place him under arrest and report what he had found to Colonel Shafter. Flipper replied, "Very well," and he was placed under arrest.

As Wilhelmi and Edmunds left the house, Sergeant Dean, 1st Infantry, was given Flipper's carbine and belt of cartridges and placed in charge of Flipper and his house and ordered not to allow anything in the rooms to be touched or moved or for Flipper to leave or communicate with anyone. Lieutenant Flipper remained quietly in his quarters after Wilhelmi and Edmunds left to see the commanding officer.

Wilhelmi and Edmunds showed Shafter the statements and letter of transmittal found in Flipper's room and stated they were certain that Flipper either had the missing commissary funds or knew where they were. Shafter agreed and ordered the search to be resumed, issuing an order for the officers "to take all money and valuables and to seal up his desk and papers and trunks and boxes so that they could not be disturbed without our knowing it." Shafter then went directly to Flipper's quarters and found Lucy Smith in the kitchen, which was in back and detached from the living quarters. When Shafter informed Lucy that he wanted to examine her in his room, she asked permission to put on a skirt and change clothes and he agreed; she then went into the sitting room and took some clothes from the trunk. Shafter then rode to his headquarters while Private Mackin, an orderly, escorted Lucy there.

When Lucy arrived at headquarters, she was taken into Shafter's office; the door to the outer office stayed open and Private Mackin stood in the doorway. Lieutenant Nordstrom, the regimental quartermaster, was called to witness the conversation; the sergeant-major and several others stayed in the outer office, able to overhear the conversation taking place.

Shafter said to Lucy, "I suppose you know there is some trouble with Lieutenant Flipper's money matters," and she replied, according to Shafter, that "she knew there was something wrong." Shafter then asked her if she had seen large amounts of money or checks around his house. She replied to that question and another inquiring "if she knew anything about it in any way." Shafter then told her that her things had been found in Flipper's quarters and ordered her to go back to Flipper's quarters, pack up her things and leave the Fort at once; a provost sergeant would come around with a cart to carry her trunk off the post.

Lucy replied that she had nowhere to go and asked if she could stay with a laundress friend down by the creek; Shafter gave her permission to do this. As she was leaving, Private Mackin asked Shafter if he was looking for papers. Shafter replied that he was and the orderly said, "That woman has some in her dress."

Shafter called Lucy back and asked if she had any papers on her and Lucy told him no, and pulled her dress open to disclose the inside of her dress. Shafter then told her to go, but Mackin insisted, "Colonel, I know she has some papers in her dress for I seen her trying to hold them up with her elbow as she came across the parade ground."

Shafter called Lucy back and as she stood close to him, he put his hand on the outside of her waist and felt some packages of paper. Shafter told her to take them out, but she refused. He insisted, saying, "You must do it. If you don't take them out, and lay them down on my desk, I will call in another orderly and have them taken from you by force. You had better lay them down, without any trouble." Lucy again refused, saying they were her personal, private papers. Shafter replied that it did not matter; he needed to look at them. Lucy reached inside her dress and pulled out two packages of papers. One of the envelopes was addressed to Major Small and contained invoices and receipts for $3,791.77, which should have been mailed in July. The other envelope contained 32 checks which totaled $2,853.56 — including the check for $1,440.43 from Flipper. None of the checks were endorsed to the chief commissary.

Shafter asked how Lucy had come by these papers. She replied, "Lieutenant Flipper gave them to me a day or two ago and told me to take care of them." Shafter asked her if she knew what they contained. Lucy replied that she had never looked inside the envelopes. Shafter then told her that he would file a complaint against her that would "probably send you to the penitentiary."

Shafter sent for his own female servant and told her to thoroughly examine Lucy's clothes. The servant, alone with Lucy, required Lucy to completely disrobe but nothing else was found. The two envelopes found on Lucy were, by this time, in the possession of Lieutenant Wilhelmi.

Meanwhile, Edmunds and Wilhelmi, along with Captain Bates, returned to Lieutenant Flipper's quarters and began a second search, taking everything of value — such as jewelry — as well as checks and official papers. According to Wilhelmi, "Money was [found] scattered all around the room in different places." The two found additional weekly statements and the telegram Small sent on August 8. Shafter came into the quarters holding the two envelopes, which he handed to Wilhelmi, and told Flipper they had been found on his servant girl and contained commissary checks. Shafter then accused Flipper of stealing commissary funds and ordered him locked in the guardhouse.

Flipper was generally silent during these events and, before he was taken to the guardhouse, searched again and his watch and chain and about $65 taken from him. Captain Bates took Flipper's West Point class ring from his finger. After the officer of the day left the quarters with Flipper, the three officers — Wilhelmi, Edmunds and Bates — compiled and signed inventories of the property collected. There were three lists made: (1) money from the desk; (2) cash and valuables taken from the trunk and Flipper himself; and (3) principal items which remained in the rooms. However, Lucy claimed the sewing machine was hers. The three officers took a napkin ring, clock and opera glass. The property and papers were then taken away and locked in the adjutant's safe. The desk was sealed, the windows nailed shut and the doors either locked or nailed shut and a padlock placed on the door which led to the hallway.

Colonel Shafter telegraphed a long report of the situation with Lieutenant Flipper to his superior, Brigadier-General Christopher C. Augur, at department headquarters stating, "The amount embezzled by Lieut. Flipper is thirty seven hundred and ninety one dollars and seventy-seven cents. The checks of officers and money recovered today will reduce that amount fifteen or sixteen hundred dollars, Lieut. Flipper has stolen. I have confined him in a cell in the post guardhouse, that being the only secure place in the post, until the orders of the Department Commander can be had in his case."

The cell where Flipper was confined was six and a half feet long by four and a half feet wide; in the hallway were 15 other prisoners. Confining an officer to the guardhouse was highly unusual; the usual forms of confinement were "open" arrest or "closed." In "open" arrest, the officer was limited to the post; "closed" arrest meant the officer was confined to his quarters.

In addition to confining him to the guardhouse, Colonel Shafter allowed Flipper to see only "respectable citizens — who might help him to restore the missing money." The only one who determined whether a visitor could see Flipper was Shafter. It is unknown how many citizens attempted to visit Flipper, but it is known that Shafter excluded two: "a colored man in town that has some official position" and "a drunken nigger that had been a servant in the garrison." Shafter ordered him to leave, labeling him "a drunken worthless fellow ... who could have no possible reason" for seeing Flipper.

On Monday, August 15, Colonel Shafter came to Flipper's cell with a telegram from the San Antonio National Bank. Shafter had requested information about Flipper's account at that bank and the cashier wired that Flipper had never had a personal account with that bank. Shafter told Flipper his check of $1,440 was not good and that, instead of his accounts being about $900 deficient, they were more than $2,000 deficient.

Flipper replied that he needed to deceive Shafter in some way and that was the way he had chosen to do it. Shafter told him that he did not need to incriminate himself, but Shafter wanted to know where the money had gone. Flipper replied that he didn't know, which Shafter thought was curious.

"It is very strange that you should be short $2,400 and not know where it is, or what has become of it," said Shafter. Flipper replied that that was true, but he simply had no explanation except that "some of them" might have stolen it.

Shafter asked what he meant by "some of them" and Flipper replied that he didn't know.

Shafter then asked if Flipper thought Lucy had any of it and Flipper said he did not think so.

Flipper then told Shafter that he thought he could make up the deficiency if he could see three or four of his friends in town. Shafter asked if he thought his friends could cover the entire $2,400 and Flipper replied "Yes, I think they can."

Flipper told Shafter he would like to see local businessmen W.S. Chamberlain, Joseph Sender, J.B. Shields and W. Keesey, and the Colonel agreed to find and send them at once. Chamberlain and Sender came first to see Shafter and Flipper; when Chamberlain and Sender asked if it would help Flipper if this money was raised, Shafter replied, "Yes, it would save him from the penitentiary." When asked if Shafter thought Flipper had tried to defraud the government, the colonel replied that he thought it was only Flipper's carelessness and bad company that had gotten him in this position. Shafter then told them that he would commit $100 himself to the fund to bail Flipper out of his dilemma.

Chamberlain raised the money, although not a single officer of the 28 at Fort Davis, except Shafter, contributed to the fund. In his book, *The Ruin of Lieutenant Flipper*, Barry Johnson notes "That none of them chose to follow the commanding officer's example is significant: they surely would have gone to the rescue of a brother officer who was socially acceptable and who was generally thought to be innocent of crime."[2]

After the money was raised, Shafter withdrew the sentinel, allowing Flipper to live in "open" arrest."

On Monday, August 15, Lucy Smith provided a sworn statement to the United States commissioner about her interview with Shafter. According to her testimony, Lucy told Shafter the following:

> [I had taken the envelopes] out of my trunk this morning when I was cleaning up. He wanted to know who gave them to me or when I got them. I told him I had taken them out of my trunk when I was cleaning up and Lt. Flipper told me to take care of his things when he went out of the house, and when I was cleaning up I was overhauling my clothes and the Lieut. knew I was cleaning up and he told me to be careful of these two envelopes because he said having so much help around the house they might get misplaced. I had them taken out of the trunk and had no pocket. I just stuck them down

in my bosom and when the girl [who was helping around the house] came after me I changed my black dress skirt and being in a hurry I never thought about them being in there anymore. I never tried to hide them or anything of the kind. I don't want them to try to think that I was trying to conceal them because they were not given me to conceal. I had always picked up everything around the house and taken care of them as far as I knew how, he [Flipper] always told me to look out for everything when he was out because you are my servant and I'll hold you responsible.

Lucy also said that Shafter asked if she had any money and that she had replied, "Yes sir, I had some," but did not know exactly how much. This was the money found in the purse on the tray in the trunk; it was $100 (including a $20 gold piece) and Shafter told her she could have it, but he remained suspicious because "I thought it was a good deal of money for a servant girl to have in her pocket book." But he had no means of identifying it, so he returned it to Lucy.

On Tuesday, August 16, Shafter received from Augur an order to "arrange for his [Flipper's] security by providing a place other than the guardhouse." That afternoon, Flipper was released and placed in "close" arrest, confined to his quarters.

Augur had forwarded to the general of the army, William Tecumseh Sherman, the report from Shafter. Sherman replied on August 23: "The arrest and suspension from his duties of Lt Flipper is right — His confinement to the guardhouse, though within the province of the Post Commander, is not usual, unless there be reasons to apprehend an escape."[3] That same day, General Augur received a telegram stating, "Both the Secretary of War and General of the Army require that this officer must have the same treatment as though he were white."[4]

Lucy remained locked in the county jail for about a week, until some citizens secured her release. By this time, Flipper had also been released from the guardhouse, so she returned to Flipper's quarters as his servant.

Within two weeks after Flipper's arrest, Shafter notified army officials that Flipper had provided all the money for which he was responsible. These funds were sent to Major Small in San Antonio with the request that the checks found on Lucy Smith be kept by the bank for future evidence. Although the funds had been replaced, the army still had to determine if Lieutenant Flipper was party to the missing funds; also, Flipper had to face the fact that he had engaged in a serious breach of discipline with his deceptions.

There is no doubt that he had lost the confidence of Colonel Shafter by this point and Shafter was determined to obtain answers to these questions. Further, the military is established along top down lines, and the commanding officer is responsible for the men under him. If an officer has missing funds and then lies to cover that up, that officer must answer for those discretions; but the commanding officer is on the line as well. Colonel Shafter was in a vulnerable position at this point: His lax administration was part of the problem and he had to make sure his own career was not ruined. Lieutenant Flipper had created the situation that placed Shafter in this position.

On August 29, Colonel Shafter filed two charges against Flipper; the first was for embezzlement of $3,791.77 and the second was for "conduct unbecoming an officer and a gentleman." There are two kinds of embezzlement defined by the Articles of War: "Actual embezzlement" involved the deliberate misappropriation of government funds, while "Constructive embezzlement" meant the responsible person — for whatever reason — failed to deliver or account for government funds upon demand. The wording on Shafter's charge accused Flipper of "Actual Embezzlement."

The second charge, "conduct unbecoming an officer and a gentleman," had five specifications. The first four each accused Flipper of lying to Shafter (on four separate dates) that the order to transmit funds to the chief commissary had been carried out, "well knowing the same to be false." The last specification was the personal check of $1,440.43 from Flipper that "was fraudulent and intended to deceive the said commanding officer." Each of the charges and specifications needed a verdict returned because they were separate offenses. For the charge of "conduct unbecoming an officer and a gentleman," the court-martial would decide the definition of conduct, which would justify or not justify this charge. It was based on the Sixty-first Article of War, which stated that "Any officer who is convicted of conduct unbecoming an officer and a gentleman shall be dismissed from the service."

Why did Henry Flipper allow himself to be caught in this situation — lying to his commanding officer and covering up the fact that commissary money was missing with no explanation? Charles Robinson believes the following:

> The only excuse that can be made for Flipper is that very early in the affair, he may have lost touch with reality, and never truly regained it. No doubt, the fact that his career was on the line traumatized him, and the fact that he was the author of his problems aggravated the trauma. The misrepresentations to Shafter and to Small compounded each other, and as Flipper sank

deeper into the mire, he began deceiving himself. The fabrications and lies built on each other until, by September, as preparations for the trial began, he had decided that his own actions had nothing to do with his arrest, that he was the victim of a conspiracy by Shafter, Wilhelmi and Nordstrom.[5]

In mid–August there was national news of an army officer with the Signal Service Department in Washington accused of embezzlement. Captain Henry W. Howgate was arrested and charged with embezzling over $40,000 during the time he was disbursing officer in the Signal Service Department. Howgate was charged with submitting vouchers in 1879 for telegraph bills which were fraudulent.[6] News of Flipper's arrest also drew national attention, often in conjunction with the embezzlement charges against Howgate. The *New York Times* reported: "Captain Henry W. Howgate faced a civil suit from the government to recover $101,257.08 which he had embezzled." (The amount had increased with new findings of more fraudulent vouchers.) A second story stated that Flipper was under arrest at Fort Davis, Texas, "charged with embezzling Government funds to the amount of $2,300." The article noted that "The announcement of this officer's fall is regarded as most unfortunate, and much regret is expressed here. His friends are inclined to make believe that his offense is technical rather than criminal, and that investigation will exonerate him from any intention or purpose to defraud the Government."[7]

The *Chicago Tribune* reported that "Capt. Howgate, the Arctic explorer," had a mistress, "Miss Burrell, on whom he is known to have lavished considerable sums of money.... She received $350 for services alleged to have been rendered the Government ... and drew a salary of $75 a month from the same source." The article admonished, "It is bad enough for a married man to keep a mistress, and steal $40,000 with which to support her, but the placing of her name on the payrolls of a Government office is an exhibition of cheek at which even those persons intimately acquainted with life in Washington will be astonished."[8] The *Atlanta Constitution* weighed in on Flipper's arrest and noted that "It wasn't his color that led Flipper to embezzle government funds. It was his connection with the republican party. There are hundreds of men in high places who are worse than Flipper."[9] A week later, that paper reported that "Flipper didn't steal because he was colored. Certainly not. He stole — if he stole at all — because he had the example of a long line of white republicans before him."[10]

The *Army Navy Journal* reported:

> It is greatly to be regretted that the only colored officer now in the United
> States Army should have been so little mindful not only of his own reputation,
> but of his responsibilities as a representative of his race, as to subject himself
> to arrest on a charge of embezzlement.... Lieut. Flipper had the respect of the
> officers of the post, and has been treated very kindly by them, though he has
> never shown a disposition to mingle with them in a social manner. The fact
> of his having retained the position of Acting Commissary of Subsistence for
> so long a time shows in what light his character and intellect were regarded.
> Being the only colored officer in the Army, great regret is expressed that
> Lieut. Flipper could not have maintained his reputation for integrity and
> high moral character; but "evil communications corrupt good manners," and
> it is said his most intimate associates of late have not been the best.[11]

Flipper's predicament was compared to that of Johnson Whittaker, who
had been assaulted at West Point in April 1880, a little over a year before Flipper was arrested. Whittaker, a black cadet at West Point who was admitted
in 1876 and roomed with Flipper during Flipper's last year at West Point, had
been beaten and tied up one night while asleep in his bed. Although he was
found unconscious, with his hands and feet tied and bleeding, a court-martial concluded that he had faked the assault.

The Whittaker case was compared with Flipper's and the *Chicago Tribune* stated:

> There is, of course, no logical connection between the case of Lieut. Flipper
> and that of Cadet Whittaker; each stands on its own merits: yet a general
> inference with regard to the value of colored youth as army officers is one of
> the first reflections that will come into most minds. Here are three colored
> cadets tried at West Point. Smith fails to pass his examinations; Whittaker is
> court-martialed for alleged trickery of a very deplorable sort; and now the
> one of the three who succeeded in getting into the army is awaiting trial for
> peculation of funds. All this does not yet justify a generalization; but it
> makes a most unfortunate train of circumstances as connected with the effort
> to introduce colored lads into the commissioned offices of the army. More is
> the pity that Lieut. Flipper seems not to have appreciated the great responsi-
> bility he was under at all times, and especially at this particular juncture, as a
> representative of his race.[12]

That same day, *The Nation* also reported: "The reported discovery that
Lieutenant Flipper, the colored officer, had been defrauding the Government
is said to have created 'wild excitement' among the garrison at Fort Davis,
Texas." *The Nation* sketched out the accusations, then stated:

> But what is Flipper's side of the story? Is he unfamiliar with the Whittaker
> case? Does he not know that the prejudice in the army against colored

officers is so intense that there would be nothing unnatural in "putting up a job" of this kind? Did he never suspect anything when they pretended to like and esteem him very much, and craftily made him commissary, and entrusted him with funds, well knowing that the negro race is not accustomed to complicated pecuniary transactions, and can easily be confused about them by means of accounts, vouchers, and the like? When he was suddenly called up to account, and stated that he had mailed his funds, did it never occur to him that his servant might have been bribed, and checks carefully prepared to look like those which have disappeared placed in his hands?... And this, too, at a distant post, surrounded by army officers who loathe him, graduates of an institution where prejudice against his race is cultivated by officers of instruction, and where the mutilation of negro cadets is regarded as a pleasant pastime.[13]

The next day (September 2) the *Chicago Tribune* reported on Captain Howgate:

He has left the service and the country at one and the same time, in company with a woman not his wife, and has abandoned his wife and family, leaving them in utter destitution. He has stolen from the United States Treasury $500,000 and left his bondsmen $40,000 short.... He made no concealment of his shame, nor did the mistress upon whom he was lavishing the stolen money nor did he think it unmanly nor she unwomanly to taunt the wife and insult her by denying all her claims upon her husband or his support.... He leaves behind him a wife and children in utter destitution, who will be objects of sympathy, except in the fact that in the loss of Capt. Howgate they have lost a depraved and worthless scoundrel.

The article then turned its attention to Flipper:

The Government has caught another embezzler squarely by the throat and is going to put him through. He hasn't been keeping a mistress, nor setting up an establishment, nor dazzling society, nor has he stolen half a million dollars. In point of fact, it is not very certain that he has stolen anything.... The new culprit is Flipper, and as Flipper is only a "nigger," it is the old story of "Hit him again, he's got no friends...." If he has stolen the regimental funds, he has only done what lots of white men have done before him, but there is this difference — Flipper is a "nigger," and the country is not used to that kind of stealing. It has never had anything but white stealing upon a large scale. If a "nigger" is allowed to steal a thousand dollars, what is to prevent the opening of the flood-gates? If Flipper, therefore, is really guilty, he should be made an example of, that the negro race may be warned in time and choked off from any further raids upon public funds. They must be taught that they have not yet been citizens long enough to claim the privileges of white scoundrels, and that it looks a little like insolence for them to assume that because they have the right of life, liberty, and the pursuit of happiness, they have also the peculiarly Caucasian right of helping themselves to the public money.... People ... will wonder why Flipper should be punished for stealing a thousand dollars — if he stole it — when Howgate, who had embezzled — white officers never steal — half a million dollars, is allowed to get away, and will wonder if Howgate is not much the blackest of the two, assuming that Flipper really is a thief."[14]

The *Tribune* also noted, in a separate comment, "The principal difference between Flipper and Howgate seems to be that Flipper stole $1,000 and is in jail, while Howgate stole $400,000 and is in Canada."[15]

The *St. Louis Daily Globe-Democrat*, a Negro newspaper, weighed in, stating, "The Democratic papers are making a great ado about Lieut. Flipper, because he was short a few hundred dollars in his accounts. He has made good the deficiency, but he is still a colored man and a Republican. Howgate, who made away with a sum compared with which Flipper's was a mere bagatelle, is not so much the subject of comment. Howgate is a white man and a Democrat. That's the difference."[16]

The *San Antonio Express* added the following:

Since the fall of Lieut. Flipper there have been many long and labored dissertations concerning the moral and intellectual status of the colored race, based upon the hypothesis that the three colored youths who obtained prominence through appointment to West Point — Smith, Flipper and Whittaker — are fair representatives of their people and that the quality of the race as members of the human family, and the possibility of their advancement, should be judged by the three men.... But a people should not always be judged by those who may happen to hold representative position.... Would the white people of this country, like to be judged by an estimate made of the character of some of their so-called representative men? Flipper ... fell, not through any lack of intelligence or sense of responsibility for offense committed, or because of any element in his nature peculiar to his people; but because of a falling, or inability for self-control that has been found in many of the brightest men of all classes and all races. "There was a woman in it." At least that now appears to be the general conclusion of those well situated to judge. If the charges against Flipper are sustained, he should be promptly dismissed from the service. He is entitled to no sympathy because he is the sole representative of the colored people among the officers of the army. The question of color should not enter into the consideration of his case; and if he is found guilty and dismissed in disgrace, it cannot be considered a reflection upon the colored people, except that portion who would shield him simply because he is of their race.[17]

The following day (September 8) *The Nation* reported:

If on the discovery of his peculations he had at once boldly denounced the whole affair as a military conspiracy to injure his race and prevent negroes from entering the army, he might at least have secured a protracted enquiry; and this would have given time for the manufacture of all sorts of theories, to say nothing of testimony which might have been of the greatest possible use to him. It might not have led to his acquittal, but it would at least have given him a national reputation and made him a representative man, and at the end of it the lecture field would have been open to him with the certainty of profitable employment. But by giving himself away, just as a white officer might under the circumstances, he has become an ordinary embezzler, differing from other embezzlers merely in having a black skin.[18]

Flipper sent letters to a number of leading "colored" men in the East, seeking help. The *New York Times* reported that, "Among the leading colored men, the sentiment is unmistakably one of bitter indignation against Flipper, and if the court-martial before which he will be tried imposes a rigorous sentence, no effort will be made on their part to mitigate the punishment."[19]

The *Army Navy Journal* reported that it had obtained a copy of a letter from Flipper and gave a rundown of his version of the situation. In the letter, Flipper says, "My 1st Lieutenant occupies the same house with me. Our rooms are separate. He hates me, and I have caught him at my window twice. He has trained his servant to watch me, and she watches me and my servant as closely as possible. Even the Colonel prowls around at night, and has been seen at my windows." The article concludes:

> Lieut Flipper says that he indubitably prefers to be tried at Fort Davis, as all his witnesses are there. He is conscious of his innocence and feels cheerful, sanguine, and in no way depressed. "I am confident that I can win my case," he adds, "and then the reaction in public feeling will make up for the hard things being said now. Of what the Colonel and the authorities have done I know only a very little, and of what they intend to do I know nothing. A trap was set for me into which I unwittingly stepped. I was taken by surprise and not allowed one word of explanation."[20]

6

The Court-Martial

Henry Flipper's court-martial was scheduled to begin on September 15, 1881, at 10:00 A.M. in the post chapel at Fort Davis, Texas. The judge-advocate was Captain J.W. Clous, of the 24th Infantry. Clous, an officer of the black 24th infantry, had served with Shafter in 1871 in the Indian wars. During the summer of 1881 Clous had served as judge advocate of several courts-martial at Fort Davis. Clous's job was to administer the oaths and question witnesses on behalf of the government, although his questions during the trial often seemed like those of a prosecuting attorney.

President of the court was Colonel Galusha Pennypacker, 16th Infantry. Pennypacker began his career in the Civil War army as quartermaster sergeant in the 9th Pennsylvania volunteers. He was promoted to captain, then major of the 97th Regiment from Pennsylvania during his first year in the army and became a full colonel on August 15, 1864. In 1865 he was promoted to brigadier general and brevetted a major general of volunteers; the next year he was appointed a full colonel in the regular army.

Others on the court were Lieutenant-Colonel J.F. Wade, 10th Cavalry; Major G.W. Schofield, 10th Cavalry; Surgeon W.E. Waters, Medical Department; Captain Fergus Walker, 1st Infantry; Captain William Fletcher, 20th Infantry; Captain W.N. Tisdale, 1st Infantry; Captain R.G. Heiner, 1st Infantry; Captain E.S. Ewing, 16th Infantry; Captain L.O. Parker, 1st Infantry; and First Lieutenant W.V. Richards, regimental quartermaster, 16th Infantry. All were veterans of the Civil War and none had graduated from West Point. Four of the men — Walker, Tisdale, Heiner and Parker — were under the command of Shafter as members from the 1st Infantry.

The case began two days late, on September 17, because Clous was delayed by the weather and bad roads. One member, Captain Parker, was dropped from the court, and by the time the first full court session took place, on September 19, Flipper was asked if he objected to any member of the court. He did not and the court proceeded. (Later, Flipper disputed the make-up of the court because three were under Shafter's command.) The court was then adjourned until November 1 so Flipper could obtain counsel.

The chapel at Fort Davis, site of Lt. Henry Flipper's court-martial (Fort Davis Historic Site).

On Monday, September 19, President Garfield died in Elberon, New Jersey, two months short of his 50th birthday. He was succeeded by Chester Arthur. Although Flipper's court-martial at Fort Davis remained national news, it was overshadowed by the news about the trial of Charles Guiteau, the man who assassinated President Garfield.

Flipper could not raise the $1,000 necessary to attract representation from black leaders in major cities and, Charles Robinson notes, "The failure of the black community to rally to Flipper's side is not as callous as it might seem. Flipper was arrogant, and his arrogance extended to the black community. He was very conscious that he was pale, urban, and educated — the 'replicated white' that, in the latter nineteenth century, formed an elite in the black community — and his writings and actions tended to denigrate those who were not. Unrefined, uneducated people could not be equal, and this extended to all races."[1]

Flipper later wrote in a memoir that he became "determined to fight my battle alone and unaided, as I had always done, when, like a bolt out of clear sky, I received a letter from Captain Merritt Barber" of the 16th Infantry, a letter offering to defend him. Barber was an army attorney and Flipper accepted the offer.[2] Earlier in 1881, Barber was on the court-martial board that tried Johnson Whittaker.

Captain Merritt Barber, Flipper's counsel during his court-martial (Fort Davis Historic Site).

On October 5 the *Atlanta Constitution* ran an article titled "Flipper's Triors: Who Are to Pass upon His Character." The article, datelined Fort Davis, states, "Many go so far as to predict that his conviction will end the connection of his race with the army in a commissioned capacity forever and not a few, both in and out of the military service, declare the whole business a conspiracy having that as its object in view."[3]

On October 6, *The Nation* reported:

> When Flipper was first accused we thought ... that it would be a good joke to predict that Flipper would appear ... as a race martyr.... Sure enough.... As soon as he could be heard from, Flipper was found proclaiming himself the victim of an elaborate white conspiracy, and his colored friends, as before, put West Point and his commanding officer "on trial".... Our suggestion that they made him Commissary of Subsistence out of far-reaching malice, with the view of basing a charge of embezzlement on his want of skill in accounts, we considered the least valuable of all our imaginings, and yet this too turned out a masterpiece, for he took it as it stood. Our satisfaction and pride were complete when the colored organ, the *Globe*, put Colonel Shafter and the Military Academy "on trial" for accusing Flipper and when Flipper became in the twinkling of an eye a kind of prosecuting judge advocate. There is nobody, however devoid of humor, but must enjoy this, because even those who do not understand joking like to see a prediction come true.[4]

In its October 15 edition, the *Army Navy Journal* printed an article from "A correspondent at Fort Davis, Texas, who signs himself 'C'" and whose article first appeared in the *St. Louis Globe Democrat*: "We the citizens, believe Lieut. Flipper innocent of any attempt to rob the Government. That he tried to escape into Mexico is all bosh. If he had had any desire to escape he could have done so, for there is not a soldier in this post, white or colored, who would not have assisted him. Lieut. Flipper had been warned to be very careful, as his brother officers were trying to get him into trouble. Whatever the decision of the court-martial may be, we shall always believe in his innocence."[5]

In the October 30, 1881, edition of the Sunday *New York Times*, there was a long article under the headline "Lieut. Flipper's Case":

> The approaching trial of Second Lieut. H.O. Flipper, Tenth Cavalry, will be of great interest in military circles, and hardly less so to the public at large. The accused officer is the only colored graduate of West Point, and the only colored man that has ever held a commission in the Army. Upon him, therefore, centered a peculiar responsibility as a representative of his race, and it is a matter of deep regret that he should have given grounds, by his conduct, whether well founded or not, for his arrest on a charge of embezzling commissary funds, as it would also be a matter for sincere congratulation, particularly after the Whittaker affair, if he should succeed in clearing himself. [After a review of the case the article states that] the case against Flipper ... is an ill-looking and serious one. The fact that he had received and had for a long time retained the position of Acting Commissary at the post would at once suggest that he must have secured the respect of his brother officers as a man of unquestioned integrity and honor, as well as of intelligence and business capacity. The next inference would be that no question of injustice could arise in this case, on the score of prejudice against color, like that which was imputed to the Cadets at West Point in their treatment of Whittaker. One rather queer statement, however, declared that "Lieut. Flipper has been treated very kindly by the officers of the post, though he has never shown a disposition to mingle with them socially." The experience of Whittaker indicates that the proper interpretation to be put upon this latter assertion is that they had never shown a disposition to mingle socially with him. In fact, the defense which Mr. Flipper proposes to offer is that if a conspiracy was not actually formed to dishonor him, at least a trap was laid by Col. Shafter, against whose professed friendship he claims to have been warned. It is enough for the present to see that his defense insists on his absolute innocence of any intent to defraud. There are so many circumstances, nevertheless, indicating prevarication, to say the least, that the case as a whole looks bad for him. It would be a very agreeable relief, not only for his own sake, but also and chiefly for that of his race, if the trial should result in his complete vindication.[6]

On November 1, the first day of Flipper's court-martial, the *St. Louis Daily Globe-Democrat* noted that "Underneath the charge of embezzlement there is what is, to the West Point notion, the still graver offense of being a 'nigger.' Between the two we wouldn't give much for Mr. Flipper's chance of wearing regimentals in the near future."[7]

When the court convened on November 1, Colonel James van Voast had been added, but Flipper objected, saying he had accepted the court and that "a new element is infused into the court, which I had no reason to expect, and which I could not and did not take into consideration."[8]

Barber stated, "The record shows that the accused was satisfied with the court.... Now some motive must have influenced a change in its composition, and the accused has a right to feel that the motive must have been adverse.... One member entirely changes the composition of the court, because [Flipper] did not consider that member." Colonel Van Voast then retired from the trial.

On November 2 Flipper was served with two additional charges consisting of nine specifications; those two concerned the desertion of scout Charles Berger, who left the post with a horse in January, and the other related to Sergeant Ross's loan to Flipper, which had not been paid as soon as Flipper received money. Both of these charges against Flipper were weak and indicate a desire by Shafter to lay as many accusations as he could against the young lieutenant. However, Judge Advocate Clous said the first trial should be completed before the second charges were presented, although if Flipper wanted "to save time and the ordeal of two separate trials" and would waive the right of challenge, then both charges could be tried at the same time. Barber obtained a recess in order to consult with Flipper on the second set of charges. Clous objected. Then Barber asked for a list of property and papers that had been taken from Flipper's quarters when he was arrested to determine which witnesses to call for the trial. Shafter had given the list to Clous, but Clous had not given it to Barber or Flipper. Clous argued that "if Barber wanted any papers or witnesses, he should make proper application" and, until such application, "There is no use of taking up the time of the court about this matter and lumbering up the record."

Barber stated he believed Clous had information and documents material to the defense and asked the court "to instruct the judge-advocate or request him" to supply the list. Clous angrily told Colonel Pennypacker, "It is not competent for this court to take any action upon that subject until I have failed to do my duty, and I consider the request as a reflection upon me in a matter upon which I have not been asked to act. On the contrary, when I came here first to try this case, I showed him every paper I had in my possession, and

81

since that [time] I have informed his counsel outside of court that whenever he wished to ask me about any paper I would be very glad to show it to him, and I ask the court to be cleared now to settle the matter." Then Pennypacker made an announcement: "The time had come to arraign Flipper on the original charges." The arraignment was set for the following morning.

The court generally sat each day — Monday through Saturday — from 10:00 A.M. until 3:00 P.M. in the chapel at Fort Davis. All the members of the court wore full dress uniforms, the president of the court-martial (Colonel Pennypacker) seated at the head of the table with members seated in descending order of rank down both sides of the table. Lieutenant Flipper wore a full dress uniform without sidearms (the others probably leaned their swords against the table) and sat with his counsel at a separate table. The judge advocate sat at the foot of the table with Lieutenant Flipper to his right; witnesses who testified sat in a chair on his left.

Flipper agreed that both charges could be tried at the same court-martial and waived the right of challenge; however, Clous decided to try him only on the original charges of embezzlement and conduct unbecoming an officer and a gentleman, with five specifications — essentially lying to Colonel Shafter about the missing funds. Flipper pleaded "not guilty" to each charge and specification.

Clous presented Flipper's financial accounts for June, July and August, and Flipper verified them. Then Colonel Shafter was called as the first witness by Clous. Shafter recounted the events until the point when Major Small notified him the money had not been received in San Antonio. According to Shafter, when Flipper was asked why Small's earlier message on missing funds had been withheld, Flipper said "that he thought it was only some temporary delay in the mail, that [the money] would reach San Antonio soon, and that it was not worthwhile to trouble me about it. I think all that I said to him then was that I preferred to be troubled about such matters and that he should have notified me." Shafter then told of Flipper's explanation of the mailing of the checks and invoices and that he had relieved Flipper of his duties as A.C.S.

Barber produced weekly statements from Flipper for June for Shafter's signature but none had been signed. When asked to explain this, Shafter said, "I am positive that I always signed the statements when I examined the funds, and at no other time. It is possible that it may have been entirely forgotten and the Sunday passed by without me counting them, but if I was at the post, and my name on the weekly statement, I know that I counted the funds rendered on that weekly statement."

Shafter admitted that the month of June had passed with nobody's signature on the weekly statements, which meant the funds may not have been examined by command. Shafter said that Flipper told him he'd "taken that package containing those inclosures to the post office and had deposited it there with his own hands, and in that way accounted for the letter not being entered in the letter book at the commissary office as other letters had been when funds were transmitted; that it was done in the evening after office hours and in order to get it off he had taken that course and had neglected to keep a list of the checks and had failed to have that letter of transmittal entered in the letter book."

Captain J.W. Clous, judge advocate of Henry Flipper's court-martial (Fort Davis Historic Site).

Shafter stated that on the morning of August 13 he'd sent for Flipper "and asked him why he had failed to give his list of checks that I had called for a day or two previously.... I also sent for him and told him that I was going to have his quarters searched, that I believed he was lying to me about sending off the checks, and I was going to act accordingly."

The next day Barber asked Shafter why he had obtained from his officers a list of checks for those who had made commissary payments.

"It was taken because at the time — that I believed that the checks had been mailed, and by some means they had been lost in transit to the chief commissary at San Antonio, and I wished to get a list of the checks so that I could ... have payments stopped on them," replied Shafter. Shafter continued that the failure of Flipper to include his own $1,400 check "was among the things which caused him to think the checks had not been sent," and "learning that there had not been any stage robbery was another, Lieutenant Flipper's manner was another."

According to Shafter, he instructed Wilhelmi and Lieutenant Edmunds to search Flipper's quarters and if they "found anything suspicious, to place Lieutenant Flipper in arrest.... I did not want any trifling about it, that I wished them to act just as I had been talking to Mr. Flipper, that it was no halfway measure, that it was to be a thorough search."

Shafter recounted his conversation with Flipper:

> Mr. Flipper came into the office. I said, "Mr. Flipper, why did you not — you presented to me a very large check for commissary funds." He said, "Yes, one for $1,440." I said, "Why was not that in the list of checks a day or two ago when I sent around for it?" He said, "I forgot it, sir." I said, "Fourteen hundred dollars is a very large check for a man to forget under the circumstances, and now I will say to you that I don't think you have ever sent those checks. I may be doing you an injustice. If I am, I shall be very sorry for it and will apologize and make all amends that I can to you after I am through, but I am going to treat you just as though I knew you had stolen those checks." He said, "Colonel, you are doing me a very great injustice, as I did mail those checks just as I have told you." I said, "Very well, I hope you did and I shall be found to be in the wrong in the matter." I then turned to the officers and told them to go to Lieutenant Flipper's quarters and search them thoroughly, that I did not want any foolishness about it.... I also told Lieutenant Wilhelmi ... to place Mr. Flipper in arrest if anything suspicious was found.

Barber asked what the officers found, and Shafter replied:

> They reported to me that they had found weekly statements and funds for the month of July with my signature that should have been forwarded weekly. They also found some subsistence funds enclosed in various places in his room in envelopes, that from the letters accompanying them were known to be commissary money, and they were so certain that Mr. Flipper had the money, or knew where it was, that they had called in a sergeant that was standing near by and gave him a carbine and told Mr. Flipper to consider himself under arrest and told Mr. Flipper not to move out of the room, and that not a thing or paper was to be touched in the house until they returned.

After the officer reported back to Shafter on what they'd found, Shafter said, "I told the officers to return to Lieutenant Flipper's quarters and continue the search, that my impression was that they would either find the checks or they would find that he had burned them and to look through the burned papers that were in his fireplace.... I continued on to Lieutenant Flipper's quarters with Major Bates, or about the same time as I had been told that the trunk and clothing of Mr. Flipper's servant woman was found in his bedroom, I determined to examine her, and directed her to go to my office, and told my orderly to take charge of her and conduct her there."

Shafter stated that, after talking with the officers searching Flipper's quarters, he returned to his office "and had a conversation with the servant woman, which resulted in my finding the checks." Shafter said he told the officers "to take all money and valuables and to seal up his desk, and papers, and trunks, and boxes so that they could not be disturbed without our knowing it. I intended to put Mr. Flipper in confinement and I wanted things made secure so that he might get them again if proper, and if not that I would have them and know where they were."

Barber asked Shafter if his orders "included his watch, his finger rings, his shirt studs, his sleeve buttons, his shoe buckles and other articles of personal use and ornament that were found on his person at the time." Shafter answered, "There was nothing designated. I directed them to take possession of everything of value."

"Did the scope of your orders intend to justify the taking of those articles of personal use and ornament which he had on his person at the time? Do you mean to be so understood?" asked Barber.

Shafter answered, "I do mean to be so understood. That I meant that they should take everything that he would not require in the guardhouse, as that was where I intended to place him and, as I did not want him to have his valuables there, and took them for safekeeping."

Barber then asked why Flipper's belongings were not given back to him when he was released from the guardhouse. Shafter acknowledged that Flipper had applied for them, but "I sent him back an endorsement or a message that I had just discovered one or two new steals and as soon as that money was made good he could have his things. Mr. Flipper said that if he could be permitted to go to town he would raise the money that he had obtained of the commissary sergeant and...."

Barber interjected, "Are you using his language?"

Shafter replied, "I am using my own. I am using Mr. Flipper's language as given to me, as reported to me by an officer that I sent over to see him."

Barber stated, "Ah! You don't pretend then to give it of your own knowledge — the language of Lieutenant Flipper?"

Shafter answered, "I do not, but I will tell you what occurred. I did give Lieutenant Flipper permission to go to town. He did so and paid the money, and then the officers went over to his quarters and told him he could have his things and he declined to take them except through civil proceedings. The things are left there yet, and I determined not to turn him over the things unless he called for them."

Barber asked why he gave an order to his officers to search for burned checks and Shafter replied, "It was a mere theory of mine ... that Lieutenant Flipper had stolen the money and that he had burned or destroyed the checks."

Barber then asked, "You afterwards found the checks?" Shafter replied, "I did." Barber countered: "Therefore your theory was wrong?" Shafter said, "So far as the necessity of searching the fireplace, it was shown to be unnecessary."

Shafter said he had an exchange of telegrams with the bank and informed Flipper in the guardhouse that the officer "had no personal account with the bank and consequently his check for $1,440 was good for nothing and that his deficiency, instead of being about $900, was perhaps something like $2,300 or $2,400." Flipper replied, according to Shafter, "Yes, Colonel, I had to deceive you in the matter in some way and I took that way to do it." Shafter said he then told Flipper, "You need not incriminate yourself—I don't want you to do so unless you choose to, but I should like to know where that money has gone to, if you are willing to tell me." According to Shafter, Flipper replied, "Colonel, I don't know where it has gone to." Shafter replied, "It is very strange that you should be short $2,400 and not know where it is, or what has become of it."

"Yes, that is so," Shafter said Flipper replied. "But I can't account for it unless some of them have stolen it from me." Shafter said he then asked, "Who do you mean by 'some of them'?" According to Shafter, Flipper replied he did not know. Shafter then said he asked if he thought Lucy Smith had some of the money and Flipper replied, "No, sir, I do not."

Flipper then requested, according to Shafter, that the commanding officer meet with some area merchants and citizens of Fort Davis who might help make up the deficit. They were, according to Shafter, "a member of the firm of Senders & Siebenborn — I never have known just which one it was — Mr. Shields, and Mr. Chamberlain and Mr. Keesey." The merchants visited Flipper in the guardhouse and then asked Shafter what would happen to Flipper "if the money were repaid." Shafter replied, "It would save him from prison and that as soon as the amount was repaid, I should release him from the guardhouse and place him in his quarters as I would any other officer that was under arrest. They said they would try to raise it and started out the door. On the afternoon of the 16th they came to my office with Lieutenant

Flipper, and Lieutenant Flipper turned over $3,791.77, the amount named as being in transit to the chief commissary."

Under Barber's cross-examination, Shafter stated he had relieved Flipper as quartermaster "almost immediately after assuming command of Fort Davis." However, Flipper continued to serve as commissary until August 10.

Shafter testified that sometime around July 1 he informed Flipper he intended to relieve him of his duties, "not because I was dissatisfied with him, but it was because I thought he ought to be assisting other cavalry officers in performing their duties in the field."

Barber then asked, "If I understand you correctly, that up to the occurrence of this matter, the conduct of Lieutenant Flipper in the transaction of his official business with you was not only satisfactory but praiseworthy?"

Shafter replied, "I say so, as far as I knew."

Barber asked, "Do you know anything about whether the funds had been regularly transmitted monthly prior to your administration here?"

Shafter answered, "I do not."

"You have records and accounts showing whether they were or were not?" asked Barber

"I can't state. I have not looked to see," said Shafter.

Barber pressed Shafter about a variety of things, and Shafter admitted he "did not know about procedures at Fort Davis prior to his assuming command, and did not even know whether records or accounts for the previous command existed, because he had not bothered to look for them." Shafter also admitted he had not received any notice of deficiencies in Flipper's transmissions prior to July and added, "Up to that day there was no reason to think but that they were all straight."

Shafter admitted he did not know about Small's order "to hold funds at Fort Davis" but knew it came "two or three months before the funds were ordered sent." Shafter then stated he inspected the funds "Every week when I was present, every Sunday morning — the funds on hand, not his bank account."

In regards to the personal check for $1,400 written by Flipper, Shafter told Barber, "I had perfect confidence in Mr. Flipper at that time and did not question it anymore than I should do other officers at the Post whose checks were there."

Shafter admitted he had approved and signed Flipper's reports and had seen money or checks to verify the accounts. When asked what he did with them, Shafter answered, "I can only judge that I handed them back to

Lieutenant Flipper from the fact that they were found in his possession. I should have sent them forward myself. I had always made it an invariable rule after signing them to hand them back to the commissary officer to transmit instead of handing them to the adjutant as was proper, as it was my paper after signing it."

Barber then questioned Shafter about Flipper's guardhouse confinement, asking, "What orders did you give in regard to the confinement of Lieutenant Flipper?"

Shafter answered, "I directed that the cell be swept out, bed put in it, Lieutenant Flipper confined in that cell and kept there until further orders from me."

"What orders, if any, did you give in regard to his communicating with anybody?"

"That he should not be permitted to communicate with anybody whatever. To receive no messages or to deliver any and that if he wished to see any person, the sergeant of the guard was not to receive his communication further than to receive his wishes."

"Any order forbidding his speaking to the persons who brought his meals?"

"Yes, sir. He was not permitted to speak to any person except the sergeant of the guard in the first instance. Make known his wants to him and he was to report to the officer of the day."

"Any sentinels additional placed over him?

"An additional sentinel was placed in the rear of the guardhouse to prevent any person from communicating with him through the window, with orders to keep all persons away from there."

"Do you not know that no bedding whatever was sent to his cell until he asked for it, and that then sufficient bedding was not sent, and that he applied a second time before the proper bedding was furnished?"

At this, Clous objected, saying, "I do not see what bearing the matter has upon the subject under investigation, or what bearing it has upon the direct examination. Supposing for argument sake for a moment that Colonel Shafter has treated this accused severely, for argument's sake only, gentlemen, I say, is this the proper place, is this the proper time, is this the proper opportunity to seek redress for it? Grant it was so, does it palliate any of the offences with which the accused is charged with having committed...? Whom are we trying? This witness or this accused?"

Barber answered, "We are not endeavoring to put the witness on trial before this court, but we are endeavoring to show that the treatment which has been administered to us has been the severest punishment that has been administered to an officer of the army since its organization."

The objection by Clous was overruled.

Barber noted that "the charge of the Sixty-first Article of War, concerning conduct unbecoming an officer, required an examination of all circumstances of the case." Barber stated that an officer — Flipper — who had not been convicted of any offense, was "confined in a felon's cell" for five days in August, the hottest month of the year, with sixteen common soldier prisoners.

"I scarcely know how to present a reply to a member of the court, excepting to hope that no member of the court will feel that he has any other duties more important than those to defend and guard the integrity and honor of a brother officer in the army," said Barber.

Barber continued to question Flipper's confinement in the guardhouse. Shafter admitted "that no one could visit Flipper without his permission, but the citizens of Fort Davis could visit as often as they wished, to discuss ways of making up the missing funds." The colonel stated, "I did think it best to permit him to be interviewed on the subject matter of his shortage, and continued it as long as it was necessary. I don't recollect of giving any permission to see him on any other subject"

Barber asked if he recalled denying anyone permission for a visit with Flipper. Shafter replied there had been "a number of persons." The only one he could specifically recall was "A colored man in town that has some official position asked to see him.... I asked him what he wanted. He said he wanted to see him. I told him he could not do it. I don't recollect any other, although there might have been."

"Do you remember any persons bringing a note of introduction from the United States commissioner, who requested to see Lieutenant Flipper?"

"I do not."

"If such occurred, would you remember it?"

"Perhaps I might and perhaps not," replied Shafter. "I don't recollect it at this time."

Barber then produced the note and handed it to Clous for examination. Shafter asked for the note to be read aloud, then stated he "still did not recall the incident, but added that based on the note alone, permission would have been denied."

"Do not you remember that a man presented that note from the commissioner, asking for an interview with Lieutenant Flipper, which you not only denied but sent the man out of the garrison?" asked Barber.

Shafter replied, "I know positive that there was no man sent." Then he hesitated before adding, "Well, I should like to amend my answer. I recollect the whole thing now. There was a drunken nigger that had been a servant in the garrison. He came to me drunk and asked to see Flipper.... I told him he could not see Flipper. He was a drunken, worthless fellow that was very much intoxicated at the time, who could have no possible reason for seeing him. I cannot give his name without some person can tell it to me. But that is a fact."

Barber pressed Shafter, who admitted that his memory was "faulty on some points," adding he only remembered "important events in the day to day administration of the post."

"You don't consider that the denial of a person in the guardhouse the privilege of seeing his friends, or the denial of his friends of seeing him, worthy of your recollection of the administration of the post?" asked Barber.

Shafter replied, "I think I said that I did not recollect every little incident connected with the command of my post. I do now recollect this occurrence and I did not consider it a hardship, or that it was a hardship for Lieutenant Flipper not to see this particular man; and I did not intend, as I have said before, that he should see any person unless I knew about it, and it was on proper business."

Barber continued questioning Shafter, who testified that he asked Flipper, in his cell, "if he thought that his woman servant had stolen it." According to Shafter, Flipper replied, "No, that he believed she was honest."

Barber asked, "What influenced you to release him from the guardhouse?" Shafter answered, "I received a dispatch from the department commander directing me to find some other secure place in the garrison in which Mr. Flipper could be kept."

"When released from the guardhouse, what measures were taken in regard to his confinement or safekeeping?" asked Barber.

"I had the front room of his quarters made what I considered tolerably secure and placed a sentinel on the porch where he could look in at his window," replied Shafter.

"Will you please state to the court what care you took, or was taken to make that room tolerably secure?"

"I had the door fastened — back windows fastened and a hasp and lock put on the front door. I think the back door was fastened by putting pieces of board across and fastening them in the walls or by nails or screws. The window in the same way."

When asked about his conversation with Lucy Smith in his office, Shafter stated he told her there were problems with money and Lieutenant Flipper, and "she said she knew there was something wrong." Shafter then said he asked Lucy, "Have you ever seen any large amounts of money about his place or any checks?" She replied, "No sir, she never had." He then informed her she had to go to the garrison and, before she did so, to return to Flipper's quarters to pack up her things in her trunk, which would be taken off the post. According to Shafter, Lucy told him "she had nowhere to go outside and asked me if I had any objection to her going down on the creek or to staying with a laundress—a friend of hers."

But as she was leaving, according to Shafter, his orderly asked, "Colonel, are you looking for papers?" When Shafter replied he was, the orderly said, "That woman has some in her dress." Shafter testified that he called her back:

> "Lucy, have you any papers about you?" She said, "No, sir, I have not." She said, "You can see I have not," and she pulled her dress open and disclosed the inside of her dress. I said, "Very well," I simply looked as I sat across my desk. She was three or four feet off. I said, "Very well, you can go." When my orderly said, "Colonel, I know she has some papers in her dress for I seen her trying to hold them up with her elbow as she came across the parade ground," I said, "Come back here, Lucy." She came back and stood up close to me and I put my hand on the outside of the waist on the opposite side of the one that she had shown me and felt a couple or three packages of papers. I told her to take them out. She said those were her papers, "and she would not do it." I said, "You must do it. If you don't take them out and lay them down on my desk, I will call in another orderly and have them take them from you by force. You had better lay them down without any trouble." She again declined, saying that they were her own private papers. I said, "It made no difference; I had to see them." She then put her hand inside of her dress and handed out two packages of papers. One of them contained a letter of transmittal.... The other contained the missing checks, or checks to the amount of $2,800, and some odd dollars, and were the identical checks, or a part of them were the same checks that I had seen on the 8th day of July in Lieutenant Flipper's possession and counted them as public money.
>
> I said, "Lucy, where did you get these? How did you come by these papers?" She said, "Lieutenant Flipper gave them to me a day or two ago and told me to take care of them." I said, "Did you know what they were?" She said, "No, sir, I have never looked in the envelopes to see." I said, "Very well, I shall make complaint against you and it will probably send you to the penitentiary."

Shafter stated that he then filed a complaint before the United States commissioner against Lucy Smith. Barber pressed Shafter about his examination with Lucy, asking, "Did you not use very violent language in your intercourse with Lucy on that occasion.... Did you not curse her?" Shafter replied, "I did not."

"Did you not threaten her?" Shafter replied, "I did not.... I don't think I used an oath during the whole examination, although I am liable to.... On the contrary, I am sure that I talked very quietly to the girl."

On further questioning, Shafter admitted, "There is one thing that occurs to me. I did not care to examine her myself and I did not care to have the men do it, so I sent a man to my house for my female servant, and told her to examine her and see if there was any funds or papers belonging to the commissary department. They went out in the other room and she said there was nothing on her."

Barber then asked, "Did you direct her to strip Lucy ... order her to be stripped naked?"

Shafter replied, "I did not tell her to be stripped but I did tell the woman to examine every part of her clothing and see that there was nothing under them." Asked if this was done, Shafter stated, "She told me that she made her take all her clothes off."

Barber asked where this was done and Shafter replied, "In my own office."

"How many persons were around the office?"

"There was no person about the office whatever but the two women. About the building there was probably the regimental quartermaster, sergeant major, my orderly, and perhaps others."

"Do you know whether there was any soldiers outside about the windows?"

"I don't know. I am very positive none were at the front windows and I don't believe there was any at the back."

Barber asked, "Did not you tell her during that interview that if she would tell all she knew about Flipper, and tell the truth about this matter, she could have a house in the garrison, or quarters in the garrison here, and have friends among the officers, and that you would go around and see her yourself once in awhile?"

Shafter replied, "I did not tell her any part of it, nor anything that could be tortured into it."

"You have stated that you did not use any violence or abusive language during that interview.... Did not you say to her during that interview, 'Yes, God damn you, I have got him where I want him?'"

"No, sir, I did not say anything at all like it except to tell her that she would probably wind up in the penitentiary, or would probably go to the penitentiary for her share of the transaction; but as far as cursing her, or swearing about Lieutenant Flipper to her, I did not do it."

Barber asked Shafter what was in Lucy's pocketbook which led him to think the money was stolen. Shafter replied:

> The amount of money, which was something in the neighborhood of $100, I think I stated something over $80, there were three twenty dollar bills and a twenty dollar gold piece. I thought it was a good deal of money for a servant girl to have in her pocketbook and from the fact that Lieutenant Flipper had presented to me week after week a solitary twenty dollar gold piece with his subsistence funds. I had no means of identifying either the bills or the gold and cannot do so, but there was no gold, that I knew of or as I am aware of found by the officers who made the search, and this twenty dollar gold piece was found in a little pocketbook that she claims was her money and given back to her.

7

The Trial Continues

The sixth day of the trial began with an argument lasting forty minutes between Clous and Barber about the means and methods for summoning defense witnesses. The court ruled for Barber but Clous then insisted he had a headache so severe he could not "sit here any longer." Colonel Pennypacker suggested an adjournment but Clous asked for a recess; the court was then recessed for an hour for Clous to rest and then Shafter was summoned again.[1]

Shafter was asked if he had any idea how Flipper would have used the missing money. Shafter replied, "Mr. Flipper's habits had been such that he had not used it up himself. He was not a gambler, or was not known to be, and was not a drunkard, or was not known to be, and I knew no way how he could have got away with that amount of money, and consequently it was a mystery to me then and is to a very great extent now."

Asking about the citizen fund drive to raise money for Flipper, Barber said, "Was not their action in making up this amount of money influenced by your belief in the innocence of any guilt on the part of Lieutenant Flipper conveyed to them on that occasion?" Shafter replied, "I don't know what influenced them to do it." Shafter added that, "while he personally was convinced of Flipper's guilt, and had been at the time mentioned, he might have said something to the effect that he did not know how Flipper had done it."

Barber then asked Shafter why he thought Flipper "was going to escape to Mexico" when he was seen at Mr. Sender's store with horse and saddlebags. Shafter replied:

> I was riding out just at sundown, or just before sundown, on the evening of August 10 and saw Lieutenant Flipper's horse standing in front of the store in town with saddlebags and saddle. I knew that he had something over two thousand dollars in money and it occurred to me right then and there that if there was anything wrong he would have an opportunity of getting away if he saw fit, and I determined — I had intended to relieve him the next morning — and I determined that he should turn his money over at once and rode back — I was very nervous about the matter as I could not conceive what had become of it as I did not suspect him of embezzling it at that time. It was simply a wonder as to what the matter could be and I thought I would be on

the safe side and get possession of what was in his hands and do it before night. I sent out to bring him in and to tell him on the way in that I was not satisfied, that I considered him very careless and I was going to take his funds that night. Mr. Flipper had the money out on his desk immediately after he came in. It should have been in the safe. Whether he had it on his horse or not I cannot tell but he had no opportunity to go to his safe but he did have his money spread out on the table, as I am told, within two or three minutes from the time he entered the house.

Barber asked, "Do you not know that Lieutenant Flipper from the date that he first took charge of the department at the post kept the subsistence funds at the house?"

"I did not know it and at that time had no idea that he did keep it in his house," replied Shafter. "The only time that I did inspect his money at the office, it was in his office. I have been told since that he never kept it in his safe, that it was kept in his house."

On the tenth day of the trial, a Wednesday, Barber finished his cross-examination of Shafter, then Clous asked a few questions.

Major Small, the departmental chief commissary of subsistence, was then called. Small had become commissary on December 20, 1880, and stated, "To the best of my knowledge, up to the time Lieutenant Flipper got into this trouble, [the business of the commissary] was well conducted.... I had no reason to be dissatisfied with the administration of the Subsistence affairs at this post up to the time Lieutenant Flipper got into trouble in any manner, shape or form."

The next witness, George Davidson, the chief clerk in San Antonio, answered some questions about handling funds in San Antonio during Small's absence. Then John Withers, cashier of the San Antonio National Bank, was called to the stand and testified that Flipper did not have an account at the bank Flipper had written a check on for $1,440.43. He did acknowledge, however, that Flipper had maintained a quartermaster's account at the bank for about three months, but he had closed it in March. On August 17, the date he notified Shafter that Flipper had no personal account in his name, Withers stated the bank was holding a certificate of deposit for $74 in his name, which were royalties from Flipper's book, sent by the publisher.

The next day, Lieutenant Wilhelmi was called and testified that on July 3 he overhead Flipper and Shafter talking about the $1,440 check and that Shafter said, "Is not this check for $1,440 a very large amount for an officer to have?" According to Wilhelmi, Flipper replied, "Yes, I had a lot of small checks which I did not wish to transmit, or could not, to the chief commissary of the department, and I sent them to the San Antonio National Bank for deposit. This check represents that amount." Wilhelmi stated he was positive of the date because "the following day was the fourth and Lieutenant Flipper had issued a circular asking the Mexicans about Fort Davis." At that, he was stopped by Barber's objections. Clous overruled him and Wilhelmi continued, "to bring their burros here for a race" on July Fourth.

Wilhelmi said that on August 10 Shafter had seen Flipper's horse tied in front of Sender and Seibenborn's store in town and, because saddlebags were on the horse, Shafter believed Flipper "might leave the post, and the country." Wilhelmi was ordered to ride over and tell Flipper he had been relieved as acting commissary of subsistence and bring him back to the post. Wilhelmi was also told to tell Lieutenant Edmunds to get the commissary funds from Flipper and give him a receipt.

After Wilhelmi had carried out his instructions, Edmunds went to Flipper's quarters for the funds. In the search of Flipper's quarters, Wilhelmi stated that in Flipper's desk he found weekly statements from May, June and August; "money was scattered all around the room in different places," and a number of checks in an envelope were also found.

He continued:

> I searched his desk in which was some jewelry, ladies jewelry, bracelets and so on.... I searched the trunk that was standing in the corner.... It was partly filled with the clothing which was afterwards claimed by the servant of Lieutenant Flipper as her own. In the wardrobe in the back room, clothing of Lieutenant Flipper and his servant was all mixed up. Her skirt was hanging over a pair of pants, or a pair of pants under a skirt and a coat over a skirt — there were three pieces of clothing on the same hook. Hairbrushes and combs were on the washstand which were claimed by the servant of Lieutenant Flipper. An old toothbrush and an old comb was there, and also some bedding on the bed which she claimed belonged to her. A sewing machine was back there. It was near the bed in the main quarters.

Wilhelmi and Edmunds then searched Flipper, asking him to turn out his pockets. According to Wilhelmi, "The first pocket that we examined was the pocket on the right hand side of his blouse. He pulled out a handkerchief and at the same time a check flew out which had been on the top of the handkerchief— of $56.00.... It was a check which I had given him on the tenth of August. It was a personal check for my commissary bill for July."

On cross-examination, it emerged that the burro race had been organized by two other officers on the post who asked Flipper to prepare the circular because he knew Spanish. Wilhelmi had been among the officers who contributed prize money. The race was organized by Captain Bates and Captain Viele, who had Flipper write out some posters in Spanish.

Questioned about the idea that Flipper might leave the country, Wilhelmi stated, "I think it was after the arrest of Lieutenant Flipper that Colonel Shafter said it would have been an easy matter of Lieutenant Flipper to have gone to Mexico."

Barber asked, "When you returned from bringing Mr. Flipper back did you say anything to Colonel Shafter about the idea of Mr. Flipper escaping to Mexico?" Wilhelmi replied, "I think not." "Before starting to go for Mr. Flipper did you or not, and since your report to Colonel Shafter after your return, have you not talked with him on that subject?"

"I had no conversation on that subject before starting to bring Lieutenant Flipper into this post on the evening of the tenth of August, nor when I made my report to Colonel Shafter on that evening," answered Wilhelmi. "At the time that Colonel Shafter said that it would have been an easy matter for Lieutenant Flipper to have gone to Mexico, I said that I believed that that was his intention on the night of the tenth, had the money not been taken from him [by Lieutenant Edmunds]. That conversation occurred after the thirteenth of August and after Lieutenant Flipper was placed in arrest."

"Then you are the originator of that Mexican theory, are you not?" Wilhelmi answered, "Not at all."

Wilhelmi then testified Shafter had removed Flipper, that Wilhelmi and Captain Bates inventoried the checks, and then Lucy Smith had come in and taken her clothes and other personal articles from Flipper's quarters. Wilhelmi stated that Smith's jewelry and money had been kept separate from Flipper's and had been returned to her. Lucy Smith was not allowed to claim the sewing machine or bedding until she could prove ownership. After the officers completed the search, they nailed down the windows of Flipper's quarters, nailed and locked the door, and put an extra padlock on the front door of Flipper's side of the building. Flipper's personal articles and papers were put in a safe in Shafter's office.

Wilhelmi stated that as he was going through Flipper's desk, "the commanding officer came into the room and handed me two envelopes, saying that there are the checks that I have been looking for. I have taken them from the person of the servant of Lieutenant Flipper.... I counted the checks and found that there were thirty-two." He testified that Flipper had been taken from the room during the search, and "After the inventory was made, the servant of

Lieutenant Flipper came there and took her clothes out of the wardrobe, packed them in the box and trunk, took her toilet articles from the wash-stand and the shoes that were behind the wardrobe. She claimed some of the bedding which was under the mattress, under the bed and on the bed, but I would not allow her to have it until she proved it was hers; neither would I allow her to remove the sewing machine until she proved it was hers. The box and trunk which contained the effects which she claimed to belong to her were taken by her."

The next morning, Barber requested to see Flipper's personal property from Shafter and Wilhelmi. Clous asked what the defense hoped to accomplish, and Barber said he wanted to see if the list of items corresponded to the items in hand. He noted that Flipper had never been given an inventory and had to guess at what had been taken. "He wants to know where it is and what it is," said Barber of Flipper's personal property. Clous objected to this as irrelevant, but Barber countered: "The property is here in court, and the witness is here in court. It would not take three minutes to verify this property with the list, and then proceed with the witness, and if there are any articles about which he has testified that are missing, we can show where they are."

Clous then asked, "What possible bearing ... will this subject of identification of the property have to enlighten you and to aid you in determining the guilt or innocence of this accused upon the subjects that I have already mentioned — the different specifications and the charges? Why should you, the gentlemen of the court, sit here and permit this accused in court to verify this list? Why can't he step up like a man to his commanding officer and ask for his property...? Was he not offered the property twice? No inventory would have been necessary, had he taken the property at the time when it was offered to him. This court would never have been troubled with the subject." Clous added that "The subject would be kicked out of court" in a civil proceeding.

Barber replied, "Everything connected with this case is proper to come before this court. What is the penalty for embezzlement? Fine and imprisonment. How much fine has he already paid? Where is the property...? We could have been halfway through with the testimony by this time. It looks to me as if the judge-advocate is laboring under a terrible state of mind, that something terrible is going to take place at some other time."

The court overruled Clous and the examination was allowed. Then Clous announced he had been directed to return the property to Wilhelmi and

Shafter's custody. Wilhelmi continued his testimony of the search, stating that in addition to himself, Edmunds and Flipper, another man was present at the search: "I don't know who it was. [I] know it was a Mexican and I told him to get out of there.... They came in while we were there. There were one or two others in the back room. While we examined the back room, the Mexican came into the front room, but he was in my sight all the time, and he did not take anything while we were there or touch anything. I took particular care to observe him in that respect."

When asked if Flipper and the Mexican had spoken to each other, Wilhelmi replied, "I think there was something said — just a few words.... It was in Mexican and I did not understand it. I can't tell what it was."

It emerged that during the search there were several people in the back room of Flipper's quarters; but neither Wilhelmi nor Edmunds noted who they were or what they were doing, and allowed them to come and go as they pleased. Wilhelmi wasn't certain if Lucy Smith was among them, or whether the others were Mexican or black. He noted that Flipper spoke with them in addition to helping with the search.

Wilhelmi testified he had also been at West Point, and first saw Flipper there in June 1873. He was a class ahead but had been turned back to Flipper's class, where he remained until he resigned from the academy in December for health reasons. He stated he never spoke with Flipper nor knew him personally during that period. Wilhelmi stated that after his resignation he went to Philadelphia, then went into the insurance business before entering the army on October 15, 1875.

Barber asked, "After you left the Point and up to the time that you were appointed to the army, were you at any time engaged in any detective business?" Wilhelmi replied he was not, whereupon Barber asked, "This matter was your first experience?" "Which matter?" asked Wilhelmi. "This matter with Lieutenant Flipper." Barber then withdrew this question after Clous objected, stating, "I hope the judge advocate will not scold me anymore than he can help and not take up the time of the court." Clous answered, "I am not scolding. I am simply attending to my duty, and I am responsible for no one here for it, least of all, the gentleman who represents the defense."

The testimony continued with Wilhelmi stating he first encountered Flipper in March 1881, when he was transferred to Fort Davis. He described their relationship as "friendly." When asked to define "friendly," Wilhelmi stated that he had a working relationship that was cordial but that they never visited each other socially.

Clous then cross-examined Wilhelmi, who recalled a conversation with Flipper in the guardhouse after the arrest in which Flipper supposedly explained his lie to Shafter, stating "Well, you know how the colonel is, an erratic sort of man, and when he ordered me on the eighth of July to send the money off, I reported it so on the ninth."

Lieutenant Edmunds was the next witness called, and he testified he found "a large amount of money piled indiscriminately on his desk, currency and silver ... [in] no regular order," and that during the search of Flipper's quarters conducted by Wilhelmi and him, they found "considerable money in the desk scattered around in different places, a great many private papers were in the desk, letters and other papers."

Edmunds reported he said to Flipper, "Good gracious, you don't keep all this money in your quarters, do you?" and Flipper replied he did.

Clous presented a letter written to Wilhelmi from Flipper, dated August 17, "asking for the return of Mexican currency and personal effects which had been taken during the various searches of his quarters." In the letter, Flipper states the Mexican money "has been in my possession for a long time as curiosities and it is my wish to preserve them." Flipper said he expected his personal property would be returned once the deficit had been made up and defined his property as "my jewelry of every sort and description. I do not refer to papers of any kind."

Clous then introduced Flipper's weekly statements for May; Barber noted the charges and specifications against Flipper were against misconduct in July and August, concluding, "They have no right to come before the court as illustrative of testimony — they illustrate nothing."

Clous wanted to prove the deficiency went back as far as May. Further, some of the weekly statements for May had been erased in order to hide the deficiency. He said, "I shall attempt to show you that there was a studied attempt on the part of the accused to deceive his commanding officer from May on to July as to the real amount of funds he was responsible for." Barber objected but was overruled.

Clous asked Edmunds if the reports were in the same condition when they were found in Flipper's quarters. Edmunds replied they weren't, because some of the original entries had been erased.

Clous then said, "I will make one further remark. Is it not plausible to presume ... that these weekly statements for June were never presented to any commanding officer, that having made so many erasures in May that the matter could not be continued all the time without attracting attention?" Clous then accused Flipper of making two sets of commissary statements, one clean and the other to cover his mistakes. This led to speculation presented by Clous that the clean, erased copies did not have the colonel's signatures.

Under Barber's cross-examination, Lieutenant Edmunds stated he had been Flipper's French instructor at West Point from around September 1873 until February 1875 and they had not met again until both were at Fort Davis in May 1881. Edmunds stated he believed Flipper's character was "above reproach" until his arrest.

Barber asked Edmunds if, on the night he relieved Flipper, he noticed "anything about the latter's dress, appearance or manners, or anything in his quarters that might be suspicious" to lead him to believe he was going to Mexico. Edmunds replied, "No, sir. I can't say there was. Simply the large amount of money that was there. That attracted my attention and that was the only thing that did."

Edmunds told Flipper that all his personal property, except his watch, which Colonel Shafter was keeping as collateral for his loan, would be returned. Soon Shafter offered to return the watch, too. Flipper declined, saying he wanted to consult his attorney or civil authorities before he accepted the returned property.

On November 14, 1881, the trial for Charles Guiteau began in Washington and dominated the national news. However, there was also national coverage of Flipper's trial, although on November 17 *The Nation* reported:

> It is curious to see how little interest some of our esteemed contemporaries take in the trial of West Point and Colonel Shafter, which is now in progress down in Texas in the Flipper matter.... Flipper's charge against West Point and his commanding officer is almost the same as Whittaker's, and the defendants are trying to meet it in precisely the same way — that is, by making the most shameful accusations against a poor colored boy. Whittaker had the uproarious support of some of our most esteemed contemporaries, and the services of one of the most stentorian lawyers in the world at Government expense, while Flipper is left to push his case himself, and, as far as we can see, has no newspaper backing but that of the *Evening Post* and the colored *Globe* of this city. There is something very mysterious in this silence. So is there also in the long delay in promulgating the finding of the court-martial in the Whittaker case. It was sent in six months ago, and nothing is heard of it. If West Point has been found guilty, the world ought to know it. If it has been acquitted, Whittaker ought to have his pay stopped and be released from the United States service for some larger field of usefulness.[2]

The court-martial of Johnson Whittaker began on January 20, although the actual trial began in February and was completed on June 10, 1881. The verdict against Whittaker was "guilty," but this had to be reviewed by the president, who had not made his decision yet.

The testimonies of Shafter, Wilhelmi, and Edmunds took up the longest part of the Flipper trial. After their testimony, the trial moved along fairly quickly. Lt. S.L. Woodward answered some questions about the transfer of funds from Fort Quitman and Captain Bates was called as a defense witness. Bates said he and Capt. C.D. Viele had organized the burro race for the Fourth of July and stated Flipper helped only in forming the starting line "because I could not make those Mexicans understand me."

Viele also testified he had noticed Flipper's horse with the saddlebags. Walter David Cox, Flipper's orderly, testified that Flipper "customarily carried the bags attached to his saddle, and that during the entire period since February, removed them only once, when they were repaired by the company saddler." He also said "the bags were empty when he saddled Flipper's horse and took it to him on the day Shafter ordered him back on post."

J.B. Shields and A.W. Keesey, both merchants at Fort Davis, were character witnesses for Flipper and had loaned money to cover Flipper's deficit. Shields stated there were "plenty of other citizens who would have contributed, but it happened at a very dull time, when very few except the storekeepers had any money to contribute." When asked why he helped Flipper, Shields stated, "The first was because I believed he was innocent of what he was charged with. The next was I thought he was rather crowded and that it was a pretty hard place for an officer or any other man to be in a cell closed up, and from his intelligence and good behavior, I liked the man and tried to help him if I could."

Shields also admitted that Flipper had provided him and his family with food during a food shortage the previous spring and that it was from Flipper's personal mess rather than the commissary.

Keesey had given $200 for Flipper's deficit, "although it left him short of needed cash." Keesey also said he "had advanced goods to the post commissary, not only under Flipper, but under every commissary officer at Fort Davis for the previous eighteen months to two years." The goods were reimbursed when the army resupplied the commissary. Keesey said he'd met often with Flipper and he found him a man of integrity who "did not gamble or indulge in 'habits of disipation.'"

On November 29, the twenty-fifth day of the trial, Lucy Smith was called to the stand. She stated she lived in Chihuahua and that on the tenth of August she was living on the post, working for Lieutenant Flipper as his servant. Barber asked her where she lived while she was working for Flipper and she replied, "I worked at the house every day."

"Where did you room?"

"In Mrs. Olsup's."

"Did you room with Mrs. Olsup all the time that you were working for Lieutenant Flipper?"

"Yes, sir."

"You did not have any room at Lieutenant Flipper's house?"

"No, sir."

"Where did you keep your clothing?"

"I kept some of them in a chest and some of them in the trunk."

"Where was that trunk of yours stored?"

"In the tent — my trunk."

"Did you keep your clothes all in your trunk in the tent?"

"No, sir. I kept some of them in Lieutenant Flipper's trunk."

"What was the reason of that?"

"Because I had no room. I had no place to put my things for safety and I asked him if I could not keep them in his trunk."

"Was your own trunk secure?"

"No, sir. It had no lock on it. There was no safety in a tent."

Smith then stated she had asked Flipper's permission to store some of her clothing in his trunk.

"Where was the trunk in which you stored your clothes?"

"In Lieutenant Flipper's — in his front room."

"Were any of your clothes in any chest of Lieutenant Flipper's in there?"

"Yes, sir, into the chest into the hall."

"What did you do when you wanted to go to the trunk?"

"I asked Lieutenant Flipper for the keys."

"Did you ever keep the keys of that trunk?"

"No, sir. When I wanted them I had to ask for them."

"What occurred on the morning when Lieutenant Flipper was put in arrest?"

"I don't remember what occurred."

"Did you go to the trunk?

"Yes, sir. I went to the trunk to take some of that clothing out of the trunk and put into the chest and hang some up, and to put away Lieutenant Flipper's things."

"How did you obtain the keys to that trunk?"

"I asked Lieutenant Flipper for them in the morning."

"What did he do?"

"He gave me the keys."

"What did you take out?"

"I had taken out a dress, or two, and taken his cuffs and his handkerchiefs and things out and folded them up and put them back."

"Did you take out any papers and envelopes?"

"I taken out two envelopes."

"What did you do with these?"

"I put them in my bosom."

"What was the cause of your taking out these envelopes?"

"Because I was in this trunk and I had taken some things out and because I had a woman in there working that was not very honest."

"When Lieutenant Flipper gave you the keys, what did he say about locking up?"

"He said, 'Lucy, don't go away and leave that trunk open, be very careful and keep it locked and when you go away give me back the keys.' That's what he always told me."

"Did he state anything to you in regard to these papers?"

"No, sir."

"Then you took them out without his knowledge?"

"Yes, sir.... He knew nothing about my taking the envelopes out."

"Who was there at that time? Who did he go out with?"

"I think he went out with Mr. Chamberlain."

"Where had he come from just before that?"

"From his breakfast."

"Who took breakfast with him?"

"Mr. Chamberlain, he boarded with him."

"After putting away these clothes, what did you do with the keys?"

"I think I laid them on the table. I had not finished putting away all the clothes."

"Where did you go to after you had changed the clothing and taken these envelopes and put them in your bosom?"

"I don't remember where I went to. I was cleaning up. I was around the house there."

"You remember Colonel Shafter coming there?"

"I don't remember anything about it."

"Did you see Colonel Shafter that morning?"

"I don't remember whether I seen him or not. I was so scared."

"Do you remember Colonel Shafter coming there to the kitchen and speaking to you? Did you go over to Colonel Shafter's office?"

"I don't remember whether I went over there or not. I was scared to death."

"Where did you go to during that day?"

"I went to jail for one place."

"Where were you when you were taken to the jail?"

"I don't know, Captain, because I was so scared I don't know where I was taken from."

"What scared you?"

"I can't tell you that. I don't know what scared me. I was scared through."

"How long had you been living with Lieutenant Flipper then?"

"I had been living there I think about two months, since I come up from Stockton. I don't remember how long exactly it was."

"During the time that you lived with Lieutenant Flipper, had he ever given you anything in the way of presents or anything besides your monthly pay?"

"There was a little ring laying on his desk one day that I asked him if I could have and he said, 'yes.' That is the only thing that Lieutenant Flipper ever gave me, and that he would not have given me if I had not asked him for it, I don't guess."

"What became of those envelopes?"

"What became of them?"

"Those envelopes which you say that you took out of the trunk?"

"I don't remember what became of them."

"Were they taken from you?"

"I don't know, Captain. I was so scared I don't know whether they were taken away from me or not."

"Do you remember anything about the transactions?"

"No, sir, I don't remember nothing at all about it."

"After you left Lieutenant Flipper, after getting the keys from him, when was the next time that you saw him?"

"I never saw him any more until after he got out of the guardhouse."

"That was how long afterwards?"

"I don't remember that, how long it was."

"Then if I understand you, you took possession of those checks without any authority from anybody whatever?"

"I did them two envelopes."

"During the time that you had been working for Lieutenant Flipper, how long had you been accustomed to keeping your clothing in his quarters?"

"Not long. This last time that I came back from Stockton. I had no room."

"Did you live with him before?"

"Yes, sir, I did."

With this, Captain Barber finished his questioning and the judge advocate began his cross-examination.

"Do you remember when you were arrested?" asked Clous.

"I hardly do remember it. I was scared to death."

"Do you remember that you were arrested?"

"I kind of remember I was in jail."

"You remember the time that you were examined out here before Judge Harnett?"

"No, sir, I can't remember nothing."

"Did you not state to Judge Harnett, or United States Commissioner Harnett, on the 15th day of August last when you were examined out here that Lieutenant Flipper told you to take care of his things when he went out of the house, to be careful of these two envelopes because there was some help around the house and they might get misplaced?"

"No sir, I remember nothing about it."

"On the 13th of August last at this post when you saw Colonel Shafter, did not he ask you whether you had any papers about you, and did not you answer him you did not have anything about you?"

"I don't remember anything about it for I was frightened to death. That is the way of it."

"You don't remember what you said before United States Commissioner Harnett?"

"No, sir, I do not."

"Do you mean to say that you don't remember anything now about that occurrence?"

"No sir, I don't remember anything about it because I ain't got over my scare yet."

Clous continued to ask her questions, but she could not remember anything, repeating that "I was frightened to death" and "I don't remember anything about it." She claimed she didn't even recognize the envelopes taken from her. Then Clous asked if Flipper talked to her "about his business?"

"No, sir, it was not his place."

"You say you roomed at Mrs. Olsup's?"

"Yes, sir."

"Well, in the morning did you dress yourself at Mrs. Olsup's or make your toilet at Mr. Flipper's?"

"No, sir, I dressed myself at Mrs. Olsup's."

"Did not make your toilet in Mr. Flipper's bedroom?"

"Oh! No, sir."

"How could you dress yourself at Mrs. Olsup's when your clothes were at Lieutenant Flipper's?"

"Well, did not I have to wear clothes down to Mrs. Olsup's? I had to put them on in the morning, I am sure, when I got up."

"Were you still cleaning when Colonel Shafter came there?"

"I don't know; the very sight of Colonel Shafter frightens me ... scares me nearly to death."

"Where are you now living?"

"Living in town."

"What is your occupation?"

"Working."

"Still keeping house for Lieutenant Flipper yet?"

"I do his cooking, washing and ironing."

Clous asked Lucy if they ate together and she replied they did not; "I do his work."

"Cook for him, do you?"

"Yes, sir."

"Did not you on the 20th day of August, while you were in jail in Chihuahua, go before Judge Harnett and make an affidavit before him?"

"An affidavit. What is that?"

"Did not you have a paper made out in reference to your release from jail?"

"No, sir. I was frightened to death. How could I remember?"

"You were still frightened on the 20th of August?"

"Yes, sir. I am frightened yet."

The judge advocate then presented Lucy Smith's affidavit to the court, but Barber objected "as it is manufactured evidence." This objection was overruled. Clous continued to question Lucy, but she could not remember a thing.

Clous asked, "Did you ever sleep or spend a night at Mr. Flipper's quarters?"

"No, sir. I went to a dance once and after I came home Mrs. Olsup and I went into the kitchen and staid [*sic*] there all night because we danced to three o'clock. Mr. Flipper did not know I was on the place."

"That was the only time you was ever there?"

"Yes, sir."

"And Mrs. Olsup was with you?"

"Yes sir."

That ended the questioning of Lucy Smith.

In his book, *The Court-Martial of Lieutenant Henry Flipper*, author Charles Robinson notes that Lucy "was a black woman in trouble with the white man's law. It is more than likely, also, that she knew a great deal about the missing money, which would have aggravated her fears. Either way, it would have certainly been traumatic for her."[3]

Robinson further observes:

> On the other hand, Shafter had also suffered from convenient attacks of amnesia any time something came up with might make him look culpable. Lucy had a much better chance of doing the same and getting away with it; given the racial stereotypes of the time, the sight of a frightened black woman, wringing her hands and wailing in fear and confusion, would have raised no suspicions among the white officers of the court or the two white attorneys. Lucy's testimony, in full, shows a definite craftiness. She had contradictory memory lapses covering an entire period of several days. It is impossible to believe that of all the things that happened — her search by Shafter, her arrest, her incarceration, her statement before U. S. Commissioner Hartnett, the filing of federal charges against her — that she would not remember at least something. In short, one must conclude that she was lying all the way through.[4]

The defense made no effort to bring in the others who were in Flipper's quarters when it was searched for questioning, even though it seems obvious they may have known something about the missing money. After Lucy's testimony, Joseph Sender took the stand. Sender ran the mercantile establishment Flipper was visiting when Wilhelmi arrived to bring him back to post. Sender said he'd known Flipper for about a year and that the Lieutenant had come in "twice or three times a week" and that "I have always found him to be a straightforward man, of good character." He never saw him gamble or "indulge in any form of extravagance."

Sender stated that "Shafter told me then that he did not think for a moment that Flipper tried to defraud the government out of a cent. It was only through his carelessness and bad company, or something to that effect, he had about his house." Clous asked Sender if he was an "Israelite." Sender said he was and that he had contributed $500 to help Flipper cover his deficit.

W.S. Chamberlain, a watchmaker at Fort Davis, was then called to testify. Chamberlain was boarding with Flipper at the time of his arrest and had gone to other merchants and citizens fund-raising to help Flipper. Chamberlain said he'd heard Flipper caution Lucy about the security of his room and papers.

Chamberlain went to his shop the morning Flipper was arrested and did not see him until the following Monday. Chamberlain had gone to Shafter and asked if reimbursement of the money would help. He testified that Shafter said, "Yes, it will save him from the penitentiary.... I will buck up a hundred dollars myself." Within a couple of days, Chamberlain and Sender had come up with the cash to cover Flipper's shortfall. He testified Shafter told him "he always thought Lieutenant Flipper to be an honest man, and did not believe that he was guilty, that there was someone else to the bottom of it.... I think his remark was that there was some 'damned nigger' at the bottom of it." Chamberlain also testified that Flipper was frugal, allowing only "a dollar or two dollars" a week to attend Mexican dances.

J.M. Dean, the Fort Davis attorney who represented Lucy Smith in her hearing with Commissioner Hartnett, said he'd overheard Shafter remark "he would get Flipper or he was on his trail, or made some remark of that sort, that he was getting more evidence on him."

Barber asked, "Did he say anything about piling it up on him?"

Dean replied, "Yes, sir, he said he was piling it up on him.... I had been led to believe that Colonel Shafter was acting as the friend of Lieutenant Flipper and was disposed to act square towards him, but after I heard him make that remark, I came to the conclusion that he was playing him double."

"Do you know whether or not Lieutenant Flipper at that time had confidence that Colonel Shafter was acting in a friendly manner toward him?"

"Yes, sir, I thought that Flipper was putting considerable confidence in Colonel Shafter."

Dean testified that Flipper "led me to believe that he thought Colonel Shafter was his friend, and I told him that ... from what I had heard Colonel Shafter say, that I thought it would be to his interest to conduct this matter without Colonel Shafter's assistance ... that I had never heard Colonel Shafter say anything in Flipper's behalf, but on the other hand had been against him."

Major N.B. McLaughlin then testified to Flipper's "upstanding character and performance as a soldier." Barber wanted to enter a letter from Colonel

Grierson, who did not want to be a witness but wrote a letter vouching for Flipper's character. The letter stated that Flipper's "veracity and integrity, have never been questioned and his character and standing as an officer and a gentleman have certainly been beyond reproach."

The letter continues:

> General Davidson [Flipper's commanding officer at Fort Sill], Captain Nolan, and others under whom he has served, have spoken of him to me in the highest terms, and he has repeatedly been selected for special and important duties, and discharged them faithfully and in a highly satisfactory manner. Being, as an officer, the only representative of his race in the Army, he has, under circumstances and surroundings the most unfavorable and discouraging, steadily won his way by sterling worth and ability, by manly and soldierly bearing, to the confidence, respect and esteem of all with whom he has served or come in contact. As to Lieutenant Flipper's late trouble, or alleged offence for which he is now being Court-martialed, I have no personal knowledge, but from all information I have been able to gain relative thereto — although he may have been careless and indiscreet, and may have committed irregularities, from want of experience — my confidence in his honesty of purpose has not been shaken, and my faith in his final vindication is still as strong as ever.... I, as his Colonel — believing in his great promise for future usefulness; knowing that his restoration to duty would give great satisfaction to the regiment — most heartily and earnestly commend him to the leniency of the Court and reviewing authorities.

The Court was adjourned until December 6 so Flipper could prepare his statement to the Court.

8

The Verdict and Dismissal

Henry Flipper never took the stand in his defense and, according to Barry Johnson, this allowed him "to shut out a great amount of detail about his household which would probably have been elicited in cross-examination." Barry Johnson brings up these questions:

Who were "some of them"? Were they the three Mexicans, or other parties about the house?

Who was the woman "who was not very safe" but who was nevertheless in there helping Lucy? Why was it necessary to have so much help around the house?

Was there ever any degree of security in the place: were the doors ever locked? Was the desk (presumably the roll-top type) ever locked?

Were the checks and cash often left in books and other odd places?

Could anyone wander in, like the Mexicans, and perhaps equally casually wander out with a few hundred dollars of the government's money?

Why was a check supposedly made out to meet a deficiency discovered on July 8 but dated May 20?

When did Flipper first contact Homer Lee, and why was he so disastrously wrong in his estimate of how much was due him?

Why did he fail to get checks from Company "A" on July 11?

Who told him that Shafter was intent on getting him into trouble, and when was he told this?

When did he begin to give credit to soldiers and laundresses, and why was no record kept of these debts?

Johnson surmises that "if the Court had been asked what Flipper should have done when he first discovered an unexplained deficiency, the members would surely have answered: 'Step up like a man to his commanding officer and tell him what happened.'" But then, Johnson adds, "would all the circumstances, as they were known to Flipper, have allowed him to do this?"[1]

Instead, on the twenty-eighth day of the trial, Henry Flipper read his prepared statement:

I declare to you in the most solemn and impressive manner possible that I am perfectly innocent in every manner, shape or form; that I have never myself nor by another appropriated, converted or applied to my own use a single dollar or a single penny of the money of the government or permitted it to be done, or authorized any meddling with it whatever. Of crime I am not guilty. The funds for which I was responsible I kept in my own quarters in my trunk.... My reason for keeping them there were that, as I was responsible for their safety, I felt more secure to have them in my own personal custody.... I had no reason to question the honesty of any of the persons about my house as I had never missed anything that attracted my attention, and when the officers searched that trunk and failed to find the funds which I had put in there three days before, I was perfectly astounded and could hardly believe the evidence of my own senses. As where that money went or who took it I am totally ignorant.

Sometime in May the actual cash on hand did not meet the amount for which I was responsible. I was owing a considerable bill myself which it was not convenient to pay, and as there was a large amount due me from men and laundresses, I believed that my shortage was accounted for in that way, but as the funds were not to be transmitted for some time it did not occasion me any uneasiness, as I felt confident of getting it in by the time it would be required.

On the morning of the 10th of August I took what checks I had to the commissary sergeant and directed him to make a letter of transmittal of them and directed him to ... search for checks to meet the money I had, expecting daily a deposit from Homer Lee & Co., but there were no checks to be produced and no deposit was made. On the 13th of August when I left my house with Mr. Chamberlain I have every reason to believe and do believe that all the funds for which I was responsible was in the trunk and in my quarters except for the $1,440 check, which I have already explained, and the amount of my commissary bill for July which I had not paid. As to their disappearance, I have no privity or knowledge and am not responsible except to make the amount good, and that I have done.

As to my motives in the matter alleged in the first specification of the second charge, I can only say that some time before, I had been cautioned that the commanding officer would improve any opportunity to get me into trouble, and although I did not give much credit to it at the time, it occurred to me very prominently when I found myself in difficulty, and as he had long been known to me by reputation and observation as a severe, stern man, having committed my first mistake I indulged what proved to be a false hope that I would be able to work out my responsibilities alone and avoid giving him any knowledge of my embarrassment.

After Flipper finished, Barber, gave his summation:

[Flipper] is struggling for his crown; for the spotless record of nine long years, and he could not do otherwise than fight the battle inch by inch and steel to steel.... Regarding his pleas and testimony together, you will observe that the accused does not present his action under the second charge [conduct unbecoming an officer and a gentleman] as blameless, but he presents it just as it is, placing before you as nearly as he can his faults and his motives and asks that they be weighed together. The first charge and its specifications [embezzlement] the accused denies in toto.... He confidently challenges the prosecution and the world to show it or even the shadow of such an act....

You will bear in mind that the accused is not required to prove, under the 60th Article of War, that he did not embezzle the money, but it is for the government to prove that he did embezzle it, and that he did knowingly and willfully misappropriate it and apply it to his own use and benefit. Have they done so? Where, when and by what testimony? There is not a syllable of proof of it.

The accused has told you his error and has given you his reasons and his motives and submitted them all to your judgment, asking you to consider his error with its surroundings, his mistake with his surroundings, and he appeals with confidence to your charity that you will measure his offense and its palliation together.

From the time when a mere boy he stepped upon our platform and asked the privilege of competing with us for the prize of success, he has had to fight the battle of life all alone. He has had no one to turn to for counsel or sympathy. Is it strange then that when he found himself in difficulties which he could not master, and confronted with a mystery which he could not solve, he should hide it in his own breast and endeavor to work out the problem alone as he had been compelled to do all the other problems of his life? Is it strange that he should withhold his confidence from his neighbors, whose relations with him had been such as not to invite that confidence, and as he saw his expectations of relief fading one by one and his embarrassments thickening around him, to hold with all the more tenacity to a vague hope which is the guiding star to those who have to fight life's battle by themselves?

The question is before you whether it is possible for a colored man to secure and hold a position as an officer of the army.

Judge Advocate Clous then gave his closing statement:

Gentlemen, the government provided the accused with a strong, heavy and secure safe, over which after hours a sentinel stood guard, the regulations of his department required to keep his public funds in that safe, but for weeks and months, on innumerable occasions, he did so keep his funds; and now at this late day he comes before you, in order to make up a plausible story, to account for his deficiency, that he considered his trunk — a portable affair, kept for the joint uses of himself and his female servant, accessible at all times to both — a more secure place of deposit than a strong iron safe, a safe which it would take the joint efforts of a body of men and draft animals to remove.

The Accused, like his female servant, Lucy, is ignorant of what became of the funds he claimed to have had in the envelope which was by him deposited in the household trunk. And yet, gentlemen, according to the statement of the accused and his servant, they were the only persons who had had access to that trunk or possessed the keys of the same up to the time the accused was seated near that trunk when the search commenced on August thirteenth. Strange ignorance indeed? But not so strange when we consider the fact that Lucy Smith is still the accused's servant or housekeeper.

The accused, in effect, tells us that having made one false entry and told one falsehood, the stern character of his commanding officer compelled him to repeat the offense.

I claim that the prosecution by the testimony adduced has made quick work of the charge of conduct unbecoming of an officer, and concluded the case for the United States.

At this point, the court dismissed Flipper and went into closed session to decide his fate. They voted, from least senior member to the most senior member, and a simple majority ruled; there was no record kept of courts-martial deliberations or votes.

Before the verdict was known, the *St. Louis Daily Globe-Democrat* reported, "It is very evident ... that Lieut. Flipper has been guilty of falsehood in stating that he had already remitted funds which he intended to remit, but never did. He discounted, in his assertions, occurrences which he hoped and presumed would come to pass. As to the charge of dishonesty, that does not seem to have been so clearly established as the charge of lying.... It must be admitted that even if Lieut. Flipper's general reputation for integrity, honesty and good habits survives this trial, he has been guilty of false statements and of gross carelessness and inefficiency in his commissary duties."[2]

After a break for deliberation, the men reentered the courtroom and presented this verdict on December 7, 1881:

The Court, having maturely considered all the evidence accrued, finds the accused, Second Lieutenant Henry O. Flipper of the Tenth Regiment of U. S. Cavalry, as follows:
  Charge I.
  Of the specification, "Not Guilty"
  Of the first charge, "Not Guilty"
  Charge II.
  Of the first specification, "Guilty"
  Of the second specification, "Guilty"
  Of the third specification, "Guilty"
  Of the fourth specification, "Guilty"

Of the fifth specification, "Guilty"
Of the second charge, "Guilty"

And the court does therefore sentence him, Second Lieutenant Henry O. Flipper of the Tenth Regiment of U.S. Cavalry, to be dismissed from the service of the United States.

Flipper had been acquitted of embezzlement but had been found guilty of "conduct unbecoming an officer and a gentleman." However, no officer could be dismissed without an order from the president, so the report of the findings and verdict had to go to Washington before the case was finished.

The court met for the last time the following day, December 8, 1881, at 10:00 A.M. and approved the proceedings of the previous day, then adjourned at 12:30 P.M. During a period of almost three months, the court had met for thirty days. According to author Charles Robinson:

> In view of the evidence presented, there were really no other verdicts the court could have rendered. For all his references to law, Clous had failed to establish that Flipper had stolen the money. As Barber maintained throughout the trial, he was guilty of no more than carelessness, and the government had recovered its money primarily through Flipper's good standing in the community of Fort Davis. Yet, try as he might, Barber could not excuse Flipper's conduct when Small and Shafter had called for an accounting. He had falsified reports and he had lied. Barber could hope for leniency over what he considered Flipper's peculiar circumstances, but he could do no more than hope. The case for conduct unbecoming an officer was airtight under any interpretation, and that is how the court saw it.[3]

Robinson noted that the court "could have given Flipper a lighter sentence, or could have recommended him to the clemency of the reviewing authorities. This, it seems, again in view of Flipper's peculiar circumstances as well as Shafter's culpability, would have been the proper course. This was not done, and the reasons will probably never be known.... It is charitable to think that the members of the court simply followed the regulation requiring dismissal, believing that at some point between themselves and President Arthur [who had to approve the verdict], the sentence would be reduced."[4]

In his book, Barry Johnson asks, "Why did a well-educated officer, who had published an autobiography at the age of twenty-two, whose record everyone agreed was spotless, who averred that he was perfectly innocent of crime, and whose career was threatened with imminent ruin, why — the members must surely have asked themselves — did he not take his oath, explain to them fully and candidly all that had happened, and then submit himself to cross-

Fort Davis in 1887 (Fort Davis Historic Site).

examination, and perhaps to their own questions? Faced with his silence—apart from the 2,000 word statement—they can have felt no inclination to do anything for him, beyond the finding of 'not guilty' on the main charge."[5]

Johnson notes that when a court thought the terms of a mandatory sentence were too harsh, they usually made a recommendation for clemency and gave their reasons. However, in Flipper's case, the members of the court did not give any recommendations. This leads to the assumption that they believed dismissal from the service was appropriate.[6]

The case was first reviewed by General Augur, the department commander, who stated in his report, "The proceedings are approved.... The sentence is approved."[7]

On January 9, the record of the case and the report reached the desk of Judge Advocate General David G. Swaim in the Bureau of Military Justice in the War Department. Before the Civil War, Swaim had been an Ohio abolitionist; during the Civil War, he was a member of an Ohio brigade formed by Senator John Sherman, brother of General Sherman. Swaim became a member of the Judge Advocate Corps in 1869 and served as James Garfield's private secretary before President Garfield named him judge advocate general.

A month earlier — on December 1, 1881 — Swaim had recommended dismissal of the guilty verdict in the court-martial of Johnson Whittaker. In his report, Swaim stated, "On the whole my conclusion is that the prosecution has fallen short of sustaining the charges and specifications by adequate legal proofs, or such as would be sufficient in law to justify a jury in uniting in a conviction, and that the proceedings, findings and sentence should be, therefore, disproved."[8]

It took Swaim two months to hand in his recommendation on the Flipper court-martial. Swaim was severe with Shafter, stating, "It would also seem that the advance of the $100 was for the purpose of diverting attention from the illegal and arbitrary action of Col. Shafter in confining Flipper in a cell in the guardhouse." Swaim criticized the officers who searched Flipper's quarters because they did not take a full and accurate inventory. He pointed his finger at Lucy, saying, "Notwithstanding Flipper's confidence in the honesty of this woman, there is some reason to believe that she made away with part of the funds found to be deficient." Swaim concluded, saying, "It is clear that Lieut. Flipper did not intend to defraud the government out of any of its funds but that his conduct is attributable to carelessness and ignorance of correct business methods." He recommended "that the sentence be confirmed but mitigated to a less degree of punishment."[9]

Normally, the report from Swaim on the Flipper case would have gone to General Sherman, head of the army, but Sherman was not in Washington at the time, so Swaim sent his recommendation on March 10 to Secretary of War Robert Lincoln, son of the slain President, that "the sentence be continued but mitigated to a lesser degree of punishment." Lincoln sent this on to President Chester Arthur.

On March 16 *The Nation* reported the following: "The record on the Flipper court-martial case, together with Judge-Advocate-General Swaim's report, have been submitted to the President. General Swaim is understood to recommend a mitigation of the sentence of dismissal, on the ground that Flipper, while convicted of certain violations of the army regulations, was acquitted of the criminal acts charged against him. The general impression is that the sentence will be mitigated."[10]

An article in the *New York Times* on May 27 noted, "It is now understood that Secretary Lincoln approved the recommendation of Judge-Advocate General Swaim for mitigation of the sentence of Lieut. Flipper, who was convicted of a gross violation of Army regulations and sentenced to dismissal from the service. The President will not act upon the case until he has had time to dispose of important questions of state now claiming his attention, but it is learned that he is disposed to grant the mitigation recommended by the Judge-Advocate General."[11]

Chester Arthur became president in September 1881, when James Garfield died from an assassin's gunshot. According to Barry Johnson, in many cases, friends and family of officers facing dismissal brought any mitigating circumstances to the attention of the War Department. Also, they would attempt to enlist the help of politicians and other public figure to bring their influence to bear on the president, ... "but nothing of the kind relating to Flipper has survived." Johnson added that Flipper's timing was also bad because the Hayes Administration, which directly preceded Garfield's, had been notably lenient with court-martial cases. This led to the House of Representatives looking into the matter. "As often happens, a mild policy was followed by more stringent measures; and Arthur appears to have taken a firmer line in confirming sentences of dismissal."[12]

Johnson adds one more twist to this story. Swaim was lucky to be then-President-elect Garfield's good friend. "He was promoted three grades and, within about the same number of years, became the only Judge Advocate General in American history to be court-martialed while holding the office! The court convicted him of attempting to defraud a firm of Washington bankers to the extent of five thousand dollars; and of making statements about the transaction which were 'calculated and intended to deceive the Secretary of War.'" President Arthur thought that dismissal was the correct punishment but finally agreed to the court's recommendation of suspension on half-pay for twelve years, until Swaim could be retired for age.[13]

The secondary charges against both Swain and Flipper were nearly the same, and it is possible the president and the secretary of war both concluded that General Augur had been correct in believing Flipper was guilty of embezzlement. This might explain why the president's endorsement completely ignored the findings in Flipper's case and was as uninformative as it possibly could have been, stating only, on June 14, "The sentence in the foregoing case of Second Lieut. Henry O. Flipper 10th Regiment of U.S. Cavalry, is hereby confirmed."

The June 16 edition of the *New York Times* gave this report: "The President has approved the sentence in the case of Second Lieut. Henry O. Flipper,

Tenth Cavalry, tried by court-martial on charges of embezzlement and conduct unbecoming an officer, and sentenced to dismissal from the service. An order to that effect will be issued by the Secretary of War in a day or two."[14]

Flipper spent his last six months as an army officer at Fort Quitman, Texas. At the noon hour on June 30, 1882, with no fanfare or ceremony, Lt. Henry Ossian Flipper ceased to be a soldier in the United States Army. With this decision, only an act of Congress, approved by the president, could reverse this sentence.

Charles Robinson, in his exhaustive study of Henry Flipper's court-martial, concludes as follows:

> The Flipper Affair was disgraceful only in treatment of the officer in question during the initial investigation and ultimate sentence. Otherwise, the conduct of the trial and the verdicts rendered were entirely appropriate to the charges, and the charges were appropriate to the investigation. If during the course of the trial, the board erred, it was in failing to pin down Lucy Smith about her alleged memory lapses.... If anyone stole the money, it was Lucy, either alone or together with any of the other shadowy figures who, testimony revealed, apparently had routine access to Flipper's quarters.[15]

The same day that Henry Flipper was released from the army, Charles Guiteau was hanged in Washington, D.C., for the assassination of President James Garfield.

9

Into the West

Lieutenant Henry Flipper was twenty-seven years old when he was dismissed from the Army. He promptly sold his horses to Lt. Nordstrom and his other personal property to civilians and made plans to leave Fort Quitman. Flipper boarded a train to El Paso, probably with his lady friend, a black woman named Florida J. Wolfe, and arrived there on July 3, 1882. One account states that, after they were in El Paso, Flipper "deserted her and she was forced to accept employment as a barmaid," while another states that she worked "for three years as a housekeeper for a wealthy rancher." At any rate, Lady Flo became well known during her lifetime as the common-law wife of British aristocrat Lord Delaval Beresford.[1]

At the time Henry Flipper arrived there, El Paso was a wild and wooly town, presided over by Dallas Stoudenmire, who was appointed deputy U.S. marshall the same month Flipper arrived. Stoudenmire had served in the Confederacy during the Civil War, then as a Texas Ranger; he moved to El Paso and became city marshal on April 10, 1881. Four days later, while having lunch at the Globe Restaurant, a ruckus caused by a drunken, loud John Hale broke out on the street. Stoudenmire ran outside and gunfire erupted. His first shot killed an innocent Mexican bystander, who died the next day, but his second shot killed Hale. Stoudenmire also shot George Campbell, who died the next day.

This caused bad blood to flow; and the next Sunday Stoudenmire and his brother-in-law, Doc Cummings, were walking the street when they were ambushed by Bill Johnson, a friend of Hale and Campbell. Stoudenmire and Cummings gunned down Johnson and chased away other ambushers who were hiding. On December 16, Stoudenmire survived another ambush.

Stoudenmire was often drunk; this caused him to resign after about a year. But in July 1882, he received an appointment as deputy U.S. marshal. On September 18, Stoudenmire had a run-in with some old enemies, the Manning brothers, at Manning's Saloon. A fight erupted. Manning slugged Stoudenmire and the two wrestled. During the fight, Stoudenmire managed to shoot Manning with a small pistol before Manning pulled out his .45 and plugged Stoudenmire in his head behind the left ear. A raging Doc Manning pistol-whipped the dead Stoudenmire until law officer Jim Gillett pulled him away.

Stoudenmire had been heard to say, "I don't believe the bullet was ever molded that will kill me." That fight with the Mannings proved he was dead wrong.

El Paso is seated in the western-most part of Texas on the north side of the Rio Grande, with a bridge crossing to Mexico and bordering New Mexico, then a territory. After he arrived, Henry Flipper obtained a job in a laundry and wrote some articles for the *El Paso Times*. A number of other blacks lived in El Paso, many of them former Buffalo Soldiers.

Henry Flipper had a decided advantage. He was well educated, bright, literate and a former army officer; within the black community he was a hero. He studied Spanish at West Point, then practiced it in Texas. He had also studied engineering at West Point and had practical experience during his time in the army.

In early November 1882, a reporter for the *St. Louis Republican* spoke with Flipper about his court-martial. The reporter noted that Flipper was a "clerk in a laundry and was surrounded by Chinese and negro experts." The reporter asked, "Is it a fact that your case will be brought up before Congress in December?" Flipper replied, "Yes, sir. My friends will endeavor to have my commission restored." Flipper continued:

> My sentence was not only illegal but unduly severe, and I refer you to the case of Paymaster Reese, who in 1876, while on duty in New York, was tried upon a similar charge. He had overdrawn his public bank account for a period of two years, and at one time was $10,000 overdrawn. During the whole of this period, he misrepresented his public bank account in his returns to the government. The charges against him were embezzlement and conduct unbecoming an officer and a gentleman, and when convicted he was simply sentenced to four months suspension. He was an officer, an experienced business and military man who was convicted upon both charges, while I was an inexperienced lieutenant — a mere boy at the time — and was acquitted of the more grave charge of embezzlement, and yet I was dismissed from the service for the latter charge.
>
> [I was] found guilty of conduct unbecoming an officer and a gentleman. The specifications on the latter charge contained clauses which could not be sustained inasmuch as I had been acquitted upon the charge of embezzlement.... Now, it is a rule in the military service that to sustain a finding of guilty to a specification to a charge, every averment to that specification must be proved or the parts not proved excepted. I was charged with embezzlement

(active embezzlement) and tried for constructive embezzlement under a section of the Revised Statutes of the United States and fully acquitted, so that the concluding words in the specification on the charge of conduct unbecoming a gentleman should have been stricken out, and it is upon this that I base my right to another hearing and setting aside of the sentence.

The reporter asked Flipper, "Do you know who stole the money for which you were held responsible?"

"Yes, but knowing a thing and proving it are two very different things," replied Flipper. "Early in July 1881, a scouting party left Davis to run down" some Indian problems. According to Flipper, a first lieutenant (Wilhelmi) told some men "that he had found a way to get rid of the nigger. I was thus warned of impending danger and I suspected that the attempt to hurt me would come from the white commissary sergeant who occupied quarters opposite to my office. So I removed my funds from the safe and took them to my private quarters where I secreted them.... The cash was stolen but the checks were left." Flipper stated that he expected "to be reinstated upon the ground of illegal finding of the verdict."

Henry Flipper around the time of his dismissal from the army (Autry National Museum).

The reporter also spoke with Major Anson Mills, who was temporary commander of Fort Davis because of the absence of Colonel Grierson. Mills said of Flipper that the lieutenant "was a rather popular man, kept his place and did not obtrude. I do not think he was treated exactly right, but I would not for a moment advocate his reinstatement in the army. His commission made him an officer and a gentleman, but then, you know, one couldn't meet a colored man on social equality."

Another officer noted the following:

Col. Shafter was as much to blame as Flipper, for it is the

duty of the commanding officer to go over the accounts and cash of his commissary before they are sent to the chief commissary. Shafter did not do this, but let Flipper run and then jumped him, scaring him into telling the lie about the funds being in transit. He had no right to place Flipper in the guard-house, as officers and non-commissioned officers are only placed under arrest, the privates being sent to the guard-house. Flipper's points are well taken and if he were a white man he would upset the verdict and sentence; but he is a colored man, and I for one would not vote for any colored man being an officer in the United States army. Our wives and daughters must be considered.[2]

A year later, in November 1883, an interesting notice was published in the *St. Louis Republican*. The "notice" was a telegram about the movement to reinstate Flipper in the army. The paper stated, "Flipper's friends are doing him poor service in encouraging hopes of reinstatement. He ought to be thankful that he suffered so little for his misconduct. A young white officer is now serving his time in a Kansas penitentiary for an offence of almost exactly the same kind, and since the supreme court shattered the civil-rights bill there has been no law making a colored man any better than his white brother. Flipper got off easy on account of his color, and he ought to open his eyes to that fact."[3]

After a little over a year in El Paso, Flipper was hired by A.Q. Wingo, a former Confederate, to work for the Chicago-based firm of Harrison, Kneeland, Beall, and Zimpleman (who were all ex–Confederate officers) as an engineer. This firm was connected to a large real estate firm in El Paso and had a contract to survey Mexican government lands in the state of Chihuahua, just across the border from El Paso.

Flipper and Wingo went to the town of Chihuahua, which had a population of about 22,000 but not a single restaurant or hotel. They traveled about forty miles south of Chihuahua, to Santa Rosalia, where they camped while doing their surveys; however, they hired a cook, and obtained two four-mule wagons.

Since Flipper knew Spanish, he could communicate in Mexico. In his *Memoirs* he notes that, in Santa Rosalia, "No young girl ever went out on the street without a relative or a duena, generally some old hag who never hesitated to sell her charge at any time, as was often done."[4] Flipper also made some other pungent observations about the Mexicans. He said, "On Sundays the people gathered in the plaza (park) and promenaded, the men going one way and the women the opposite way. You never saw a couple together unless they were husband and wife. The people were intensely Catholic, externally, and were in the churches all the time. When a man passed in front of a church, he took his hat off. With all that, the people were and are the most immoral I ever saw. There was a street called the Street of the 11,000 virgins, given wholly over to the unregenerated Magdalenes. Gambling was common."[5]

Flipper, Wingo and their party left Santa Rosalia until they reached a salty lake, where they camped. The next morning they awoke covered with snow and moved on, but their helpers were freezing. Flipper and Wingo looked for mesquite trees to cut for firewood, but could find none; finally they found some black walnut logs and brought them back to camp.

Flipper and Wingo surveyed the boundary line between the states of Chihuahua and Coahuila, arriving at the Rio Grande on Christmas Day of 1883. There, they crossed the river to look at an old house; they entered it "and found it full of corn, pumpkins and other things, among them some dried venison." Flipper later said, "We had not seen a human being for many days, but we helped ourselves to pumpkins and venison."[6]

The surveying party traveled to the town of Meoqui, beside the railroad, where they rented a house. But, according to Flipper, "We had not more than got our things in the house before I was arrested and thrown into a filthy Mexican jail." Wingo contacted the manager in Chihuahua, who saw the governor — who also happened to be a stockholder in the company — and Flipper was released. "I did not know why I had been arrested till later," remembered Flipper. "It was to the effect that a priest was living openly with his daughter and had two or three children by her. This priest was a near connection to a leading family in Chihuahua and the richest in Mexico." Flipper wrote about this priest in a letter to a friend of his in El Paso, a barber named Bainbridge, and Bainbridge showed it to a newspaper editor, who printed it. The priest received a copy, and that's how Flipper came to be arrested.[7]

Flipper was disgusted by the morality in Mexico. In addition to the priest who lived openly with his three daughters and had children by all of them, there was a wealthy resident in Chihuahua who lived openly with his sister. This man applied to the legislature for permission to marry his sister but was refused.

Flipper and Wingo dined once with the governor in Chihuahua, which prompted Flipper to observe dining customs in Mexico. "When there are guests in Mexico, in a Mexican family," he said, "the women do not sit at the table with the men, but wait and eat alone.... There were no two plates alike, no two knives and no two forks. They served something like whipped cream and it was put on the table in a cigar box.... They generally ate with their fingers and tortillas. With a piece of tortilla they will scoop up beans and chopped meat, etc. Meat is usually served cut in small pieces to facilitate this. If the meat be in large pieces, they break it with their fingers."[8]

After they finished making their maps in Meoqui, they took them to Chihuahua, then traveled to the western part of the state where they worked throughout 1884 and 1885. In 1886 Flipper remained in Chihuahua, making maps for Banco Minero until the fall of that year.

For some blacks, the West was a chance for a new beginning, a land of opportunity where many fled to escape Southern hostility and violence. However, blacks soon discovered that the racism prevalent in the eastern United States was just as prevalent in the West. There were laws against blacks (like the Black Codes of the South), and a number of former Southerners carried their racial hatreds into the West. But in a land so vast, with law enforcement so lax and sporadic, blacks often escaped persecution. Still, blacks were lynched at the slightest provocation, they were tarred and feathered, and they could not find protection with the law; indeed, a number of lawmen actively singled out blacks for persecution. Overall, whites in the West simply did not want blacks around; therefore, they did all they could to discourage blacks from settling in the West.

There were Africans in what became the United States before there were white English settlers; a black man came over with Columbus, and in 1501 a group of African slaves were brought to America by the Spanish. Spanish explorer Vasco Núñez de Balboa had 30 Africans with him in 1513 when he sighted the Pacific Ocean; there were also Africans with Hernando Cortés during his expedition in 1519. But these Africans were slaves. The only difference between the Africans in the early 1500s and the Africans in the early 1600s is that the Spanish brought the former over to the Southwest and West, whereas the latter were brought over by the English on the East Coast.

The most famous early African in what became the United States was Estevan (sometimes called Esteban, Estavanico or Stephen Dorantes), who was a slave and accompanied the 1527 Spanish expedition that began in Florida. Estevan survived and gave the Spanish their first reports of what the Southwest was like (he claimed to have found the Seven Cities of Gold). On the first white American exploration into the West, York, the slave of William Clark, accompanied the group on the Lewis and Clark Expedition. When fur traders entered the Rockies to trap beaver, two famous trappers — Jim Beckwourth and Edward Rose — were black. Beckwourth discovered Beckwourth

Pass just north of what is now Reno, Nevada, and guided settlers through that pass.

By the time of the Civil War, blacks accounted for about 20 percent of the population in the United States but it was unevenly distributed. In New England blacks were about 2 percent of the population but in the Deep South they could be 70 percent of the population in certain areas. During this period, some blacks ventured west. One George Washington, born to a white mother and a black father, was given to a white family who moved from his native Virginia to Ohio, then to Missouri and then to Oregon Territory, where he married the black widow, Mary Jane Cooness, and founded the town of Centerville. Another black, George Washington Bush, came to Oregon Territory in 1844 and introduced the first sawmill, gristmill, mower and reaper to the area; one of his sons served in the Washington state legislature twice. Aunt Clara Brown became a leading citizen in Central City, Colorado, and, through her work as a laundress and nurse, earned enough money to sponsor a black wagon train from Fort Leavenworth to Denver and to help establish a church.

Although these are good and noble stories, they are the exception and not the rule. Western territories quickly enacted laws against black migration. People at the time believed that blacks were inferior, and whites simply did not want them as neighbors. Even the pro- and antislavery forces had one thing in common: Both wanted to control blacks. The slavery question was of great political concern to the South because Southerners depended on slaves for their economic power. Southerners wanted to keep their strong political base so they could continue slavery; many other politicians opposed slavery not for the benefit of blacks but as a way to diminish or abolish the power of white Southern politicians. The culture of slavery was important to the Southern states because they needed slaves for the large plantations that grew cotton and tobacco and other labor-intensive corps. Slavery did not fit into the West because these crops were unsuited to the West.

Blacks first came to the West as Spanish slaves; later, they mixed through marriages and, as Spain lost Mexico to independence, became free. In 1790 about 18 percent of Californians were black or mulatto; in fact, Los Angeles was founded by 44 persons (11 families) of whom 26 were black. Pio Pico, governor of California from 1845 to 1846, was the son of a mulatto mother.

That did not help the freed blacks who came to California in the gold rush beginning in 1849. (About 2,000 blacks joined the Forty-niners.) In the goldfields, blacks found themselves discriminated against, unable to file claims or obtain any legal protection. Whites who brought black slaves to the goldfields caused laws to be enacted that barred blacks from the diggings. At issue was the "unfair advantage" of having slaves help dig while other miners had to swing a pick and shovel on their own. The only advantage that blacks had in the goldfields was that 17,000 Chinese were also there in the diggings and whites feared the Chinese more than they feared the blacks.

Because Texas was a slave state, there were a number of blacks there at the end of the Civil War. Since the state was so decimated (about a fourth of the white male Texans who served in the Civil War were killed or wounded), blacks were involved in early cattle roundups and trail drives. On these trail drives, blacks enjoyed less discrimination than anywhere else. On ranches or on drives, it was impossible to have segregation; and the trials of the trail forced a man to prove himself regardless of color. On the trail, white cowboys came to know black cowboys as individuals, so there was much less violence. But there was discrimination in the towns, although the early cattle towns enforced a rather easygoing discrimination. Black cowboys were expected to gather at one end of the bar and were not allowed in white prostitution houses. Still, the early cattle drives treated blacks fairly well. About 5,000 blacks went up the Chisholm Trail; and on most early crews of eight men, about two would be black.

Like white settlers, blacks dreamed of owning their own homesteads and establishing their own communities. Since violence and hatred were so prevalent in the South during Reconstruction, a number of blacks fled to the West, especially Oklahoma (Indian Territory) and Kansas, where they established communities. These "Exodusters," led by Benjamin "Pop" Singleton, migrated into Kansas in such great numbers (20,000–40,000) that they overwhelmed local communities. The black migrants managed to purchase 20,000 acres of land and build 300 homes. Their most famous town was Nicodemus, Kansas, established in 1877, the year Henry Flipper graduated from West Point.

Although Kansas initially received the most Exodusters in the westward movement of 1870–1910, in general the black population in western territories doubled during this period. In Montana, Idaho, Wyoming, Colorado, New Mexico, Arizona, Utah and Nevada, the black population increased 13-fold, while in Washington, Oregon and California it increased five times. By 1910 there were almost a million blacks living in the West, although Texas, with 690,000 blacks, and Oklahoma, with 137,600, had the majority. In the Mountain and Pacific states blacks accounted for only 0.7 percent of the population.

The Apaches were among the most violent of all the Indian tribes. They were nomads, very brave but very cruel, and were feared by other peaceful, settled Indians such as the Pueblo because of their raiding and killing throughout the southwestern area of the United States. In 1875 most Apaches were rounded up and put on reservations, although some continued to raid until the surrender of Geronimo in 1886.

Geronimo became famous in the 1880s because he was the last Apache to surrender to the government, leading a band of renegade Apaches in the mountains of southeastern Arizona. Mexicans gave Goyahkla (One Who Yawns) the name Geronimo, or Jerome. The Mexicans killed Geronimo's mother, wife and three children during a raid, so the Indian hated Mexicans with a vengeance his whole life.

Geronimo joined the Chiricahua band through marriage and served under Cochise as a warrior. When Cochise died in 1874, Geronimo took over leadership among the Chiricahua. The U.S. government rounded up the Chiricahua in 1876 and sent them to the San Carlos Reservation, but Geronimo refused to go. The U.S. Army sent General George Crook to capture Geronimo and he did so twice. Each time the Apache fled, which prompted Crook's resignation, so the U. S. Army assigned General Nelson A. Miles to the task. In September 1886 Miles captured Geronimo, who spent the rest of his years on reservations.

Flipper was doing his survey work in Mexico before the Apaches had been captured but managed to avoid them, although he was aware of their presence. Flipper wrote in his *Memoirs*:

> Often I have rode up on dead bodies still warm that had been killed and mutilated by the Indians. I had a young American engineer as assistant. He was taken very sick once and I went into a little town by the name of Aconchi and got rooms for him and myself, my men camping in the back yard or corral. We remained there two weeks. The man of the family had to go to Bisbee, Arizona, where he had a contract for packing wood and we traveled together for several days. I was going to Fronteras to continue my work. At Bacuachi I received a courier asking me to send in my monthly statement of expenses. I remained there all next day to make out this statement, write up my mail so as to send it all in by the courier. The Mexican, his wife and four or five children, proceeded and at about 11 o'clock were attacked by Indians and all killed and horribly mutilated. I passed the following day and saw it all. It was horrible and I shuddered to see what I had miraculously escaped.[9]

Flipper worked in Sonora for three different companies, surveying land. From Sonora he went to Yuma, Arizona, where he and his assistant obtained rooms at the hotel, with plans to go back into Mexico for more surveying work. Told there was an American farming near the border, Flipper hired a horse and buggy and drove there and found a family named Hill. Flipper arranged for room and board at the house and set up camp just below the river; the farm straddled the border. Hill worked for Flipper, hauling supplies and going for mail.

"Frequently at meals Mrs. Hill and I and the children were alone," remembered Flipper. "One day she asked to do my washing. I had no washing except underclothing, an occasional woolen shirt and some handkerchiefs and one of my Mexican men usually washed them in camp. I gave the washing, however."

"They were poor white trash and he was shiftless and so was she," observed Flipper. "One day when she and I were alone at the table, she asked me if I knew who she was. Of course, I had to say I did not. Then she startled me by saying: 'I am a niece of Jefferson Davis. We are from Mississippi, but I belong to a poor branch of the family.'" Flipper was astounded. "Think of that!" he said. "A niece of Jefferson Davis cooking and washing for a Negro and eating at the same table with him, working for him for wages!"[10]

After he finished in Sonora, Flipper returned to Nogales, Arizona, to finish his maps and reports. This was in 1891. Flipper was hired by the town of Nogales to prepare a land grant case for the Court of Private Land Claims.

Nogales is located on the border between Arizona and Mexico, due south of Tucson. Henry Flipper first arrived there in October 1885, and lived there almost 16 years, until July 1901. Here Flipper established himself as a leading citizen in the Southwest.

In 1887 Flipper bought some property in Nogales; that same year he learned of the death of his mother from a newspaper article. In 1889 Flipper purchased a second piece of property in town. In September 1891, Flipper "married" Luisa Montoya through a legal contract; since Arizona law forbade Negroes marrying non–Negroes, Flipper could not marry Montoya, a Hispanic, in a regular ceremony. So the two arranged a legal contract between themselves. However, the marriage apparently did not last longer than a year.[11]

Flipper was hired in 1891 to translate Mexican documents and survey lands to settle disputes over the ownership of tracts of land. The Mexican government awarded large land grants to individuals and the United States agreed to honor these grants in the Gadsden Purchase.

The Gadsden Purchase, negotiated by Secretary of War James Gadsden, sought to settle the border dispute between the United States and Mexico that

The International Hotel in Nogales, Arizona, c. 1877 (Arizona Historical Society, 43900, B3739).

lingered after the Mexican-American War in 1848 and to provide a southern route for a transcontinental railroad. The Gadsden Purchase fixed the boundaries of the continental United States, although boundary disputes continued to arise because of shifts in the Rio Grande River. There were problems encountered because of sloppy surveying, documents in Spanish located in Mexican cities, claims for the land made by land speculators and real estate attorneys, and the question of which land grants were legitimate. This meant that no resident of Nogales could legally own property and be assured that what they purchased had a clear, legal deed.

A leading citizen of Nogales was John Slaughter, the legendary lawman of Cochise County, Arizona. Slaughter had brought a herd of cattle from Texas in 1879 and purchased the San Bernardino grant from the heirs of Ignacio Perez, who, in 1822, had been awarded the land grant from the Mexican government. The estimates of the size of the grant ranged from 13,000 to 250,000 acres, which were part of Mexico until the Gadsden Purchase of 1853.

These were the days of open range, so Slaughter wasn't overly concerned about the property's boundaries. The important thing was to control the water; however, as settlers moved in, the homesteaders pressured the United States Court of Private Land Claims to fully establish legal boundaries and determine who owned what land. Since Flipper had surveyed boundaries in New Mexico and Arizona, as well as having conducted surveys in Mexico for President Porfirio Díaz, he was hired to go to San Bernardino with a four man crew and determine the boundaries of the Perez land grant that lay within the United States. Of special concern was the establishment of the boundaries in Cochise County, where John Slaughter lived and ruled.

John Slaughter became sheriff of Tombstone, the county seat, in 1887. The lawman was born in Louisiana, then moved to Texas where he served in the Confederate army. He moved to Arizona Territory with his family and cattle, bringing along some African Americans who were former slaves of the Slaughter family.

John Slaughter cleaned up Tombstone and restored law and order to Cochise County. He was a strong, tough man who stood up to outlaws and horse thieves. Henry Flipper and his four man crew arrived at Slaughter's ranch just before supper. Flipper introduced himself to Slaughter and told him why he was there. Slaughter brusquely invited Flipper to eat in the kitchen with Old Bat and Nigger Jim — his two black hands — while the white crew members were invited to eat supper with the family.

The next morning, Flipper was straightforward with Slaughter; the grant boundaries would be established and the chips would fall where they might. When Flipper finished his surveying, John Slaughter owned a little over 6,000 acres, but he never appealed Flipper's decisions.[12]

Henry Flipper spent almost a year finding and translating documents related to the land grants as well as surveying the area. His book from this work, *Mining Laws of the United States and Mexico and the Law of Federal Property Tax on Mines with Regulation Thereunder and Other Laws Relating Thereto*, compiled and translated from Spanish, was published in Nogales by P. Aguire Press in 1892. Another book by Flipper and Matthew Reynolds, a naval academy graduate who served as attorney for the Special Court of Private Land Claims while Flipper served as special agent, came from this work in the Southwest. *Spanish and Mexican Land Laws: New Spain and New Mexico* was published in 1895 by Buxton & Skinner Stationery Company in St. Louis.

When the case for Nogales went to court in August 1892, Flipper provided expert testimony based on his translations, surveys, and knowledge of Mexican land documents. The case was tried in Tucson and lasted until the end of December 1893, at which time the court decided that the Mexican land grant in question applied only to Sonora, the state in Mexico, and not any lands included in the Gadsden purchase. The court decision was a victory for Nogales, in Arizona Territory, because it meant that its citizens could legally own their property, including homes and businesses.

Flipper continued to work as a civil engineer, surveying in Nogales in 1896, then surveying planned roads in Mexico. A Republican paper, the *Sunday Herald*, was the only newspaper in Nogales. When the owner and editor was elected to the territorial legislature, Flipper was left to run the paper. This was in late 1896, when Grover Cleveland's term was finished and William McKinley would soon be sworn in. Since Cleveland was a Democrat who had appointed the Democratic Arizona territorial governor, the Republican legislature wanted to wait until Republican President McKinley was in office to avoid having the sitting governor appoint Democrats for four-year terms in territorial offices. In order to avoid this situation, they passed a resolution to spend sixty days examining territorial institutions (the legislature could only legally meet for sixty days each year). During this four month period, Flipper "ran the *Sunday Herald* and had great fun with it."[13]

Meanwhile, the Nogales case had been appealed and was heard by the United States Supreme Court in 1898; Henry Flipper went to Washington, D.C., in the spring of that year to provide expert testimony in the case.

The land grant cases were fought bitterly by those who made various claims to the lands against the court of private claims. Flipper himself was under attack, his work and his character questioned. During his time in Nogales, Flipper had served as assistant postmaster and was accused of embezzling money from the post office; he was innocent but these and other attacks on him took their toll.

"The grant claimants fought me bitterly," remembered Flipper. "The attorneys of the great Cameron family of Pennsylvania, which claimed a big grant in Arizona, filed charges against me alleging that I had done a job of surveying in Sonora for which I had received $1,500, that I had returned to Nogales, got drunk and remained drunk till every penny was gone. These charges were investigated, but every man, woman and child in Nogales knew I never drank liquor of any kind."[14]

The opposing forces also tried to use Flipper's army court-martial against him to discredit his testimony. "The same attorneys in another case waited till their case reached the U.S. Supreme Court," said Flipper, "and in a brief to that Court charged that I had been cashiered from the Army, that I was not therefore eligible to hold any position of honor or trust under the government and that all I had done in the land grant cases was illegal and should be ignored and expunged from the records." The U.S. attorney, Richard Olney, answered these charges in a letter, and the Supreme Court's ruling "ignored the charge absolutely." Flipper states, "As a matter of fact I was not cashiered but dismissed. The difference is an officer cashiered is barred from any official position of honor or trust under the government. The officer dismissed is not under any such prohibition, but cashiering was abolished in our Army years and years before I ever saw the Army."[15]

In his letter, U.S. attorney Oleny supported Flipper: "Mr. Flipper was the best equipped, most efficient, competent, reliable and trustworthy man to perform the duties necessary to be performed on behalf of the government.... He has been more sinned against than sinning." He added that "no successful attack can be made upon his honesty, his integrity, and his reliability." The letter continued: "Having little in common with his race by reason of his talents, attainments and education; sensitive in the extreme and fully understanding the social lines which the conventionalities of society have drawn against him; compelled by this ostracism to seek his books for companionship and recreation, he has equipped himself both in head and heart so as to obtain the respect and confidence of scholars and men of learning who know him or have examined his works."[16]

During the time these cases (there were a number of challenges to the land grants) were tried before the Supreme Court in Washington, Flipper often sat in the courtroom and watched the trial. The Nogales case led to Flipper's appointment as special agent of the Department of Justice, where he once again translated Spanish documents and interpreted Spanish land law.

In July 1901, Flipper received a telegram from the manager of the Balvanera Mining Company, based in New York, requesting an appointment for a meeting in El Paso on a certain date. Flipper was requested to be prepared to go to Mexico with the manager in the position of resident engineer of the company. The president of the company was William G. McAdoo, who later became the son-in-law of President Woodrow Wilson and secretary of treasury in his cabinet.

Flipper did not go down to Mexico until August because there was a disagreement in the company over who should be the general manager. Each faction had a candidate and refused to approve money until their own candidate was named. The company limped along like this for about a year, then suspended operations; however, the money generated from the mines was enough to pay the employees.

Flipper was placed in charge of the mines while the on-site manager of the operation went to New York to try to settle the situation. When the manager arrived in New York, the opposing faction sent a man down to evict Flipper from the property. When the man arrived, Flipper provided him a room for the night and "next morning, when he got up, he told me who he was and ordered me off the premises and out." Flipper "didn't waste any words with him but [I] told him I had possession and if he got obstreperous I would put him off."

Henry Flipper circa 1890 (Arizona Historical Society).

In addition to Flipper, there were two other men in the house. The argument continued for a while, then the interloper "went up town to get his breakfast and when he came back, he found his baggage in the street and one of my men watching it till his return. He never got on the premises again." The gentleman tried to oust Flipper through the courts, and Flipper "learned one day that he had bribed the judge to put me out by force." Flipper "went at once to the judge and told him what I had heard and it so scared him he did nothing." The gentleman stayed "five or six months," then "got tired and left." "I never had anymore trouble," said Flipper.[17]

The Spanish American War was instigated when the American battleship *Maine* exploded in the harbor at Havana, Cuba, on February 16, 1898; on April 21, war was declared against Spain by President McKinley, who called for 125,000 volunteers for the army. Recruiting offices were swamped, and Flipper sent a telegram to the War Department stating, "As graduate U.S. Military Academy, class seventy-seven, my services are at disposal of War Department in any capacity in which they can be utilized in event of war." A number of other former soldiers did the same. This war prompted Flipper to apply to Congress to restore his position in the army while he was in Washington during 1898.

"I had a bill introduced in Congress to restore me to the Army," said Flipper. "I paid a colored man, Charles Alexander, to make campaign speeches to elect a white man to Congress from Maryland. He was elected and introduced a bill for me, but nothing more was done. I have had no end of disillusionments, many bitter disappointments."[18]

According to Flipper:

[Lyons, the registrar of the treasury,] was going to get me right back into the Army, no doubt about it, he knew all the Congressmen and had the necessary influence. What did he do? If you will pardon the slang, he "pulled my leg" and nothing more. He would come to me and say: "I have an appointment with Senator ___ at the Shoreham tonight to discuss your case. He'll order the drinks and cigars and, of course, I'll have to correspond. Let me have a ten or better a twenty. I'll report tomorrow. Run up to the office about eleven." I'd go to his office in the Treasury building only to learn he had failed to see the Senator for this reason or that. He got two or three hundred dollars out of me in this way, and there never was any result whatever. Once he came to me and told me he had arranged for an interview with the President and we were to go to the White House on a certain day and talk the matter all over, with all the time necessary. I was greatly elated over this and was on time the appointed day at Lyon's office. We went to the White House, Lyons expatiating all the way on how well he had arranged the interview, how much influence he had, etc. When we arrived we were shown into the waiting room and I noticed there were fifteen or twenty other persons there, also waiting to see the President. By and by a flunky came in and showed us into another room. We stood in line with our backs to a wall. In a moment a door opened near one end of the line and President McKinley entered. He said: "Good morning, gentlemen. I am glad to see you," shook hands with each and passed out at a door at the other end of the line. The whole thing did not last two minutes and no one spoke a word except the President. The flunky showed us out and this was the end of the interview. Lyons made all sorts of excuses and explanations and promised to arrange another interview but it never materialized. It dawned on me finally that he had never made an appointment at all. He was just bleeding me.[19]

Another offer to help came from Professor W.S. Scarborough at Wilberforce, who sent Flipper a letter saying he "personally knew the two Senators and all the Representatives in Congress from Ohio, had considerable influence with them" to help Flipper and asked for "$50 for expenses, etc." Flipper stated he "bit" and "sent the $50 and $10 and $20, and various sums at various times, but if he ever did anything, I never heard of it." Flipper noted the man "had found a sucker and bled him to the limit."[20]

Someone who did help was Barney McKay, an ex-sergeant of the 9th

Cavalry (colored) who lived in Washington. McKay came to Flipper's hotel and introduced himself, and Flipper "took a liking to him instantly." McKay "came to urge me to move and he had the first bill introduced by a Congressman from Wisconsin. He worked like a Trojan, held interviews with Congressmen, took me to call on Congressmen." McKay arranged an interview with General Joe Wheeler, known as "Fighting Joe" when he had served with the Confederates during the Civil War and then as a congressman from Alabama. When Flipper finished telling his story to Wheeler, the congressman replied, "That is the damndest outrage I ever heard of and I pledge you my word to make your case a personal case and to push it through the House."[21]

No doubt Wheeler would have been good at his word, but the following day he was appointed a major general in the army by President McKinley and sent to Cuba for the Spanish-American War. Flipper "never saw him again" and Wheeler died shortly after returning from Cuba.

McKay had also introduced Flipper to the son of Kentucky senator Breckenridge, who also promised to help; but this young man was also sent to Cuba for the Spanish-American War.

The preceding versions of Flipper's reinstatement came from Flipper's "Memoirs," which he wrote to Anna White Shaw while he lived in El Paso. However, Barry Johnson has done a great deal of research into Flipper's attempts to get back into the army and points out that, many officers in Flipper's situation would have gone immediately to Congress if it was in session or would have made arrangements to have their bill introduced as soon as possible if it was not. However, Flipper waited 16 years after his dismissal, even though he received a copy of his court-martial record in March 1883 — 15 years previously.[22]

Aware that the long delay would harm his efforts, Flipper, in his petition, wrote:

It might be pertinently asked why have I not, prior to this occasion, sought the rectification of the wrong which I conceive has been done me, why have I suffered quietly the contumely of this sentence and allowed myself to appear before the country in a position that reflected on my integrity.

To these questions I will say:

1. I was thoroughly humiliated, discouraged, and heart-broken at the time of my dismissal from the service.

2. On reflection, I saw clearly that I was not sufficiently removed from the excitement and prejudices of the time.

3. I was aware that I had no political or army influences sufficiently powerful to present my case in its true aspect.

4. I preferred to go forth into the world and by my subsequent conduct as an honorable man and by my character disprove the charges.

Having been educated by the government of the United States, being the first of my race to be so educated, and feeling it my duty in the crisis in which the country is now situated, to apply the training and ability acquired by me at the Military Academy to the service of the government, I venture to come before your Committee and ask, at your hands, the just and impartial consideration of the facts I have presented.[23]

The "crisis" was the Spanish-American War.

The *Washington Post* ran an article stating the government was considering the formation of a negro cavalry comprised of volunteers, with Flipper as colonel and Charles Young, the third Negro graduate of West Point (Class of 1889), as lieutenant-colonel. Flipper notes that "I never knew what truth there was in it, it was never done and I made it plain I was not seeking a commission in either the regular or volunteer Army." What Flipper wanted, and tried to get, was "a clearing up of my Army record, which meant restoral to the regular Army with the grade and rank I would have attained had I not been dismissed." If the original appeal had been approved, Flipper would have received back pay and qualified for a retirement pension.

One of the most enthusiastic volunteers in the Spanish-American War was Under Secretary of the Navy Theodore Roosevelt, who organized the Rough Riders and charged up San Juan Hill in Santiago on July 1 supported by troops from the 10th Cavalry (colored), Flipper's old troop. Also at the battle was First Lieutenant John J. Pershing, an officer with the 10th Cavalry, and Fighting Joe Wheeler. The Spanish fleet was defeated July 3, Santiago surrendered July 17 and Puerto Rico surrendered on July 28. In a related battle, Manila and the Philippines fell to the United States, led by Admiral George Dewey of the navy, on August 13. On December 10, in Paris, a treaty was concluded that gave the United States control of Puerto Rico, Cuba, Guam and the Philippines. This ended what Secretary of State John Hay called "a splendid little war."

The first bill for Flipper was introduced by Wisconsin Republican congressman Michael Griffin, when Republicans controlled both houses of Congress. Griffin was a member of the House Military Affairs Committee. The bill was introduced on April 13 and sent to the War Department for a copy of the court-martial proceedings and any other relevant information. The adjutant general, Corbin, sent it to the secretary of war, who wrote a brief note: "This office cannot recommend the restoration by special legislation of any officer dismissed by due sentence of court-martial approved by the President" before sending it to the House committee. According to Johnson, "This was the official view of the Department and it was a view which never wavered throughout Flipper's bid for reinstatement; it amounted to a blank refusal to discuss the merits of any individual case, while of course providing the basic information which Congress requested."[24]

According to Johnson, "The War Department had long been opposed, on general principles, to the reinstatement of dismissed officers; and the prospect of a former second lieutenant, who had been out of uniform for sixteen years, suddenly returning to command a troop of cavalry would have made the department even more reluctant to consider his case sympathetically."[25]

In May, Flipper submitted a brief to the committee, and several friends in Arizona and New Mexico sent letters of support. According to Johnson, they increasingly brought up race, "so that the precise details of the case — whether by design or by accident — were eventually buried deep in the debris."[26]

Congress adjourned in July with no action taken on Flipper's bill; on December 5, 1898, a new session opened which ran until March 3, 1899. By this time, Flipper was back in the Southwest; however, he had printed a 78-page pamphlet, which he sent to the committee and apparently distributed widely to the media.

The bills to reinstate Flipper were reintroduced in the 56th Congress, which convened in December 1899, and were both reported from committee. There is a discrepancy between what Flipper told the court-martial and what he told Congress. In his "Statement of Case," Flipper states, "When called upon to submit my funds for special inspection on July 8, 1881, I discovered a discrepancy of some $200 or $300. This caused me no uneasiness as I knew the discrepancy arose from unpaid bills owed by officers serving on detached service outside of the post.... Some of these bills were not paid until after I was relieved.... I borrowed money for the occasion as the commanding officer refused to inspect my funds till they were all in ... completed the amount for which I was responsible and submitted it for inspection.... I also submitted the check for $1,440.43 NOT AS A PART OF MY FUNDS, but in compliance with the suggestion of Colonel Shafter to make such a check and let him see it, made by him when he suggested depositing my funds in a bank in San Antonio, Texas, and drawing a personal check against them. The check was never out of my possession, and was found in my quarters when searched in August."[27] There is no mention of Lucy Smith in this brief or in the one submitted in 1922. Flipper seems to indicate that the missing funds were due to other officers.

Kansas senator William A. Harris, a former Confederate staff officer, reported for the Senate Military Affairs Committee that "The War Department has refused to recommend on several occasions the restoration by special legislation of this officer, and no reason is given why such action should be taken." New Jersey congressman Richard W. Parker reported for the House committee, stating, "Most careful consideration has been given this case to be sure that the dismissal was not caused by prejudice and fully justified by the facts. The record of the court-martial occupies many hundred pages. It fully proves the charges of which he was found guilty."[28]

The report goes on:

> The court acquitted him of embezzlement, but found him guilty of fraud in these statements, which are admittedly untrue.... Lieutenant Flipper waited eighteen years, and at last, at the Fifty-fifth Congress, second session, introduced a bill to restore him to the Army. These facts are all from his own brief. His case is one of admitted falsehood, and the conviction was of fraud. His own oath alone denies the latter. The suggestion of robbery is the common refuge of embezzlers. Under these circumstances we see no reason for a special bill to restore him to the Army by an exception to general law. No new facts are alleged. No new evidence is offered. Public policy demands the utmost care that legislation should not interfere with the army discipline that demands honor and truth in all its officers, an honor and truth that were admittedly absent in this case.[29]

This same bill for Flipper's reinstatement was introduced an additional four times between 1903 and 1908 but was never again reported from committee. During this time, Sergeant McKay was the major instigator; Flipper was in El Paso during this time.

10

Flipper and Mexico

The Balvanera Mining Company was sold to Colonel William C. Greene, the "Cananea Copper King," in 1905. After the sale, Henry Flipper received a telegram from attorney Albert Fall, vice president of the company, offering him a staff position in the legal department. Flipper accepted the offer and began his professional relationship with Fall.

Albert Bacon Fall was born in Frankfort, Kentucky; his father was a teacher who became a Confederate soldier during the Civil War. Fall then left Kentucky and became a cowboy, helped drive a herd up a cattle trail, and became a cow-camp cook. From there he became a bookkeeper in Clarksville, Texas, then went into gold and silver mining. In 1883 he moved to Mexico and learned rudimentary Spanish while he worked at mining; in 1885 he moved to Kingston, New Mexico Territory, in hopes of better mining prospects. He was joined by his brother-in-law, Joe Morgan, and Edward L. Doheny; those three spent a good deal of time together staking mining claims, dodging Apaches, and prospecting. In 1887 Fall moved to Las Cruces, still mining with Morgan and Doheny.

The mining ventures never quite panned out, so Fall sold real estate in the Mesilla Valley, then started work in N.M. Lowery's law office. For years Fall had been reading law; at that time someone had only to pass the bar to practice law — there was no schooling requirement. When Lowery died, Fall took over his law practice; he was admitted to the New Mexico Territory bar in 1889 after passing the bar exam.

In 1888 Fall ran for the New Mexico Territorial Legislature as a Democrat in a heavily Republican area controlled by the "Santa Fe Ring," which was comprised of Republicans who dominated political offices in the area. They controlled these political offices because the president appointed men to territorial offices before New Mexico became a state, and eight of the ten presidents during the 1869–1885 period were Republicans.

In addition to controlling federal and county positions, the "Ring" also controlled the lucrative contracts for supplying beef, food and clothing to the army and the Indian reservations. But their greatest power came from their control of the appointments of judges and justices of the peace and in the selection of grand and petit juries. The "Ring" was dominated by ex–Union soldiers, one of whom was Albert J. Fountain.

After the Civil War, Fountain came to New Mexico Territory as an Indian fighter. He was wounded in a skirmish and went to El Paso to recover. He was discharged from the army in El Paso and remained there. He joined the New Mexico Territorial Militia, passed his bar exam, and became a lawyer in New Mexico Territory; he was also elected to the Texas state legislature. In 1875, after a gunfight in which he killed lawyer B.F. Williams and Judge Gaylord Judd, Fountain moved to Mesilla, New Mexico.

Fountain sided with the big cattlemen and other moneyed interests, while Fall took on many poor clients, including Mexicans, and won cases for them in the territorial courts. Doing this, Fall built up popularity with voters. He also learned the old Spanish laws concerning land and water.

In the 1888 election, Fountain defeated Fall by twelve votes out of 3,000 cast. During the next few years, the two squared off in the courtroom in a number of cases. This rivalry developed into open hostility and bitter enmity. In the November 1890 election for territorial legislature, Fall defeated Fountain; from this time forward, Albert Fall never lost another election. When Grover Cleveland, a Democrat, became president, he appointed the 32-year-old Fall as judge of the Third Judicial District of Southern New Mexico.

Albert Fall was part of the old Wild West, where the law and lawless citizens mingled in a gray area that sometimes meant that a man had to defend himself with a gun. Fall proved himself a man to be reckoned with, a man who could stand up to the barrel of a gun as well as to a court of lawyers. It was a time when physical courage was demanded of those who succeeded, and Fall had his share of Wild West adventures.

Albert Fall and Joe Morgan were in Las Cruces on Saturday night, September 14, 1895, around 10:00 P.M., standing on the east end of Main Street beside a lamppost, talking about a horse with a man named Albert Ellis. Trouble came walking down the street when Ben Williams, Oscar Lohman and another man (thought to be Joe Cunniffe) appeared. Lohman and Cunniffe crossed the street when they recognized Fall and Morgan, but Ben Williams kept coming. Williams had been deputy United States marshal and worked with the Cattle Association, whose attorney was Albert J. Fountain. Fall managed to get Williams removed; Williams vowed revenge. Also, Williams and Fountain were both connected to the "Santa Fe Ring," which wanted to get rid of Fall.

As Williams walked up, Fall stepped back to allow him to pass, but Williams almost ran Fall and Morgan down. Morgan, who was jumpy, pulled his pistol and fired instantly but missed; however, Williams' chin was burned by the powder. Williams yelled, leaped from the board sidewalk, and fired from the hip; the bullet grazed Morgan's arm. Williams then ran across the street to Sam Bean's Tip Top Saloon, firing several more shots as he ran. At the door of the saloon, Williams raised his left arm and rested his pistol on it to take aim; Albert Fall's shot hit Williams' elbow and ran up his arm. Williams' pistol went off as he fell backward and the bullet hit the top of the door. That was the last shot fired by Williams; Fall's final shot struck the bar as Williams fell.

At a drugstore, Fall and Morgan tended to the latter's arm, while Williams was placed in a chair by some bystanders. With blood flowing, Williams sat in the saloon doorway with his gun and swore he would kill Fall and Morgan when he saw them. Meanwhile, a hanging party quickly gathered with the intention of stringing up Fall and Morgan, but they were stood down by Acting Sheriff Manuel Lopez. About two weeks later, on September 27, Fall and Morgan were "no billed" by a grand jury for their actions in the gunfight that Saturday night.

As a lawyer, Albert Fall was involved in three famous Old West trials that contributed to his legend.

El Paso in the 1890s was run by peace officer John Selman. Selman served with the Confederacy during the Civil War but had deserted. He moved to Texas with his family in 1869 then moved to Colfax County, New Mexico, then back to Fort Griffin, Texas, where he was close friends with rustler John Larn. Larn was sheriff of Shackleford County and often deputized Selman. In 1876 Selman killed a deaf man, wanted by the law, who kept walking away when Larn ordered him to stop. Later, Selman hid and watched a mob kill Larn on June 22, 1878.

Selman and his brother, Tom, went to Lincoln County, New Mexico, in 1878, during the period of the Lincoln County War, and robbed stores and rustled cattle. This gang became known as Selman's Scouts. Selman killed one gang member who was eating at the time and another during a poker game. He moved back to Texas and rustled cattle until he caught smallpox. After his recovery, he organized a gang of rustlers and robbers who terrorized the Fort Davis–Fort Stockton area. He moved to El Paso, and in 1892 was elected city constable. He killed the legendary Bass Outlaw in El Paso on April 5, 1894, when the drunk Outlaw shot at Selman, who was in a sporting house.

Selman was hit several times; but his return shot was deadly, hitting Outlaw in the chest.

John Wesley Hardin was one of the most notorious gunmen in the West; he supposedly killed between 30 and 40 men. He escaped the law in Texas and was living in Florida when he was captured on a train by the Texas Rangers in 1877. He served his time in the Huntsville, Texas, penitentiary, where he studied law. After his release in February 1894, he moved to El Paso, where he wrote his autobiography and practiced law.

Hardin's girlfriend was Mrs. Beulah Morose, a former prostitute and wife of cattle rustler Martin Morose; she had been arrested drunk and disorderly by John Selman, Jr. This caused friction between Hardin and the Selmans. On August 19, 1895, the elder John Selman walked into the Acme Saloon, where Hardin was at the bar drinking with his back to the door. Selman pulled his gun and shot Hardin in the back, killing him.

Selman hired Albert Fall as his lawyer and Fall successfully argued that the mirror behind the bar where Hardin was standing reflected the room behind him. Therefore, according to the lawyer's argument, Hardin saw Selman come in and was going for his gun when Selman shot him — in self defense!

There was an appeal of the "not guilty" verdict, but before Selman came to trial again, he was killed by George Scarborough. Scarborough also had a connection to Martin Morose. Morose and Scarborough were crossing the bridge over the Rio Grande in 1891 when Morose was killed by Texas Ranger Frank McMahon; Selman accused Scarborough of stealing money from Morose's body. Around 4:00 A.M. Easter Sunday morning, April 5, 1896, Selman was in the Wigwam Saloon in Deming, New Mexico, drinking when Scarborough came in. The two went out in the alley to talk; but Scarborough pulled a gun and shot the 56-year old lawman in the neck, then pumped three more shots in him as he lay on the ground. Selman never pulled his gun. He died the next day, but Scarborough was acquitted of murder. However, he was later killed by Harvey Logan, a member of Butch Cassidy's Wild Bunch.

Another famous trial involved the death of Fall's longtime nemesis, Albert J. Fountain. In January 1896, A.J. Fountain brought charges of cattle rustling against three ranchers: Oliver Lee, James Gilliland, and William McNew. On Saturday, February 1, of that year, as Fountain and his eight-year-old son, Henry, were driving in a buckboard from Lincoln to Las Cruces, they disappeared; their bodies were never found. Sheriff Pat Garrett had the three ranchers arrested and the ranchers hired Albert Fall as their attorney.

During the trial, Fountain's older son accused Fall of complicity in his father's death. However, when the trial ended, Lee, McNew and Gilliland were acquitted; the mystery of the disappearance of Fountain and his young son was never solved. Further, it was known to be dangerous to even discuss the case in that area for a number of years.

The final controversial case that Fall was involved with was the death of Pat Garrett. The six-foot-four-inch Garrett was a legendary Wild West figure. He had moved to Fort Sumner in 1878 and was elected Lincoln County Sheriff in 1880 to restore order.

The Lincoln County War in New Mexico was fought in 1878–1879 by gun-toting factions. After several bloody showdowns (the big battle came on July 15–19, 1878), it continued until the deaths of Billy the Kid in 1881 and rancher John Chisum (probably the largest cattle rancher of his time) in 1884. During 1878–1879, former Union general Lew Wallace was territorial governor; during his time there, he wrote his novel *Ben-Hur*.

On July 14, 1881, Garrett went to Fort Sumner in search of Billy the Kid. The Kid came into a dark bedroom where Garrett was sitting and the sheriff killed the Kid. After his stint as sheriff, Garrett became a rancher; then, in 1896, he joined in the hunt for Fountain's killers. He was later named customs collector in El Paso.

Garrett's son leased a ranch Garrett owned to Wayne Brazel. Brazel raised goats, which Garrett hated, so Garrett attempted to evict Brazel and lease the ranch to someone else. On February 29, 1908, Garrett was in a buggy with Brazel and Carl Adamson — who had agreed to lease the ranch from Garrett — when he stopped to urinate. While Garrett had his back to the buggy, he was shot in the back of the head. He turned and caught a second bullet in his belly, fell to the ground and died moments later.

In April 1909, Brazel was brought to trial, defended by attorneys Albert Fall and H.B. Holt. Brazel admitted the killing, but claimed self-defense; he was acquitted in a trial that lasted less than one day.

Albert Fall remained a Democrat until 1902 when, at the urging of President Theodore Roosevelt, he switched to the Republican Party.

For a year, William Greene's Gold-Silver Company did no mining. Instead, Greene raised money by inviting potential investors to visit the mines, hoping to convince them to buy stock in the company. Greene ordered Flipper to play host to these investors, so Flipper hired a Chinese cook and helper, established a kitchen and dining room, purchased chickens, eggs, wines and other provisions from Chihuahua, and entertained these guests, presiding over excellent meals with hospitality.

Eventually, there was work in the mines, located in Sonora and Chihuahua, and it was Flipper's job to maintain good relations with the authorities to avoid any legal problems. One of their mines, located about twelve miles south of Ocampo, was "rich" but was located on another American mining company's land. Greene's company tried to purchase the land but was turned down. After negotiations proved futile, Greene instructed Flipper to have the courts condemn the land. The other company tried to tear down the housing Greene's company built for its workers, and some workers were arrested when attempting to install a telephone line.

Greene's company had a store that the other company attempted to close; Flipper was given strict orders to keep the store open. A lawyer from Tombstone was hired by Greene to assist Flipper; he was placed at this mine and ordered to make sure the store remained open. The next morning, Flipper received a telephone call from the lawyer saying that, after a conversation with the superintendent of the other company, he had decided to close the store. Flipper mounted his mule, went over and reopened the store. "I am stubborn as a mule and never so happy as when some one has the temerity to oppose me," stated Flipper, who fired the lawyer and ordered him off the property.[1]

The suit to condemn the land was successful; but the other company appealed, which caused Flipper to appeal to the supreme court in Mexico City. The court ruled in Greene's favor, and ordered them to pay the other company $800 in silver for a deed to the land. Flipper "walked all around and over Ocampo one whole day with a mozo (servant) carrying a sack of 800 Mexican silver dollars, trying to find the lawyer of the other company to make a tender of the money, but he hid."

"At the end of office hours I reported to the court and was ordered to deposit the money with the County Treasurer, which I did," said Flipper, "and next day the court itself signed the deed.... This stopped all trouble."[2]

In 1908 the Greene Gold-Silver Company went out of business, and its mining properties passed to the Sierra Mining Company, based in Duluth, Minnesota. Flipper remained in Mexico, working for this company, until March 1912, when President William Howard Taft ordered all American companies to bring their employees out of Mexico because of the turmoil created by the Mexican revolution. Flipper disagreed with the decision and was reluctant to leave Mexico; but he moved to El Paso, Texas, where he worked for the company until 1916.

The Mexican Revolution began in 1910 after President Porfirio Díaz was reelected for his eighth term in July, after saying he would not run again. In September, Díaz arranged for a dual celebration to commemorate the centenary of the War of Independence (September 16) and his own eightieth birthday (September 15).

President Díaz maintained peace for 34 years in Mexico, from 1876 when he first took office, and managed to get reelected every four years except 1880–1884 when his hand-picked compadre, General Manuel Gonzalez, occupied the presidential chair. Under Díaz the nation was linked by the railroad, agriculture and mining had increased, and there was a budget surplus.

But there was another side to this "progress," which involved Porfirio Díaz's willingness to let foreign firms enter Mexico and take out enormous profits. By 1910, the United States had 38 percent of the total foreign investment in Mexico and owned two-thirds of the railways. Although American business interests benefited, it came at the expense of most Mexicans, 70 percent of whom still lived in rural areas. At that time, half of all Mexican children died in their first year and 84 percent of the population was illiterate. Although around two-thirds of the population were mestizos, a result of the mixture of Spanish, African and Indian blood which led to a racial tolerance not generally known in the United States, a third of the population of 15 million was still pure Indian. About 87 percent of the population spoke Spanish and there were over 8,000 haciendas, which were "as enormous as they were unproductive ... entities that consumed their own products, closed up within themselves in time and space, more aristocratic luxuries than business ventures."[3] There was an enormous gap between the rich and the poor, and the gap was impenetrable because of the control of vast tracts of land by the wealthy.

The first leader of the unrest was Francisco I. Madero, who lived in Chihuahua. Madero had taken Porfirio Díaz at his word that he would not seek election in 1910 and formed the National Anti-reelectionist Party in 1909, with himself as a presidential candidate. Madero was a young, wealthy landowner who intensely disliked Díaz's long-running regime; he was not alone among Mexicans in his feeling towards the Mexican President. Madero wanted a free, democratic election; but after meeting with Díaz in April 1910, he realized this was impossible. In June, he was arrested by the government and in July, Díaz was elected in a fraudulent election for his seventh term.

At the time of the September celebration, Madero was in prison in San Luis Potosi; on October 4 he escaped and fled to San Antonio, where he called for a revolt on November 20. On Sunday morning, November 20, accompanied by ten men, Madero went to the border of the Rio Grande at Chihuahua. In the states of Chihuahua, Sonora, Tamaulipas, Coahuila and Vera Cruz, there was an uprising for Madero, aided by men like Pascual Orozco and Francisco Villa, who led armed troops in a grassroots revolution. In February 1911, Madera, with 130 men, entered Mexico and led an attack on Casa Grandes. By April, the revolution had spread through eighteen states, including some south of Mexico City, where the leader was Emiliano Zapata. Meanwhile, in the northern states, troops led by Orozco and Villa were winning battles against government troops. In Mexico City, the reign of Porfirio Díaz came to an end in May 1911 and in July he fled to Paris. Madero became president in November through a free election.

American Ambassador Henry Lane Wilson disliked Madero and engineered a plan whereby Madero was deposed and General Adolfo de la Huerta became president; by the end of 1912, Huerta was president of Mexico. The next year was a bloody one; General Bernardo Reyes was assassinated on February 9, 1913, and Madero was assassinated on February 22.

In 1912 New Mexico became a state and Albert Fall became one of the first two senators elected. Henry Flipper sent several letters to Fall in Washington, giving his observations on the situation in Mexico.

Because Spain was a Catholic country, their colony, Mexico, became a Catholic country after its independence. When Mexico adopted its first federal constitution in 1824, Catholicism was the only religion legally permitted. However, the constitutional convention in 1857 approved a liberal constitution which "made all individuals equal before the law and consecrated wide-ranging liberties (freedom to express ideas in public, freedom of teaching, of the movement of people, freedom of association and conscience); it extended civil protections (abolition of privileges and special courts, abolition of prison for debtors, free defense in every civil or penal trial, and especially the right of habeas corpus in cases of abuse of authority); it gave the legislative power supremacy over the executive power; and it stipulated the free elections of judges to the Supreme Court." It did not make Catholicism the exclusive religion, which brought intense resistance from the Church.[4]

In 1858 the Mexican legislature issued the Laws of Reform, which nationalized all ecclesiastical property without compensation, closed monasteries and convents, suppressed religious confraternities and monastic orders, made cemeteries national property, prohibited civil servants from taking part in any religious rites, set up civil courts to deal with births, marriages, and deaths, and permitted freedom of worship.

This led to the War of the Reform, which lasted from January 1858 until January 1861. One of the principal points was the responsibilities and perquisites of the Catholic Church. This war was fought between liberals, who based their program on the Enlightenment values of individual freedom and responsibility, and conservatives, who stood for the traditional values embodied by the church. The conservatives won, resulting in the restoration of the Mexican Empire under a European Catholic prince, Maximilian von Hapsburg, emperor of Mexico from 1864 until 1867.

After the death (by firing squad) of Maximilian, an elected president ruled the country; however, there was still a faction who wanted a Catholic monarchy. Flipper addressed this movement to return to a "theocracy," which Madero and other leaders in the Mexican revolution did not support. If the Church regained its power, it would rule the country with a divine sense of justice, which meant the loss of civil law.

On August 5, 1913, Flipper wrote to Fall:

> The Catholic Party is very strong, is united and is extremely wealthy. All the other so-called parties in Mexico are either in the formative period or hopelessly split in many factions.... The Catholic Party is working quietly, assiduously and effectively. If there is anything like a fair election in October, it is my opinion that the party will win. Then, what? They will undoubtedly begin to repeal the Reform Laws. Will the people submit to this? It is my opinion that they will.... I have talked with many Mexicans on the subject and they all believe that if the church wins in the next or any election, it will mean another religious war worse than that of 1857 and the Maximilian war of intervention.... There is a strong leaven of socialism in Mexico now and it is hostile to the church. The church in Mexico is bitterly anti–American and once in power will not wait long to show its teeth. From every point of view, I do not think the Catholic Party is the one that should dominate in Mexico. Once it gets hold of the situation, it will repeal the Reform Laws, will attempt to recover its former vast holdings or get others just as valuable and will ally itself with the wealthy class to the detriment of the poor peon.[5]

One of the most intriguing figures of the Mexican revolution was Francisco Villa, born around 1878, who grew up poor, then became a bandit and between 1901 and 1909 killed at least four men. Villa directed his rage against the haciendas, the large land-owning ranches controlled by the rich and powerful. The hacienda system, which expanded greatly under Díaz, made the rich richer and kept the rest poor. Around 1910 Villa moved to Chihuahua and worked as a butcher. After meeting Madero, Villa saw the revolution as a way to right the wrongs of social injustice, rescue the lower, working class and help the poor. In May 1911, Orozco and Villa occupied Ciudad Juárez, which provoked the resignation of Díaz.

In January 1913, Villa was in El Paso and in April 1913 he entered Mexico to avenge the death of Madero. Villa and his troops made northern Mexico a perpetual battleground. In September 1913 he seized Torreón, the key city for the railroad system. In November he captured the city of Chihuahua, then took control of the entire state of Chihuahua, assuming the governorship of the state on December 8.

Villa's exploits captured the attention of Hollywood producers, and in January 1914, he signed a contract with the Mutual Film Company to film his life story. *The Life of General Villa* starred Raoul Walsh as Villa and debuted in May of that year in New York City. In July 1915, the American government sent troops to depose President Victoriano Huerta. President Woodrow Wilson tried to persuade Huerta to resign. Huerta refused and the United States began shipping arms to Mexico to help support the army of General Alvaro Obregón. Wilson sent in the navy and marines after an incident in Vera Cruz when the American crew of a whaleboat were briefly arrested. Although the government of Huerta quickly apologized, the Americans invaded and defeated Huerta's forces. General Obregón took over as president, and Huerta went into exile. That same month, Porfirio Díaz died in Paris and was buried in the Montparnasse Cemetery.

By mid–June 1916, at least 18 American soldiers, under General John J. Pershing, had been killed by Pancho Villa's forces, which had become a guerrilla army. Pershing led 12,000 troops on a raid into Mexico to capture Villa, while 100,000 national guardsmen stayed on the Mexican border and navy warships sailed along both coasts of Mexico. In January, Villa's troops killed 16 American mining engineers in cold blood near Chihuahua City. In March, Villa's soldiers raided the small New Mexico town of Columbus, killing 19 Americans. In May, Mexican president Venustiano Carranza demanded that American forces be withdrawn; at the same time, Villa crossed the Texas border and killed four in Glen Springs. This led to calls for war against Mexico by American politicians and citizens. Military plans were drawn for a full scale invasion of Mexico by the United States Army, but German attacks on France and Great Britain led to a war in Europe and President Wilson oversaw a build-up of American armed forces while keeping Europe at arm's length.

Pershing and the American army never did find Villa, who was wounded in the leg and hidden in a cave. Eventually, much to the embarrassment of the United States, the armed forces pulled out and went back to American soil.

In March 1916, an article appeared in the *Washington Eagle* headlined, "Colored Artilleryman with Villista Forces. Dispatches from Front Say Flipper is in Mexico," alleging that Flipper was part of Villa's forces. Flipper replied two months later, stating, "I do not know Villa or Carranza or any of the leaders of the so-called 'revolution' in Mexico ... nor have I ever had any connection ... with the Mexican government.... I can conceive of no contingency under which I would fight the United States. I am loyal through and through, because no man born in the United States, who knows Mexico and has an atom of intelligence can be otherwise, as between the two countries." He asserted, "Every colored person in El Paso knows me and knows that I am not and have not been with Villa. They have seen me on the street and elsewhere in El Paso every day for the past four years."[6]

On his views of American troops entering Mexico, Flipper stated, "I am glad they have gone, regret they did not go sooner, and wish them all possible success and any aid I can give is at their service, now and always."[7] Still, rumors persisted that Flipper had joined forces with Villa and there were even some who believed that Flipper *was* Villa.[8]

Another leading figure in the Mexican revolution was Venustiano Carranza, who sought the office of governor of Coahuila in 1909; however, Díaz supported the opposing candidate, who took office in December. This led Carranza to join forces with Madero. In January 1911, Carranza and Madero met in San Antonio and Carranza was named provisional governor of Coahuila and commander in chief of the revolution in Coahuila, Nuevo León and Tamaulipas. After Madero's murder, Carranza set the stage for another rebellion against the national government. In July 1914, he became president of Mexico; on October 19, 1915, the American government recognized Carranza as the legal president of Mexico.

On February 24, 1914, Flipper wrote to Senator Fall from El Paso: "I have been very, very careful not to mix in any way in the troubles in Mexico. I am too anxious to return to Mexico to make enemies of Mexicans on either side of the controversy and far too anxious for a successful issue to my Army affair to say or do anything to which the [Woodrow Wilson] administration or any of its participants or friends might take an exception."[9]

On August 10, Fall wrote to Flipper, who lived at 803-½ So. El Paso Street: "I wish that you would endeavor to ascertain from as reliable a source as possible, just what the present situation is, what Villa is doing, etc., etc. I wish you would also ascertain for me if Lazaro Del la Garza is in El Paso or Juarez. If anything new, or if you can ascertain anything definite of interest as to the situation, wire me fully by night letter, not waiting to write."[10]

On August 15 Flipper wrote to Fall:

> It is impossible to ascertain just what the present situation is.... The papers state that Villa has recruited his army of 50,000 or 60,000 men. This is confirmed by the statement of the Mines Company of America that they have been compelled to close down their operations.... Villa's recruiting officers in his camp paid a bounty of 200 pesos and offered two pesos a day for recruits.... The bulk of Villa's army is in the small towns and ranches within a day's ride of the city of Chihuahua.... Villa's agents have been buying uniforms here, one house having a contract for 20,000 of them. Arms and ammunition smuggling has been going on as never before, especially as the smugglers can not be arrested under recent orders.... There are all sorts of rumors and reports of contemplated revolts against Carranza.... Gov. Maytorena ... of Sonora and Gov. Riveros of Sinaloa are preparing to rebel against Carranza and the rebellion will be inaugurated shortly by the seizure of Nogales, Naco, Cananea and Agua Prieta, the only points in Sonora held by Carrancistas.... He says these governors are working in harmony with Villa, who will join the revolt at the proper time and that they have the support of Mr. [President Woodrow] Wilson.... Villa publicly stated many months ago that Maytorena gave him the $1,000 in gold with which he armed and equipped the nine men with whom he began the present revolution, so that there can be no doubt of their cooperation.[11]

On October 6 Flipper wrote Fall:

> The Herrera brothers, the Arrieta brothers and Chao with their brigades have declared their allegiance to Carranza and have abandoned Villa. A Villa paymaster tells me that Villa has 52,000 men fully armed and equipped and drilled and under good discipline, while the Carranza troops are little more than undisciplined mobs. He also tells me there are several brigades of Carranza troops who will join Villa at the proper time, in case of hostilities, but which are keeping quiet until that event arises. All the arms, ammunition seized by our troops and other federal officials here from smugglers were delivered to Villa officials last Saturday and amounted to several car loads. Since then six million rounds of ammunition have been received from eastern factories, ordered by Villa, and delivered to him. He is ready to fight and if not hampered by the U.S. will beat Carranza. Carranza's action in asking his officers to decide whether he should resign or not was farcical. He had appointed all of them as well as the governors and naturally they were not going to vote themselves out of their jobs.[12]

When Carranza became president, he immediately addressed the issue of oil and mineral rights in Mexico. At that point, two foreign companies owned the most productive properties: Lord Cowdray's English company, El Aguila, and Mexican Petroleum, which belonged to an American, Edward Doheny. In January 1915, Carranza decreed that all oil exploitation would be suspended until a regulatory law was issued. In May, he sent an envoy, Pascual Rouaix, to the United States to observe the American oil industry with the intent of creating a national petroleum company in Mexico.

In March, Carranza raised taxes on foreign mining interests (80 percent of the mining companies were American owned) and the companies as well as the American government objected, saying the tax increases were unconstitutional and must be repealed. In May, Carranza imposed the taxes and license expiration dates on the large companies but granted concessions to some small mining companies. The legislature passed a law, effective August 15, 1915, that made it impossible for foreign-owned companies to resolve disputes through diplomatic means; instead, they had to bring their cases before Mexican courts.

In late 1915 or early 1916, Senator Fall asked Flipper for his views on the establishment of a branch of West Point in El Paso. Flipper replied in a letter dated January 9, 1916, listing a number of army schools, including the Army War College in Washington, D.C., the army School of the Line, Fort Leavenworth, Kansas, and schools at Fort Riley, Kansas, and Fort Sill, Oklahoma.

"Most of these are post-graduate schools for West Pointers and those appointed from civil life and promoted from the ranks," wrote Flipper. "In my opinion West Point now produces enough officers for the purely technical departments, such as the artillery, engineers and ordnance." Flipper noted that an enlistment encompassed seven years, three on active duty and four in the reserves.

Along those lines, Flipper wrote:

> I would propose that an accurate record be kept of every enlisted man, his character, education, conduct in the service, fitness to become an officer, etc., etc., and that before passing from the line to the reserves, the commanding officers recommend such men as the records show to be worthy for assignment to the post-graduate schools. Let these men take the prescribed course there and when they have completed it, give the honor graduates commissions in the regular establishment, after the West Point graduates have been placed.... The possibility of becoming officers would doubtless secure a much better class of men for enlistment in the army and make better soldiers of themselves and by their influence on the laggards who could never make anything but privates.... In a few years we should have an abundant

supply of highly trained officers and, in my opinion, that caste spirit that prevails to so great an extent in an army officered wholly by West Point graduates will have disappeared, which would be no small gain to the army itself and to the country. Under this plan there will be no need of enlarging West Point or of building a second West Point at El Paso, Texas, as was proposed recently by a visiting Texas congressman.[13]

In addition to working for the Sierra Mining Company and sending letters to Senator Albert Fall about Mexico, Henry Flipper researched and wrote several important works while in El Paso. In July 1914, his article, "Early History of El Paso," was published in *Old Santa Fe*, the forerunner to the *New Mexico Historical Review* as well as a booklet, "Did a Negro Discover Arizona and New Mexico?" about the black explorer Estevan. In 1916 Flipper wrote a manuscript, "The Western Memoirs of Henry O. Flipper," that was apparently intended for Anna White Shaw and not for publication. White's family donated the manuscript to Atlanta University where Theodore White found it in 1960 and published it later under the title *Negro Frontiersman*.

11

From the Wild West to Washington

During the time Henry Flipper lived in the West, roughly 1878–1919, that region changed from "the Wild West" to a settled, vital part of the United States.

It was the heyday of the cowboy at the time of Flipper's arrival at Fort Sill in 1878. The cowboy had been driving cattle from Texas to railheads in Kansas since the Civil War ended; the big cattle drives began in 1867 when Joseph McCoy established stockyards and a business structure in Abilene to make it the first cattle town.

The major cattle driving period was 1866–1885; there were drives from Texas to Kansas, as well as drives into Montana and Wyoming and into the Southwest. The cattle industry suffered a major setback in the winter of 1886–1887 because a severe freezing winter virtually wiped out the cattle industry on the northern ranges. By this time, the ranges were overstocked, there were more homesteaders, which took away the large open fields needed for cattle grazing, barbed wire had been introduced and fenced off property, and the railroads had linked the country, making the long cattle drives unnecessary. By the mid–1880s, the cattle drives were over; also by the mid–1880s the buffalo were virtually gone from northern ranges.

The West was filled with wild, colorful figures such as Wyatt Earp, Bat Masterson, Doc Holliday, Billy the Kid, Pat Garrett, Jesse James and Butch Cassidy and the Sundance Kid. The Earp brothers created a legend for themselves; on October 26, 1881, the famous Gunfight at the O.K. Corral took place between the Clantons and the Earps with Doc Holliday.

In 1883 Buffalo Bill Cody and W.F. Carver created the first Wild West show and took it on the road. This show took the cowboy away from the boring and mundane — though dangerous — job of looking after cattle and turned him into a romantic hero. Dime novels, written by figures such as Ned Buntline, provided entertainment for thousands of readers and helped develop the allure and mystique of the Wild West. Cody's Wild West Show toured the East and Europe and gave eastern audiences a thrilling spectacle of shootouts and Indian raids that helped create the enduring mythology of the Wild

West. Owen Wister's novel, *The Virginian*, published in 1902, created the allure of the loner-hero in the West.

In 1880 cowboy artist Charles Marion Russell moved to Montana, and Frederic Remington made his first journey West in 1881. These two documented the final days of the Wild West in authentic, real life paintings and sculptures. In Langtry, Texas, Judge Roy Bean served as justice of the peace from 1882 to 1892 as the "Law West of the Pecos." There were landmark "events" like the Lincoln County War in New Mexico 1878–1879; the Johnson County War in Wyoming in 1892; the Pleasant Valley War in Arizona 1886–1887; the Coffeyville Raid that ended the Dalton Gang in 1892; Bob Ford's bullet that killed Jesse James in 1882; the Oklahoma Land Rush of 1889; and the Wounded Knee Massacre in 1890 that ended the Indian Wars.

"The Old Glory Blowout" in North Platte in 1882 was a forerunner of the modern rodeo; other early rodeos include the one in Pecos, Texas, in 1883 and "Frontier Days" in Prescott, Arizona, in 1888. Dude ranches were started where easterners could live "the cowboy life" during a summer vacation. Historian Frederick Jackson Turner presented his "end of the frontier" theory in 1893 that stated that after 1890 the United States no longer had a frontier; there was no more uncharted, unsettled territory out West. In 1919 the Grand Canyon was established as a national park.

In 1879 John Moses Browning received his patent for the Winchester single-shot model. In 1885 he invented the lever-action repeating rifle and also the .45 automatic pistol, automatic machine gun and semiautomatic pistol, as well as the fundamental changes in firearms that helped "tame" the West.

While Henry Flipper lived in the West, the story of the "New Negro" was unfolding in the East. Because Flipper was in the West during these years, he was not part of the history of black America, which was being created and written in the part of the country lying east of the Mississippi by people like W.E.B. DuBois and Booker T. Washington.

Booker T. Washington, who was born the same year as Henry Flipper (1856), founded the Tuskegee Institute in Alabama in 1881. In 1895, Washington gave his famous Atlanta Compromise speech in which he stated "the Negroes of the South should stay in the region, accept segregation and disenfranchisement, work hard, and look to the charity of whites for help in securing a subservient role in agriculture and industry."[1] Washington "strategically conceded the superiority of whites, commended their behavior toward blacks in the post–Civil War years, and endorsed the U.S. Supreme Court's 'separate but equal' doctrine in advance, a year before its articulation in *Plessy v. Ferguson.*" In short, Washington believed "that blacks be given a truly fair and equitable share of public support within the framework of segregation."[2]

Washington was the leading voice for Negroes during his day. In 1901 he had lunch with President Theodore Roosevelt in the White House, and during the terms of Roosevelt and William Howard Taft served as the unofficial "Secretary for Negro Affairs." Washington was viewed as the leader of the black race during a period when Jim Crow sat on his throne at the center of Southern life and second class citizenship of blacks was acceptable to the vast majority of Americans, including those governing from the White House, Congress and the Supreme Court. In 1896 the Supreme Court had ruled in *Plessy vs. Ferguson* for the "separate but equal" doctrine, giving its blessing on segregation by stating that Negroes should be separated from whites but should receive equal treatment and facilities. The result was that blacks and whites were separate, but definitely not equal. Booker T. Washington seemed to accept this situation and urged blacks to learn a trade and make the best of their situation; he died in 1915.

During the decade before Washington's speech, over a thousand blacks were lynched, most of them in the South, and as the calendar turned over to the new century, about a hundred blacks a year were lynched.

In 1906 there were riots in Atlanta after the *Atlanta Constitution* headlined a front page article, "Negro Menaced Miss Orrie Bryan." The father of Miss Bryan called on a crowd of white men to lynch Luther Frazier, who had allegedly "accosted" but not touched the young lady. The city imposed martial law after mobs killed nearly fifty Negroes and five whites over the next three days; about a hundred people were injured. Around dusk on Sunday, September 22, a white mob gathered on Houston Street outside the home of George White, but White and his family managed to emerge unhurt.

Among those living in Atlanta during the time were Simeon Flipper, Henry's brother and a bishop in the African Methodist Episcopal Church, W.E.B. DuBois, a 38-year-old professor at Atlanta University, and Walter White, the 13-year-old son of George White.

DuBois graduated from Fisk University in 1888, then studied at the University of Berlin and Harvard, where he received a PhD in 1895. DuBois taught at Wilberforce, a black college in Ohio, then returned to the South in 1897 to direct a new program in social sciences at Atlanta University. In 1903 his book, *The Souls of Black Folk*, was published.

After the Atlanta riots, DuBois was instrumental in helping found the NAACP in 1909 and in 1910 moved from Atlanta to New York to launch and edit *The Crisis*, a monthly publication of the NAACP which expressed DuBois's views for the next quarter century. DuBois believed that "Meek submission and accommodation to whites in the manner of Booker T. Washington would be disastrous and ultimately fatal to all people of African descent in America."[3] He also believed that the "talented tenth" of the Negro population, an educated elite, should press for full political rights for Negroes. DuBois and others were militant in their demands for social and political justice, opposite the view of Booker T. Washington, who encouraged Negroes to make the best of the status quo.

In Atlanta, the downtown riots led to a flight of prominent white families from stately Victorian homes around Auburn Avenue; this area developed into the center of Negro life in downtown Atlanta. A cluster of Negro businesses developed in this area, including the Atlanta Life Insurance Company, the Citizens Trust Bank, and the *Daily World*, all doing business with and for Negroes. There were also prominent churches, including the African Methodist Episcopal Church, headed by Simeon Flipper, and Ebeneezer Baptist Church, headed by Martin Luther King, Sr. The most prominent houses were on "Bishops' Row" on Houston Avenue, where the AME Bishops who ran Morris Brown College lived.

The Negro insurance companies developed a market of small policies to cover medical bills and funerals. A number of sales agents were recruited to go door to door to collect the small premiums — often a nickel — from their clients each week. In this segregated world, the preacher enjoyed the greatest status. First, the ministry usually did not require schooling, only a "call" to preach. The preacher had to give himself polish and inspire others to follow him; "Success was a mixture of common sense, rigid adherence to a few well-chosen proverbs, and the projection of a successful image."[4]

The prestige and influence of the ministry developed during slavery, when the gift of oratory became valuable because it was illegal for Negroes to be taught how to read and write. The ability to speak eloquently from the pulpit became a marketable skill, the best credential for blacks aspiring to a white-collar trade. During the era of Jim Crow, "all roads converged at the Negro church. It served not only as a place of worship but also as a bulletin board to a people who owned no organs of communications, a credit union to those without banks, and even a kind of people's court."[5] W.E.B. DuBois noted, "the preacher is the most unique personality developed by the Negro on American soil"; and Taylor Branch, in his book *Parting The Waters*, states, "As a rule, the preachers had no use for church democracy. They considered themselves called by God to the role of Moses, a combination of ruler and prophet, and they believed that the congregation behaved best when its members, like the children of Israel, obeyed as children."[6]

Educational opportunities for blacks in the South from the Civil War to the 1930s were provided primarily by Northern philanthropists. This is how the Storrs School and Atlanta University, both attended by Henry Flipper, were founded, as well as Fisk University in Nashville. In Atlanta, the most prominent benefactor was John D. Rockefeller. Rockefeller heard a plea for funds to support the Atlanta Female Baptist Seminary, a school for Negro girls, during a sermon at the Erie Baptist Church in Cleveland, Ohio, in 1882. The two women who made the plea, Mrs. Packard and Mrs. Giles, had taught Rockefeller's wife, the former Laura Spelman; he pledged $250.

Rockefeller and the Spelmans went to Atlanta in 1884 to attend the third anniversary celebration of the Female Seminary. Mrs. Spelman, Rockefeller's mother-in-law, spoke, and after the ceremony the trustees voted to rename the college Spelman. Rockefeller then began buying up land on Atlanta's west side for Spelman College. He also donated land for a Baptist college for men, which was named Morehouse, after Dr. Henry Morehouse of the Baptist Home Mission Society in New York.

The white flight from the area around Auburn Avenue, and the Rockefeller land purchases for Spelman and Morehouse, caused Atlanta to have a large concentration of its black population in the southwest quadrant of the city. These institutions provided an educated elite of Negroes, or a "Negro aristocracy," in Atlanta. There would emerge a "Negro aristocracy" in other segregated cities as well.

In 1900 there were seventy-six million people living in the United States; about nine million were Negroes and less than a million of those lived outside the South. But after World War I, blacks fled the South in huge numbers, especially to Chicago and New York, where the black population tripled between 1910 and 1923 to reach over 180,000. In New York, the center of Negro life was Harlem and there the Harlem Renaissance took root.

Harlem, located between 125th and 135th streets on the east and west and bordered by Lennox Avenue on the south, was the birthplace of the "New Negro," who was self-confident, assertive, self-respecting, intellectual, and capable of great works of art, music and literature. Living in Harlem during the Renaissance were novelist Zora Neale Hurston, poet Langston Hughes, educator W.E.B. DuBois, and James Weldon Johnson, who, with his brother J. Rosamund, wrote "Lift Every Voice and Sing," which became known as the

Negro National Anthem. James Weldon Johnson was born in 1871 and graduated from Atlanta University in 1894; he was a leading black intellectual, author of *The Autobiography of an Ex-Coloured Man* and editor of a book of Negro spirituals, the first black executive secretary of the NAACP, and a Tin Pan Alley songwriter who wrote "Under the Bamboo Tree" and "The Congo Love Song." During his time with the NAACP, Johnson organized 250 local chapters; among the strongest was the one in Atlanta.

There were important publications which circulated in the Negro population. *The Crisis* was published by the NAACP, and *Opportunity* was published by the National Urban League. There were black newspapers in most major cities; one of the most important was the *Chicago Defender*, formed by Robert Abbott, and *The Messenger*, a magazine started by A. Philip Randolph, head of the Brotherhood of Sleeping Car Porters. Train porters were almost exclusively black and they carried Negro publications from city to city, providing an underground railroad for the Negro press.

These publications published news of the Negro community and cultivated self-respect. One of the most important questions blacks faced was what to call themselves. After the Civil War, the terms "black" and "negro" were disparaged because slave owners had preferred them and because these terms excluded the thousands of mulattos. "Colored" implied that whites were not colored, while "African" implied they were not really Americans. The term "Negro" became popular in the late 1800s after black New Orleans newspapers campaigned to capitalize the first letter. The NAACP adopted "Colored people" when it was founded in 1909, but in 1910 the *Chicago Defender* began using the term "Race." In the *Defender* "Negro achievement" became "Race achievement" and "Colored men" became "Race men." In polite white society, blacks were called Negroes or colored people, although they were almost always denied the courtesy of professional titles such as Dr., Mr., Mrs. or Miss. In the South, it was common to use the term "nig-ra," which blurred the line between the terms "negro" and "nigger."

There were organizations and conferences; in 1908 a group of white and black educators gathered in Atlanta to discuss "what college men can do to improve the racial situation." In 1912 the first Southern Sociological Conference convened in Nashville; beginning in 1913 it was held annually in Atlanta.

Although there was a flowering of Negro intellectual life, important contributions to popular culture through music, art and literature, and the emergence of profitable Negro businesses and the rise of an aristocracy in segregated cities, it was not a good era for black-white relations in America.

Among the top-selling books were *The Negro, A Beast* by Charles Carroll, published in 1900, and *The Negro, A Menace to American Civilization* by Robert W. Shufeldt, published in 1906. The book *The Clansman: A Historical Romance of the Ku Klux Klan* by Thomas Dixon, published in 1906, became the popular movie *Birth of a Nation* in 1916. This was the first big movie "hit" from Hollywood, and established the movies as the dominant popular entertainment in American culture. The stage version of this book inspired a resurgence of the Ku Klux Klan in Atlanta in December 1915, which celebrated its new beginning with a cross burning on Stone Mountain.

In late August 1919, Senator Albert Fall sent Henry Flipper a telegram, requesting him to move to Washington and work for the subcommittee investigating the situation in Mexico. The senator offered $150 for expenses and asked Flipper to bring along any pertinent documents and files pertaining to Mexico.

The telegram was sent to Flipper in care of Lauro A. Guirre, 2930 Nashville St., El Paso. Several telegrams were exchanged and then Henry Flipper wrote a letter to Fall:

> For about a year and a half after I came out of Mexico, the Sierra Mining Company paid me a monthly salary of $100, on which I could easily live. At the end of that time they cut it down to $50 per month. I could manage with that sum until the war began in 1914, when prices of all kinds began to go up and since then it has been impossible to do so and I have steadily been going behind without any visible means of bettering myself. There is no work here I can do and an occasional translation for Mr. Walthall or someone else adds very little to the funds at my disposal. I am wearing the same clothes I brought out of Ocampo in 1912, having never had money enough to buy others. They are worn and threadbare and I am ashamed to appear on the streets. I could not form part of your party unless properly dressed and I would need a complete outfit of clothing, shoes, underwear, etc., in order to be fit to join you in the work before your committee. It is painful to have to tell you this, but it is the simple truth, which you can readily understand, and is the reason for my reluctance to accept your offer or to ask anyone for the necessary assistance.[7]

This letter indicated that Fall had not paid Flipper for the work he had done for him from 1914 to 1919. The issue of money was settled and Henry Flipper left El Paso on September 15, 1919, to work for Fall in Washington; however, Fall backdated the appointment to September 1 for extra pay. The records show that Flipper worked for Fall from September 1, 1919, to January 15, 1920, and from February 1, 1920, to March 3, 1921.[8]

During the Mexican constitutional convention of 1917, it was established that the government had control of oil and minerals below ground. Also, only Mexican citizens could have full property rights in Mexico, although the government could grant such rights to foreigners with the proviso that foreigners could not make legal appeals to their native governments — which had been done in the past — but must present legal disputes in Mexican courts. This gave the Mexican government control of their oil and mining industries and dealt a severe blow to American companies doing business in Mexico.

The year 1917 was "the year of hunger" for most Mexican people. With a debt of 750 million pesos and no credit available, the Mexican government could meet only its military budget. From 1917 until 1920, Carranza was president, but at the end of May, 1920, the Army of the Northeast, led by Adolfo de la Huerta and backed by Alvaro Obregon, defeated Carranza's forces. Carranza fled Mexico City in April and on May 20, 1920, died in Tlaxcalantongo; at the end of the month, Adolfo de la Huerta became interim president of Mexico for six months, then in December, Obregon became president.

The bloody fighting of the Mexican revolution ended in 1920 with the presidency of Alvaro Obregon, although internal turmoil continued until 1940. General Zapata was killed on April 10, 1919, and Carranza died in May 1920. On July 28, 1920, Villa's last 759 followers laid down their rifles; on July 20, 1923, Francisco Villa was assassinated while he was driving his car, ending the military threats against the regime. Obregan's term lasted from 1920 to 1924.

Henry Flipper worked with Senator Fall in his senate office translating Spanish documents for Fall's subcommittee, which investigated crimes against Americans in Mexico, and consulted with Fall and other members of the committee to interpret the events in Mexico. In testimony before the committee, a number of people involved in the oil industry urged the United States to defend their interests against the Mexican government, which sought to gain control of the oil and mineral industries in their own country. Flipper was heavily involved in the report issued by Fall's committee, "Investigation of Mexican Affairs," which was presented to the 66th Congress in 1920.

Flipper enjoyed prominence and respect in the halls of Congress, although he worked behind the scenes providing information and advice to senators. In segregated America, it was rare for a Negro to be in such a position of honor and respect, but Henry Flipper was a rare individual.

In the 1920 election, Warren G. Harding was elected president and he named Albert Fall as secretary of the interior. On March 5, 1921, the day

Albert Fall took office as interior secretary, he appointed Flipper as special assistant at a salary of $3,000 a year.

Fall's appointment was a controversial one. A leading conservationist, Gifford Pinchot, stated at the time that Fall was "a member of the 'exploitation gang,'" adding that "it would have been possible to pick a worse man for Secretary of the Interior but not altogether easy."[9] In his book *The Politics of Justice: A.B. Fall and the Teapot Dome Scandal*, author Herman B. Weisner states, "Fall's conservation belief was typical and western: Natural resources are there to be utilized in the development of the country."[10]

At the Department of the Interior, Flipper translated Spanish and French documents and wrote reports, primarily about the oil industry. While in Washington, Flipper's book *Law Governing Hydrocarbons and other Combustible Minerals of the Republic of Venezuela*, compiled from translating Spanish documents, was published in New York in 1922.

A.B. Fall is best known in history for the Teapot Dome Scandal, which began during the Harding administration. The roots of the scandal came on May 26, 1921, when the secretary of the navy, Edwin Denby, transferred the naval oil reserves, set aside during the Taft and Wilson administrations, to the Department of the Interior. This came when there was a threat of war against Japan, at which time the navy would need to use the underground oil as fuel for their ships, which were converting from coal to oil. Officials in the navy department objected to the transfer but Harding issued an executive order authorizing the change.

There were three oil fields involved; two were in California and the other in Wyoming. The rock formation in Wyoming looked like a teapot, hence the name Teapot Dome. After the transfer from the navy department to interior, Fall, in April 1922, leased the California fields to his old friend Edward Doheny and the Teapot Dome field to Harry Sinclair. It was a sweet deal: Sinclair Oil had a guaranteed market with the United States government. Before World War I, Sinclair struck oil in Oklahoma and became the largest independent oil producer in the Midwest. Harry Sinclair has been described as a brash, arrogant man who "simply insisted on getting his way.... He got into the habit of thinking that when he wanted to do something, nothing should stand in his way. And one thing he had wanted was Teapot Dome."[11]

In the spring of 1922, Walter Teagle of Standard Oil went to see Albert Lasker, who had been director of campaign publicity during Harding's election and was then head of the United States Shipping Board. Teagle talked to Lasker about the leases, and said "it smells." He encouraged Lasker to alert

Harding about the situation. When Lasker informed Harding about Teagle's concerns, the president replied, "If Albert Fall isn't an honest man, I'm not fit to be president of the United States."[12]

Fall believed himself to be honest and working for the best interests of the country. Fall knew that oil companies could drain the reserves by drilling into the underground pool of oil while their rigs remained outside the reserve's boundaries. He reasoned that, by signing the leases, he assured the government of getting the oil in the reserves, and that by ignoring this situation, other oil companies would drain the oil fields and thus the United States would lose the reserves.

But Fall was also a man plagued by money troubles; his years of public service left him drained financially. In public he put up the front of a wealthy, successful man, while privately he struggled to pay his bills. His friends were rich and the industry he was involved with — oil and minerals — was a thriving industry. He somehow reasoned he was helping the country as well as himself by signing the leases and taking money from "friends" whom he helped, and who wanted to "help" him.

Others got wind of the deals and Senator La Follette of Wisconsin began to investigate. The investigation uncovered the fact that Fall had done extensive renovations on his New Mexico ranch around the time the leases were signed and purchased a neighboring ranch "partly with hundred dollar bills he lifted out of a small tin box." Fall claimed he'd received a $100,000 loan from Ned McLean, publisher of the *Washington Post*. McLean admitted he'd sent Fall a check for that amount, but said the check had been returned, uncashed, a few days later. Sinclair's secretary testified that his boss had once instructed him to give Fall twenty-five or thirty thousand dollars if he ever asked for it. Sinclair avoided testifying by fleeing to Europe.[13]

In August 1921, a bill was introduced by George W. Pepper, R-Pennsylvania, on Flipper's behalf, requesting a review of Flipper's court-martial. It received some support. Attorney Moses E. Clapp, a former senator, agreed to serve as counsel for Flipper before the Military Affairs Committee. This was the final bill presented to Congress on behalf of Flipper's dismissal. Fall wrote a letter in support of the bill on September 9, 1922, to Senator James Wadsworth, chairman of the Senate Committee on Military Affairs after the bill had been postponed. Part of the letter is a letter of recommendation. Fall states, "Without any hesitancy or qualification whatsoever, I can say to you that he is one of, if not the highest class colored men whom I have ever met in my life.... Mr. Flipper is a master of the Spanish language without a superior;

he is thoroughly and fully acquainted with the Civil Law of Spain and of Mexico, and was the person on whom principal reliance was placed in the investigation of land grant frauds, securing witnesses and testimony, as assisting in the preparation of all the cases before the court for trial."

In a revealing section of the letter, Fall observes of Flipper, "His life is a most pathetic one. By education, by experience and because of his natural high intellectual characteristics, he can find no pleasure in association with many of his own race, and because of his color he was and is precluded in this country from enjoying the society of those whom he would be mentally and otherwise best fitted to associate with. I have never known a more honorable man in my somewhat varied experience.... He has never presumed. He has always been assiduous in attention to his duties and performs every task willingly, cheerfully and efficiently.... He is the most reliable interpreter and translator whom I have come in contact with in any office in the public service."[14]

Henry Flipper served as assistant to the secretary of the interior until March 1923, when Albert Fall resigned. By serving as "Assistant to" instead of "Assistant Secretary," Flipper's appointment came from Fall directly, who hired whomever he chose to help him, rather than as a federal appointment from the president.

During his time in Washington, Flipper walked the halls of Congress and served a presidential administration with dignity and respect. Flipper's work was important but routine; he was influential but hidden behind the high profile of Albert Fall, who as senator and cabinet secretary of the Department of the Interior overshadowed those around him.

The Harding Administration was not particularly concerned with Civil Rights; its primary focus was on being a pro-business administration. The campaign for "normalcy" by Harding was an attempt to turn back the clock to an earlier, bygone era when people lived on farms or in small towns; but that era could never return. From 1900 to 1920 the population of the United States had increased almost 30 percent — up to 106 million. For the first time, more Americans lived in urban areas than in rural areas. By 1920 there were three cities with over a million residents and one state, California, added almost two million residents in 20 years.

The era of "Progressivism," led by Theodore Roosevelt, an activist president, had extended through Woodrow Wilson, but by 1920 the Progressives' program of government regulation and active involvement had businessmen demanding "more business in government and less government in business."

Harding named Pittsburgh industrialist Andrew Mellon to the Department of Treasury; Mellon believed that "as much capital as possible should be in the hands of the wealthy, because these people were the main risk-takers in society. They provided for expansion of the economy, which would result in an increase in jobs for the less fortunate."[15] This "trickle down" theory was promoted by businessmen and the wealthy as they demanded tax cuts which benefited them and shifted the tax burden to middle and lower class citizens. A heavily Republican Congress approved.

Under Wilson's Democratic administration, segregation was accepted and conditions for blacks had generally deteriorated. Blacks looked to the new Republican administration of Harding — and the Republican House and Senate — to help them. Harding met with black leaders, who requested anti-lynching legislation, a national commission to study race relations, black assistant secretaries in the Departments of Labor and Agriculture, and an executive order ending segregation in government service. The president supported the anti-lynching bill; but Southern senators managed to filibuster, so nothing was passed. The administration's bias towards wealth and business managed to derail the other demands. The Republican administration did not like the idea of helping individuals, although they were perfectly comfortable helping business. Harding's belief in an inactive government meant the president would not take the lead or initiative on any issues, relying instead on Congress. And Congress, with a number of Southerners in key leadership positions because of the seniority system, wasn't likely to make any changes that would benefit the civil rights of black Americans.

Flipper deserves honor and respect for his work in Washington, although history taints that honor and respect because Flipper worked for a man who comes down through history marked by scandal during an administration tainted by corruption. Albert Fall was Henry Flipper's supporter and benefactor; Flipper was loyal to him. Unfortunately, history has judged Fall as a crook, ignoring his support of a black man at a time when that support took courage and was acknowledged by black leaders at that time. While Henry Flipper as an individual is not tainted by Fall's scandal, he may have been judged guilty by association.

Actually, history has not really judged Flipper's work in the Department of the Interior because Henry Flipper was in Washington but not of Washington. He did not use his position to promote for civil rights, was not involved in any Negro organizations like the NAACP or Urban League, and did not assume a leadership role in working with other Negroes. Henry Flipper remained a good soldier who always performed his duties capably and well, carried out assignments, and accepted the chain of command. He succeeded in Washington like he succeeded at West Point, by turning the other cheek to slights, ignoring controversial issues, and working hard as an individual to rise above other's expectations of African Americans. History does not generally record or extol the work of good soldiers; history writes the stories of generals and others at the forefront. Henry Flipper always worked quietly in the background.

12

Venezuela to Atlanta

Henry Flipper was sixty-four years old when he resigned from the Department of the Interior; he was hired within a month by William F. Buckley, president of the Pantepec Oil Company in Venezuela. Buckley knew Flipper because the former had testified for Fall's subcommittee, advocating the protection of American oil interests in Mexico. Also, Flipper's publication *Law Governing Hydrocarbons and other Combustible Minerals of the Republic of Venezuela*, published the year before he resigned, established him as an "expert" on Venezuelan oil laws.

On April 7, 1923, Flipper left New York on a ship that took him to Puerto Rico, then to the Dutch East Indies before docking in Caracas, Venezuela, where he began work for Pantepec. By this time, the oil industry had changed as a result of the American government's case against Standard Oil, which had established a "trust" that controlled the oil industry. In 1870 John D. Rockefeller formed Standard Oil; by 1879 Standard controlled 90 percent of the refining capacity and pipelines in the United States. Over half the oil output was refined into kerosene; however, with the invention of the electric light by Thomas Edison, the demand for kerosene fell sharply. Oil then began to be refined into gasoline for the internal combustion engine in automobiles after the demand created from Henry Ford's mass produced automobile. There were 8,000 automobiles in the United States in 1900 and 902,000 in 1912, providing a new, huge market for the oil industry. In 1910, the market for gasoline exceeded the demand for kerosene for the first time.

The automobile continued to increase in popularity; in 1916 there were 3.4 million registered and by 1929, there were 23.1 million registered autos. By the end of the 1920s, 78 percent of all the automobiles in the world were in the United States. In addition to the demand from automobile owners, the United States Navy had begun to convert their ships from coal burning to oil burning, beginning in 1911.

Under President Theodore Roosevelt, the government brought suit against Standard Oil under the Sherman Antitrust Act, and in 1909 the federal court ordered the dissolution of Standard. The old Standard Oil empire was broken up into seven companies that eventually became Exxon, Mobil, Chevron, Sohio, Amoco, Conoco and Sun.

This laid the groundwork for entrepreneurs to form new oil companies. One of those new, small oil companies was Pantepec, formed in 1915 by William Buckley. Buckley grew up in Texas and had a law degree from the University of Texas; he set up a law practice in Mexico City after working as a Spanish translator in the Austin Land Office. In Mexico, Buckley was joined by his brothers, Edmund and Claude, in Tampico where they worked as a liaison between American oil companies and the Mexican government. This thriving law business led to Buckley forming his own oil company, which operated in Mexico.

In early 1922, Buckley was expelled from Mexico because of his opposition to that nation's attempts to control its oil industry. He testified to Albert Fall's committee about the Mexican takeover of the oil industry and urged the United States government to finance a revolution in order for American-owned oil companies to keep control of the Mexican oil fields.

At the time Henry Flipper arrived in Venezuela, the country was ruled by General Juan Vicente Gomez, described as "the cruel, cunning, and avaricious dictator who, for twenty-seven years, ruled Venezuela for his personal enrichment." Gomez seized power in 1908 and "set about centralizing power and turning the country into a personal fiefdom, his own private hacienda." Gomez was "barely literate" and "by one count, he fathered ninety-seven illegitimate children." He was an "Absolute Monarch" who had "installed his brother as his vice-president, a post the brother held until he was murdered by Gomez's son." During World War I, Gomez was "pro–German and dressed up in imitation of the Kaiser." Before this period he had dressed in "Teddy Roosevelt big game hunter garb."[1]

Venezuela itself was described as an "under populated, impoverished, agricultural nation."[2] Royal Dutch/Shell had gone to Venezuela in 1913 and began commercial production the following year. The object of interest for oil companies was Lake Maracaibo, which covered 4,200 oil-rich acres underwater. In Venezuela, the roads were so bad that most cars, and few ox carts, could travel on them. There were no accurate maps of the country and oil company workers found their way by traveling by canoe or on a mule. It was a dangerous country, with disease running rampant, while medical care was primitive at best and inaccessible or nonexistent at worst. Hostile Indian tribes populated the land.

The Petroleum Law, passed in 1922, set the terms for oil royalties, concessions and taxes. Because of the absolute rule of Gomez, the country's political situation was stable. Late in 1922, Shell's Barroso well in the Maracaibo Basin struck a rich lode. Gomez set himself, his family and his cronies up to reap the benefits of this oil strike; they received concessions from the choice areas, then resold them at a huge profit to foreign companies. Kickbacks for favored treatment was the usual way of doing business.

Venezuela became an oil rich nation during the 1920s. In 1921 the nation produced only 1.4 million barrels, but by 1929 it was producing 137 million barrels. This made it second in the world, behind the United States, in oil production. In 1929, oil exports accounted for over three-fourths of the government's revenues.

While Henry Flipper was in Venezuela, the investigation into the Teapot Dome scandal continued in Washington. In January 1924, Edward Doheny admitted he'd given $100,000 to Fall "in cash in a little black bag" but insisted it was a loan to a friend. For evidence he presented a mutilated note with the signature ripped off. Doheny explained the signature was removed and given to his wife so that Fall would not be embarrassed with a demand for repayment if Doheny should die. Fall was in New Mexico, insisting he was too sick to testify. Harry Sinclair hired a detective agency to investigate members of the jury while he was on trial for contempt of the senate after he refused to answer questions about the Teapot Dome lease.[3]

Shortly after Flipper left for Venezuela, President Warren G. Harding died, on August 2, 1923, from a heart attack while in San Francisco. He was succeeded by his vice president, Calvin Coolidge. In 1924 President Coolidge ran a silent campaign for president. During the campaign, Coolidge appointed two special prosecutors — one Democratic and the other Republican — to investigate the Teapot Dome lease. The investigation uncovered the fact that Sinclair had provided several hundred thousand dollars to Fall through the Continental Trading Company, a bogus firm, which meant that Fall received $409,000 from Sinclair and Doheny while he was secretary of the interior.

Before leaving for Venezuela, Flipper and Anna White Shaw discussed her joining him there. But Shaw had two grandchildren she was responsible for; and neither was assured that the harsh living conditions would be good for her, or that Flipper's salary could support them both, so she remained in Atlanta.[4]

Flipper was a representative of Pantepec in Venezuela, negotiating with the government for oil leases and surveying possible drilling sites. His main job involved working with a corrupt government to make sure Pantepec received favorable treatment, while the officials received the benefits of the exported oil. Again, Henry Flipper served as a good soldier, faithfully carrying out the orders from Buckley to acquire as many leases as possible for oil exploration. While he functioned at a high level with top officials in both his company and the government, Henry Flipper was never the top official himself; still, his diligence, persistence, and competence made him a valuable part of Pantepec's oil ventures in Venezuela.

The Wall Street crash in October 1929 precipitated the Great Depression in the United States — as well as a worldwide depression — and the small Pantepec company could not weather the storm. Buckley's company kept a presence in Venezuela, but Henry Flipper was terminated. He was seventy-three years old and, after his release, returned to Washington, D.C., where he remained for about a year, looking for work.

In response to the Great Depression, the American oil industry lobbied Congress to pass a tariff on foreign oil in 1932 to protect domestic interests. This drastically reduced the flow of foreign oil into the United States and hit Venezuela particularly hard. Before the tariff, 55 percent of Venezuela's oil exports had gone to the United States; after the tariff, a number of other expatriate oil men followed Henry Flipper's path back to the United States.

In 1931 Henry Flipper returned to Atlanta. The man who had gone from West Point to the Southwest — with its dry climates, rocky soil, sparse vegetation and a beauty defined by rocky mountains and big skies with an earth colored by shades of brown, grey and dull green — returned to a South of lush greens and rolling hills. He left Atlanta as a teenager to attend West Point, returned after his graduation a conquering hero, and embarked on a journey which saw him face the depths of despair in a military prison and the ignominy of a court-martial, then emerge to become a prominent, respected citizen of the Southwest with an access to power that reached all the way to Congress and the White House. But when he returned to Atlanta, Henry Flipper was a troubled man, seventy-four years old, financially broke, with the prospect of facing his final years dependent on the kindness of his family. He came to the door of his brother, Bishop Joseph Simeon Flipper, at 488 Houston Street, carrying absolutely nothing, "just himself."[5]

Fortunately, the Flippers were a relatively wealthy, prominent black family in Atlanta. Joseph Simeon Flipper was a bishop in the African Methodist Episcopal Church; Carl Flipper was a professor at Savannah State College, Emory Flipper was a physician in Florida, and Festus Flipper, Jr., was a successful businessman and civic leader in Thomasville. Bishop Flipper, former president of Morris Brown College, was still involved with that institution, which moved in 1932 to West Hunter and Tatnall Streets, the old site of Atlanta University, and near Morehouse and the new site of Atlanta' University.

It was not a good time for Henry Flipper; he was out of work with no prospects for employment at a time when Social Security did not exist. His benefactor, A.B. Fall, had been on trial for bribery since October 1929. On July 20, 1931, Fall left his El Paso home in an ambulance to begin serving his sentence at the New Mexico State Penitentiary in Santa Fe. He had been convicted of bribery for receiving $100,000 from Edward Doheny, but Doheny was acquitted for giving the bribe. As one senator remarked, "You can't convict a million dollars in the United States."[6] Fall served nine months and 19 days, leaving prison May 9, 1932. For this conviction, he lent his name to a slang term, "the fall guy."

Flipper came back to the South during the Great Depression, a time in history when the United States economy almost went belly-up, to a region so poor and backward it was almost like a third world country within the United States. Further, he was a black man in a Jim Crow South whose white population would not even acknowledge the basic dignity and humanity of African Americans, much less the innate dignity and accomplishments of a Henry Flipper.

Flipper returned to a Georgia where mule-drawn wagons were still seen on the streets, where over a third of the households did not have electric lights or indoor plumbing, a land of failed crops and five cent cotton. It was, in many ways, a feudal land whose values were rooted in stability and permanence, in hierarchy and status, in caste and class and race. Honor and duty, loyalty and obedience were the highest virtues and every member of that society — man and woman, white and black — knew their place.

In the eleven states of the old Confederacy there were about thirty million people, nine million of them Negroes. It was a poor land that held about a fourth of the nation's population but a tenth of its wealth, an area where only about a hundred or so people per state earned $10,000 a year.

The Great Depression hit America hard, but it hit the South hardest of all. By the time of the 1932 election, over 75 percent of Southerners could be called paupers — two-thirds of them on farms or small towns — with most farmers either sharecroppers or tenants, not landowners. An average farm family's total income was less than a thousand dollars. In the South as a whole, the per capita income was less than four hundred dollars. These rural families were so poor that most did not have shoes, coats or hats and lived where there was no electricity, running water or telephones, in homes with no insulation and no privacy, where two meager meals a day fed the fortunate families. Millions of people throughout the nation had no home at all; they were vagabonds, tramps and hoboes, wandering from place to place.

Three and a half million more people left the South than moved into it from the turn of the century until Henry Flipper moved back to Atlanta. Farming was the backbone of the South, but it was primitive agriculture. There were five million mules but only fifty thousand tractors, or an average of one tractor for every fifty farms. Northerners had twice as many cars per capita than Southerners, and a much better network of roads. Although these were the early years in the Golden Age of Radio, most rural Southerners did not have access to this medium because only one in twenty-five farms had electricity.

Illiteracy ran rampant in the South; only 60,000 graduated from high school in 1930. Only one in a thousand Southerners graduated from college, or about 30,000, in 1930. A third of all adults finished their schooling by the end of the sixth grade. Politicians kept the South poor and ignorant; states spent between $35 and $75 per year per pupil. If it hadn't been for Northern philanthropists, poor blacks and whites would have had virtually no access to education during the seventy-five year period after the Civil War.

Bigotry and intolerance ran rampant in the South. The Jim Crow laws and "Southern Way of Life" isolated blacks and whites, while religion pitted the churchgoers against the non-churchgoers, Christians against Jews and, even within the Christian religions, Protestants against Catholics, Baptists and Methodists against Presbyterians and Episcopalians — and vice versa.

There were racial conflicts soon after Flipper moved back to the South. In March 1931, two teenage white girls in Scottsboro, Alabama, told police they had been raped by several blacks. Nine black males, ages 13–20, were arrested and tried, and eight were convicted to die in the electric chair (the ninth was too young) within two weeks. In June 1932 in Atlanta, a 19-year-old black youth from Ohio, Angelo Herndon, was charged with insurrection for organizing an interracial protest demonstration by some who were unemployed and sentenced to twenty years in prison. The Scottsboro boys were eventually found innocent, and Herndon's conviction was declared unconstitutional by the United States Supreme Court in 1937. But the message in these trials and countless other incidents between blacks and whites sent a clear message: none but the foolhardy and suicidally reckless dared challenge or confront or cross the racial divide.

Things were not peaceful within the Negro community either, even in the area of black-white relations. Walter White, who as a 13-year-old boy living on Houston Street in Atlanta saw an angry white mob outside his door during the riot of 1906, was head of the NAACP in New York. W.E.B. DuBois was editor of *The Crisis* and the two often clashed. DuBois argued in *The Crisis* against the idea of "total integration," which the NAACP advocated. Instead, DuBois thought that blacks should build a strong economic base through black businesses, churches and organizations in segregated cities in order to obtain political and economic clout. DuBois was a passionate, eloquent writer who combined cold logic with lyrical passages; but as an individual he was usually arrogant and difficult and, as an elite intellectual, not temperamentally suited for the give and take of political debate or even socializing with a wide range of people, which included those less educated or less intellectual.

The argument between Walter White and W.E.B. DuBois was on how blacks should achieve racial equality. White pushed for full integration, while DuBois argued that Negroes should unite as a race in "voluntary segregation" in order to establish a strong economic base as a defense against discrimination. In the long run, White's idea of integration won; however, it won because, by the 1960s, blacks had established a strong economic community and social infrastructure like that advocated by DuBois which withstood attacks by the white majority on the black community.

In 1932 Walter White hired Roy Wilkins to "control" DuBois; Wilkins wanted to turn *The Crisis* into a magazine of mass appeal that would be financially self-supporting, rather than an august intellectual journal.

In 1934, DuBois resigned from the NAACP staff; he was sixty-six years old and had no savings. In his January editorial for *The Crisis*, he asserted that "Negroes should face the fact that they would die segregated ... in spite of all justice and their best efforts. Therefore, to hate segregation was inevitably to hate themselves; and it would be far better to embrace voluntary segregation in schools, colleges, businesses — both for reasons of psychic well-being and to build concentrated strength for later fights."[7] This belief was against the policy of the NAACP to push for full integration in all aspects of American life. However, the NAACP faced internal conflict when board chairman Joel Springarm stated the antisegregation policy ruled out meetings and services at Negro churches, classes at Negro schools, and fund-raising activities at all-black institutions. The antisegregation policy was then quietly reversed.

During the first six months of 1934, DuBois argued his views vehemently in *The Crisis*; finally, he left and Roy Wilkins took over the publication. DuBois accepted a position at Atlanta University, where he founded *Phylon*, a social science research journal focusing on race. DuBois was hired by John Hope, an ardent supporter who was the first black president of Morehouse College before he became president of Atlanta University. During the period 1934 to 1940 DuBois published three of his most important books: a revisionist history titled *Black Reconstruction*, a study of Africa in world history titled *Black Folk, Then and Now* and an autobiographical work, *Dusk of Dawn*.

And so, during the last decade of Henry Flipper's life, he lived in the same city as the leading Negro intellectual of his time, W.E.B. DuBois. The two certainly knew of each other. In August 1917, there was a mutiny of over a hundred black soldiers in Houston who were forced to sit in the back of trolley cars and were called "niggers" by the Houston police. A riot left sixteen whites, including five policemen, dead. After a court-martial, thirteen black soldiers were hanged on December 11 near San Antonio. DuBois defended the soldiers in *The Crisis* and wrote to Flipper to enlist his help. However, Flipper disagreed with DuBois and felt the guilty should be executed because, by law, this was mutiny in time of war. The war he alluded to was the American involvement in the Mexican revolution.

Although Flipper and DuBois knew of each other, they held differing views on racial conflict. DuBois stood up for the black race and was an outspoken advocate of civil rights, while Flipper chose to accept broad racial discrimination, believing that an individual could rise above it. Flipper believed he should be an individual example of character and achievement for his race. Through his example whites would honor and accept him and the acceptance of other blacks would follow. DuBois did not believe that racial problems would be solved by individual examples but rather by the Negro elite presenting a united front, persuading the ruling whites to accept them based on cogent arguments, group achievement, individual self-respect and economic power.

Henry Flipper lived in the midst of the thriving black community whose center was Auburn Street. The Flippers lived a few blocks from "Sweet Auburn," where the Bethel African Methodist Episcopal Church was located a few blocks towards Peachtree from the Ebeneezer Baptist Church, where Martin Luther King, Sr., preached. During the 1930s, while Flipper lived the final years of his life, a young boy called Martin Luther King, Jr., was starting his life. Less than two miles away, Margaret Mitchell was writing her novel, *Gone With The Wind*, in a house on Peachtree.

Living down the street on Houston Avenue was Flipper's fiancée, Anna White Shaw. Flipper spent his time writing letters to old friends, seeking employment. He wrote to Robert Pardo, whom he had worked with in Caracas and who remained in Venezuela, as well as William Buckley, asking for work. Buckley never answered him. Pardo shipped Flipper's books back to him and gave him suggestions on where he might find job opportunities.

Both Flipper and Pardo had purchased shares in Pantepec, but they did not yield much money; in 1931 Flipper received a total of $312.88 when he sold these shares. In 1939 he transferred his shares in the Compañía Venezolana de Inversiones to Joseph Martin, secretary-treasurer of Pantepec. Flipper had stock in Venezuelan companies registered in his name as a "front man" for friends of the president, who did not want their own names on these official transactions. It was part of doing business in Venezuela.

Franklin D. Roosevelt was elected president in November 1932 and took office in March the following year. Things had improved for blacks somewhat with his election, mostly through the efforts of his wife, Eleanor Roosevelt, an indefatigable civil rights activist. In August 1933, Roosevelt named Clark Foreman as an "advocate for African Americans." Ironically, the initial resistance to this appointment came from the black press and the NAACP, who objected to a white Southerner — and grandson to Clark Howell, the founder of the *Atlanta Constitution* — being named to this position. However, Robert Weaver and William H. Hastie, both African American, were named as assistant and assistant solicitor, respectively, which silenced the critics.

13

Final Days

During the last years of his life, Henry Flipper kept up a lively correspondence with Dr. Thomas Jefferson Flanagan, an associate editor of the African American newspaper *Atlanta Daily World.* The newspaper was one of the top African American newspapers in the country and Flanagan was an esteemed member of the black community in Atlanta.

Theodore Harris, who edited *Black Frontiersman: The Memoirs of Henry O. Flipper,* noted the letters "were expressed with a cogency that can best be described as legalistic. Always the perfectionist, the grammar, spelling and punctuation in Flipper's letters were almost flawless. Each was meticulously typewritten with every page carefully numbered. They reveal Henry Flipper as a conservative who was a strict constructionist in his interpretation of the Constitution, including issues pertaining to race relations."[1]

Henry Flipper was proud of his knowledge of the Constitution, although he held views that were considered unconventional during his time and would have been out of step during the civil rights movement in the 1960s with his advocacy of states rights.

Flipper disliked Roosevelt and the New Deal and believed the president was "an impractical theorist, idealist and dreamer."[2] Flipper believed that "Roosevelt has led the people, the unthinking element, to believe the Federal government would take care of them under all circumstances, guarantee them jobs or take care of them when no jobs were to be had, thus lowering their morale. Old age pensions should come from the State, Congress appropriating funds to aid the States under the welfare clause of the Constitution."[3] Later, Flipper was bothered because Roosevelt attracted votes from African Americans, stating, "The Negro voted twice for Roosevelt [in 1932 and 1936]. On neither occasion was his vote necessary. He was elected without it, but the Negro has been a strong factor in the election of Democratic senators and representatives in the North, forgetting that he was strengthening the hold of the Democratic party in the South."[4] Flipper disliked the Democratic party because the South was controlled by Southern Democrats, whose white voters expected and received a strong stand for segregation.[5]

In 1937, after Congress had allocated $4.8 billion for New Deal programs, Flipper criticized FDR and the New Deal, stating, "Our method of relief [welfare], considering our dual system of government, was entirely wrong. Instead of giving the President $4,800,000,000 to spend at his discretion and with which to buy votes, that money should have been allotted to the States, on condition that they appropriate an amount equal to their allotment and take care of their own needy. There would have been some stealing; there was some anyway, but the responsibility would have rested where it belonged, on the States, and the morale of the people would not have been lowered."[6]

Later that year, Flipper wrote, "The New Deal was wrong in its inception, because based on the idea that those who have must support those who have not, with the additional Rooseveltian theory that this must be done through the Federal government, that is, to get the money the Federal government must tax those who have till it hurts and use that money to maintain the shiftless, the lazy and the vice-ridden, not realizing that by depriving industry of its capital to squander on the aforesaid and their white collar distributors, it was depriving industry of the means of employing labor itself among those it sought to relieve."[7]

Georgia — and the South — was still ruled by virulent segregationists. Georgia Governor Eugene Talmadge fought against Roosevelt and the New Deal and ruled the state like a feudal lord. The fact that Franklin and Eleanor Roosevelt were Democrats, and that the New Deal was a Democratic initiative, persuaded some African Americans to become Democrats. However, there was a split in the Democratic Party; Northern Democrats were more likely to be liberal with social issues, but the Democratic Party that dominated the South was comprised of "Dixiecrats," fiercely loyal to "The Lost Cause" of the Civil War, adamantly segregationist, and rulers of a party organization that disenfranchised blacks and poor whites and kept them from voting through poll taxes, literacy tests, and violent opposition to voter registration drives. By keeping voting in the hands of a like-minded few, politicians were assured of reelection and, once in office, would not be challenged by their constituents as long as they stood strong against Yankees, Jews, Catholics, Republicans and "Nig-ras."

The Republican Party was the party of Abraham Lincoln, the man who freed the slaves. The majority of African Americans in Atlanta favored the Republican party; the Flipper family — and Henry Flipper in particular — claimed a number of times to be Republicans "through and through." There would be no significant change in this view until the election of President John Kennedy in 1960 and the resulting civil rights bills that followed.

During the election year of 1936, when Roosevelt ran for reelection, Flipper stated, "I am not a Democrat and wonder how any Negro can be one, so long as the political and economic conditions are such as they are. To elect a northern Democrat is to add strength to southern Democracy.... What the Negro needs and wants is not a mess of pottage, half a dozen fat offices for as many Negroes, but better political, economical and educational conditions. Given these the Negro will work out his own destiny."[8] Flipper was adamant that he was "not a Democrat, not till the South learns what democracy is and stops parading under a name that does not belong to it.... No Negro who knows the condition of his race can conscientiously be a Democrat."[9]

Just before the 1936 election, Flipper wrote to Flanagan, stating, "I, personally, do not believe the time has come for the Negro to choose to be a Democrat. The party is dominated by that section of it which is responsible for the oppression of the Negro and the Negro should do all in his power to keep that section out of the saddle. It is not human nature to appeal to an avowed enemy for succor."[10]

Blacks were still being lynched in the South during the Great Depression and there was pressure on Congress to pass anti-lynching legislation. Southern senators and congressmen on the whole opposed such legislation and so did Henry Flipper, who was against efforts by the NAACP to have Congress pass an anti-lynching bill."[11] Discussing efforts to pass anti-lynching legislation, Flipper stated, "It is my deliberate opinion that no American Congress will ever pass an anti-lynching law. Aside from being manifestly unconstitutional, it is ill-advised, impolitic, serving only to intensify racial antipathies. Its avowed purpose is to coerce the South, another 'Reconstruction,' like that of 1865 and the years following, for the punishment of the white South. While the white South has suffered and is still suffering from the effects of 'Reconstruction,' not altogether without its own fault, the punishment ricocheted onto the black South and it has suffered most, because a minority without political power, wealth or learning and, therefore, unable to combat it."[12]

Although President and Mrs. Franklin Roosevelt headed a national government that pushed gently for civil rights and Georgia was ruled by segregationists, Henry Flipper was a strong advocate of states' rights. Flipper stated, "States' Rights, the rights of each and all the States, are the basis, the very foundation of our government...."[13] Flipper was adamant: "I believe in the

States. They existed long before the Federal government, which they themselves made. We do not want a strong central government in this country. [Roosevelt's administration] has shown the numberless evils of such government. Every new amendment, like the Child Labor Amendment, weakens the powers of the States and strengthens those of the central government. Amendment is sometimes necessary but it should not be made at the behest of every pseudo reformer who shows his head."[14]

One of the ways that states kept African Americans — and poor whites — from voting was through the poll tax. Flipper supported this tax, endorsing a Supreme Court decision upholding the Georgia law requiring payment of a poll tax in order to vote. "There are some things in this world of ours so simple it is more than a wonder that some people will not understand them," wrote Flipper. "The vote is not a right or a privilege that one can demand; it is not from the United States but is a gift from the State, which the State can restrict as it pleases or deny altogether for any reason except race, color, previous condition of servitude or sex."[15]

Henry Flipper turned 84 on March 21, 1940, and on that date wrote a letter to Flanagan, stating, "The poll tax question is to the fore again.... As my brain sees it, the poll tax laws do not disenfranchise anyone; they put the decision up to him and let him decide it. He may pay the tax and vote or refuse to pay it and not vote. He franchises or disfranchises himself, not the State. But, if the poll tax be a menace or challenge, why not accept the challenge, pay the tax, get the vote and then use it to elect men pledged to repeal the obnoxious tax?"[16]

Flipper continued:

> It seems to me the whine against the poll tax comes with poor grace from the Negro. The amount of the taxes of all kinds paid by Negroes anywhere is insignificant as compared with the total of taxes paid by the whites and this is one reason why teachers of our [black] public schools are paid less wages than teachers doing identical work in white schools; the white taxpayer instinctively shrinks from bearing the whole expense of Negro schools as the Negro himself contributes so little. This is a shortsighted view. The State takes care of its insane and they contribute nothing nor should they. It ought also to support its schools, all of them alike, without any ulterior consideration, because an educated citizenry is the highest and best asset any State can have, and such citizenry will ultimately be the best taxpayers.[17]
>
> There seems to be much misconception, if not ignorance, of the poll tax. Why should not the man who has no taxable property but enjoys the benefits of government, pay something toward the support of that government? As he has nothing that can be taxed, why should not his person, his

head, his poll be taxed? There is no other penalty, no other sanction, than to deprive him of some one of the rights he enjoys without contributing anything to its maintenance or, as was done in Europe at one time, sentence him to serve in the army for such or such time.[18]

Flipper was also opposed to labor unions and attacked "Sit-Down Strikers," saying, "They are clearly guilty of criminal trespass. They have seized and hold property not their own, thus depriving its rightful owners of its use and enjoyment. Not even the government, Federal or State, can take private property without 'due process of law' and just compensation, and no law authorizes a citizen to do so on his own responsibility.... Strikes like all other activities must be lawful. The law permitting strikes does not permit the unlawful seizure of property nor any other unlawful acts. The law never authorizes a crime.... Labor is fast becoming autocratic and tyrannical and some sort of compulsory arbitration will have to be made into law."[19]

In September 1939, Germany invaded Poland, and Hitler's actions caused England and France to declare war on Germany. Thus World War II began in Europe. In Asia, the Japanese had been fighting the Chinese, and the aggressive military leaders of Japan were intent on ruling the Pacific. Two years before the German invasion of Poland, Flipper observed, "The coercive clauses of the Treaty of Versailles have given us Adolph [sic] Hitler and the consequent unrest in all the world."[20]

Shortly after the German invasion of Poland on September 1, Flipper stated, "Another war! What do I think about conditions? It seems to me democracy is in far greater danger now than in 1914. It also seems there are far too much hysteria and emotionalism among the American people. I believe if the war is prolonged, we shall be drawn into it; not only that, I believe we should go in now with all our might. The so-called Neutrality Act should be repealed and we should get back to international law as it existed before hysteria and emotionalism had that law enacted by Congress. Let all nations buy anything they want and can pay for but make them come and get it. We should not deliver."[21]

He continued, "In the event that the United States gets into the war, shall we have a Negro division? No. There is no Negro capable of commanding a division. The men who have commanded divisions in an army have first commanded a company, then a battalion, a regiment, a brigade and then possibly he will be fit to command a division. Many whites failed in the Civil War on both sides."[22]

At the outbreak of World War II, there was only one black officer in the army, Colonel Benjamin Davis. Davis was born in 1880, about three years after Henry Flipper graduated from West Point, although he listed his birth year as 1877 in order to enlist in the army during the Spanish-American War. Davis entered the Army in 1898 as a first lieutenant in the Volunteer Infantry, was mustered out less than a year later, then reenlisted as a private in the 9th Cavalry Regiment. After serving as a corporal, then sergeant major, Davis was commissioned a second lieutenant in the regular army in 1905. Davis rose through the ranks; he was promoted to captain in 1915, brevet major in 1917 and brevet lieutenant colonel in 1918 during World War I. After the war, he reverted to the rank of captain in 1919, then lieutenant colonel in 1920 and colonel in 1930.

After the German invasion of Poland, Flipper noted:

> We have one Negro officer in the Regular Army, Lieut. B.[enjamin] O. Davis. It is my information that he is now at Tuskegee [Institute] playing soldier with a lot of schoolboys over whom he has no control and cannot discipline and is not himself under discipline. He ought to be with his company and regiment, getting experience, elbowing with his captain and first lieutenant and other white officers of his regiment, breaking down prejudice, learning to command his company and preparing himself to command larger bodies, for that is the only way. To keep him away from his regiment in some school or college is to keep him practically out of the Army, although he wears the uniform.[23]

Davis had been assigned duty as professor of military science and tactics at Tuskegee Institute in 1920, then became instructor of the Ohio National Guard in Cleveland in 1924. In 1929 Davis was professor of military science and tactics at Wilberforce University in Ohio, then served on special duty with the Department of State, working on their affairs with Liberia. In 1931 Davis returned to Tuskegee and then, in 1937, was transferred to Wilberforce for a year before he was assigned as commanding officer of an infantry division with the New York National Guard in 1938.

Referring to an article in the *Atlanta Daily World* "on the ill treatment of colored soldiers in our Army," Flipper noted:

> We have only one such officer who is kept away from his company and regiment to the satisfaction, no doubt, of his fellow officers. He is not wholly to blame; he must obey orders, but the colleges are to blame, in this case Tuskegee. They apply to the War Department to have an officer, in this case by name, sent to the school to train a bunch of students and the War Department complies. The training he gives is confined to drilling, at such times as the students are not otherwise occupied. Its kind and amount is

necessarily limited and is more for show than anything else and is a soft snap for the unambitious officer. If Lieut. Davis himself realized what is happening and his duty to himself, his regiment and his people, he would apply to be relieved and to return to his company and regiment. The [black] colleges should be made to see the wrong they do by taking him from his military duties and should cease to apply for officers. Any sergeant could do what Lieut. Davis is doing and not be missed from his company. A better way would be to drill their students with such means as they now have and each year ask the War Department to send an officer to inspect and report on conditions. The Negro press should take this matter up and see that Negro officers are not nullified by being perpetually kept from their commands.[24]

When Flipper wrote this letter — in October 1939 — Colonel Davis was with the New York National Guard. In January 1941 he was assigned to Fort Riley, Kansas, as brigade commander of a cavalry division and in June of that year was sent to Washington, where he served as assistant to the inspector general. Davis served in Europe, beginning in September 1942, as "Advisor on Negro Problems," then returned to the inspector general's department in Washington. In November 1944, Davis was in Paris as a special assistant to General Eisenhower; after World War II he served with the inspector general again until his retirement in 1948. Davis's son, Benjamin O. Davis, Jr., became the fourth black graduate of West Point and became the first African American to become a three star general in the United States military.

Perhaps the biggest event in Atlanta — and the South — that occurred in 1939 came in December when the movie *Gone With The Wind* premiered. The Atlanta premier featured appearances by Clark Gable, Vivian Leigh and other stars in the movie who attended a grand ball after a city-wide celebration and parade. *Gone With The Wind* wasn't just a movie; it was an affirmation of "The Lost Cause," and a source of pride for Southerners who had suffered the indignity of defeat in the Civil War, then life in a depressed, backward region of the country for seventy-five years. Southern pride was kindled and blossomed full blown with the release of *Gone With The Wind*.

Henry Flipper did not take part in any of the festivities connected with *Gone With The Wind*; segregated Atlanta did not even allow Butterfly McQueen, the black star of *Gone With The Wind* who played "Mammy," or the Flippers, who had lived in Atlanta during the time period of the story, to attend the invitation-only festivities.

Flipper was concerned that African Americans rise above their station and acquire learning and manners like whites. In 1937, Flipper noted that, from March through June, a number of African American ministers and their wives had come from South Carolina to consult with his brother, Bishop Joseph Simeon Flipper, about church issues and always had dinner in Flipper's home before returning.

Flipper wrote:

> It has been a matter of keen interest to me to observe how none of them knew how to use the knife and fork and spoon, thus indicating a similar lack of knowledge of other things that might have been learned by observation, if not otherwise. These men ... have grown up in families where no one knew anything different. Grown up now themselves, their children have no other instructor than the example of their parents.... The use of the knife and fork is only one of many important things they could have learned by observation. Each now has a church and is trying to lead his people, in some things blindly, because his vision is limited. They see none of the causes and effects that affect their lives so profoundly.[25]

Flipper discussed the clergy under his brother in another letter, dated August 27, 1937. He noted the bishop received a large amount of mail from preachers in South Carolina and Florida, and "of these letters I see only the envelopes with the addresses they carry. More than fifty per cent of these addresses are written with pencils and presumably the letters inside are also written with pencils. The American Negro is possibly the only person in the world who writes his letters with a pencil, not the better educated class but still a large majority of him, man and woman.... It seems that in our schools little or nothing is taught about letter-writing, at least of the good or bad manners involved in it. I have never received a letter from a white person written with a pencil, but they come written with a pencil from many race correspondents. I do not like it!"[26]

Flipper continued, "Our great problem is ... the improvement of the condition of our people, the submerged, ignorant masses, a job for the churches, lodges, and other agencies. Comparatively few of us are civilized whereas all ought to be."[27]

On April 16, 1940, Flipper wrote a letter to Flanagan and gave the associate editor a lesson in English — spelling out the differences between "capital" and "capitol," even using the Latin root "capitolium" and "caput."

"The newspaper and especially the race paper should be a source of instruction, contain the best of good English with, generally, an exclusion of slang and with emphasis on the proper use of words. Many race papers are weak on this point. The race paper should be a virtual textbook on orthography, grammar, rhetoric and composition."[28]

Flipper was ill and infirm. Since early in 1937 he had been weak, catching a cold, losing weight, experiencing problems with his heart.

In May 1940, Bishop Joseph Simeon Flipper and his family were at an African Methodist Episcopal Church conference in Detroit; at their home on Houston Street, Henry Flipper was with Charles Rembert, the bishop's stepson. At 7:00 A.M. on May 3, Winnie Braswell, the Flipper family cook, rang the doorbell. Henry Flipper had always answered the door. The eighty-four-year-old military man still stood erect and rose early, usually at 5:00 A.M. But this morning he did not answer.

In his room, Braswell and Rembert found him lying across his bed, fully dressed except with one shoe off. He had died while getting dressed.

Bishop Flipper was contacted and came back to Atlanta. On the death certificate under "Occupation," the bishop wrote "Retired Army Officer." On May 5, 1940, Henry Flipper was buried in the segregated Southview Cemetery in an unmarked grave.

14

Conclusion

Henry Flipper's grave is now surrounded by a brick wall with an iron gate in the Old Magnolia Cemetery in Thomasville, Georgia. Flipper was carried to this grave in a mule-drawn wagon with a riderless horse following on February 11, 1978, attended by a crowd estimated to be around 500, with 18 family members and dignitaries from the U.S. Army and the Georgia government following an honor guard from Fort Benning. His body had been exhumed in Atlanta and brought to Thomasville for this occasion.

Henry Flipper had been mostly forgotten for 35 years after his death, until Ray MacColl, a student at Valdosta Community College, stumbled across Flipper's court-martial while doing research for a college paper. Flipper's story lit a fire in MacColl, who gathered information on Flipper and wrote to the Pentagon, hoping to have Flipper's court-martial overturned and his army record reflect an honorable service.

MacColl spent several years of his life — and considerable personal expense — to right what he believed were the wrongs done to Henry Flipper by the army. MacColl's letter to the Pentagon came to the attention of Minton Francis, an African American graduate of West Point who was a member of the board of trustees at West Point. At that time, Francis served as assistant defense secretary. With the support of Flipper family members, Francis submitted the letter to the Army Board for Correction of Military Records, which reexamined Flipper's court-martial and upgraded Flipper's dishonorable discharge to "honorable" in 1976. The board did not have the authority to overturn Flipper's criminal conviction.

The reexamination of Flipper's court-martial brought the story of Henry Flipper to light. On March 21, 1977, which was the 121st anniversary of Henry Flipper's birth, there was a proclamation for "Henry Flipper Day" in Georgia. That same day, there was a ceremony honoring Flipper at Atlanta University. In October of that year a bronze marker commemorating "Flipper's Ditch" was installed at Fort Sill, Oklahoma. The Henry O. Flipper Memorial Award was established at West Point for a cadet "who demonstrates the highest qualities of leadership, self-discipline, and perseverance in the face of

Henry Flipper's grave in Thomasville, Georgia (Jack Hadley Black History Museum).

unusual difficulties," and a bronze bust of Henry Flipper was installed in the library at West Point.

Still, the guilty verdict from the court-martial of Henry Flipper remained. Minton Francis contacted Judge Eugene Sullivan, an associate judge on the Federal Court of Appeals for the Armed Forces about Henry Flipper, and Sullivan assigned his clerk, Barbara Burley, to investigate the Flipper case at the National Archives in 1991. Sullivan sent a report to military historian Thomas Carhart, who enlisted the help of Jeff Smith, partner in the Washington law firm of Arnold and Porter, who took the case to the White House.

On Friday, February 19, 1999, President Bill Clinton — with 16 descendants of Flipper present — signed a posthumous pardon for Henry Flipper. At the signing, Clinton stated, "We must recognize that [freedom and equality] represent difficult goals that must be struggled with every day to be realized. In 1882, our government did not do all it could to protect a man's freedom."[1] An article about the event noted that "An ugly scar has been removed from our nation's judicial records" and "the president has righted a very old wrong."[2]

Since that time, there have been other honors for Henry Flipper. A PBS television drama, *Held in Trust: The Story of Lt. Henry Ossian Flipper*, was shown in February 1996. The film was introduced by General Colin Powell and was narrated by Ossie Davis. (During his time as chairman of the Joint Chiefs of Staff, Colin Powell kept a portrait of Flipper in his office.) El Paso artist and actor George Robert Snead, who had developed a one man show on Henry Flipper, portrayed Flipper.

In 1999 a post office in Thomasville, Georgia, was named after Flipper and in 2000 a bust of Flipper was placed in the museum at Fort Davis, Texas. In February 2003, a Texas Historical Marker honoring Flipper was unveiled in El Paso. A number of articles and even some dissertations and master's theses have been written on Henry Flipper. There is a large archive of material on and about Flipper at the Fort Davis Historical Site, and the city of Thomasville, the birthplace of Flipper, has embraced his memory.

The Ephraim Ponder House still stands on North Dawson Street; it is a private residence. Henry's brother Festus Flipper lived on Lester Street in Thomasville and his home also remains; it too is a private residence. There is a "Thomasville Black Heritage Trail Tour" which features Flipper's grave, a Lt. Henry Ossian Flipper Park on North Broad Street, and in the Thomas County Public Library a "Flipper Room" where a bronze bust of Lt. Henry Ossian Flipper is prominently displayed.

The interest in Henry Flipper and his court-martial is part of the reexamination of the history of African Americans in the United States. American history is clouded with racism and injustices heaped upon African Americans. The reexamination of Henry Flipper's story is part of America's attempt to correct the wrongs of the past. But was Henry Flipper "wronged" in his court-martial? Was the guilty verdict a product of racism?

The Flipper court-martial was well-covered by the national media during its time. In some ways, Flipper's race helped him, because army officials were well aware that the eyes of the nation were on them as this case progressed. A number of articles and studies have pointed out that the verdict on the original charge of embezzlement was "not guilty" and therefore Flipper should have been allowed to remain in the army. Further, the charge of "conduct unbecoming an officer and a gentleman" sounds like a judgment call in the twenty-first century, subject to be based upon the prejudices of a court. However, the charge was leveled at Flipper for lying to his commanding officer, a very serious charge.

Lieutenant Henry Flipper was clearly guilty of lying to Colonel Shafter and falsifying documents. As he told several lies to his superior officer, he weaved a web for himself which he could not escape. As is often the case, it was the cover-up, not the crime, that created his downfall. Further, during his court-martial, Flipper did not take the stand, and this was surely viewed as an admission of guilt — or at least having something to hide — by his fellow officers on the jury. The court-martial found him guilty, and that guilty verdict meant an automatic dismissal from the army.

From this point, a web continued to be woven where Flipper was caught in a set of circumstances. Judge Advocate General David Swaim recommended a lesser punishment than dismissal from the service. However, Swaim had two strikes against him: (1) he was a close friend of President James Garfield and (2) he was court-martialed himself. After Garfield's death, Chester Arthur became president and was saddled with two problems: (1) President Rutherford Hayes had been lenient with soldiers court-martialed and this had brought on a congressional investigation, and (2) a discredited Swaim was the judge advocate general who recommended leniency for Flipper. President Arthur probably felt that leniency in the Flipper case wasn't worth the potential problems it could cause him.

Henry Flipper waited 16 years to appeal to Congress for his reinstatement and this long wait hurt his appeal. Further, there was no separate court in the armed services to hear these cases. It was dependent upon Congress to reverse a military judgment, and Congress routinely rejected these appeals because the War Department rejected them. They felt that overturning a verdict undermined the legal authority of the military court-martials, and they had a valid point.

Additionally, Flipper's appeals presented a version of his story not entirely in line with the court-martial records. Flipper continued to insist he was innocent of embezzlement and that race played a factor in his dismissal. However, the men in Congress who examined his appeal were attorneys who had access to the court-martial proceedings, and that record showed Flipper had been given a fair trial and was guilty of lying several times to his commanding officer, which action was responsible for the guilty verdict on the charge of "conduct unbecoming an officer and a gentleman."

The court-martial does not obscure the fact that Henry Flipper was the first African American to graduate from West Point and that in itself is a great achievement. The honors he has since received at West Point, and an award named in his honor for the graduating senior who has overcome hardship and difficulties, are certainly appropriate. He achieved success after he left the army, but it was not on a national level and not in the area of civil rights, which was the great story for African Americans of the 20th century.

Flipper's own views on race and civil rights did not fit well with the civil rights activists of the 1960s. Henry Flipper was a conservative, and black conservatives have been dismissed by mainstream and liberal African Americans as being out of touch with black concerns. Still, Flipper did not arrive at his political beliefs in a cavalier manner; he was a well-educated, well-read African American when most African Americans were not.

It is difficult to sum up the life and career of Henry Flipper because he was, in many ways, a complex man whose life is not easily laid out in a few words. He was a private man in the public spotlight, a black elitist during a time of Jim Crow laws and practices in America. Although he failed to achieve his most cherished goal during his lifetime — a career in the United States Army — he has been recognized and honored by the army after his death for his life and achievements.

The life of Henry Flipper spanned 84 years; he was born a slave before the Civil War and died after World War II began in Europe. He lived through 14 presidencies — from Franklin Pierce to Franklin Roosevelt. He was born before the telephone, radio or phonograph were invented and died when all had become a part of American life. He was born a slave, graduated from an elite institution of higher education, had a promising career in the army, was court-martialed, achieved success in the Southwest, then in Washington, as an assistant to a cabinet secretary, worked in the oil industry when that was becoming an essential part of the national economy, died in poverty during the Great Depression, and was honored years after his death.

For those who live only in the moment, history offers no consolation when it bestows rewards after death. But history records the story of the long race, and in the long race, Henry Flipper has emerged in a place of honor, a symbol to many, an inspiration to some, and certainly an individual worth knowing.

Chapter Notes

Chapter 1

1. Franklin M. Garrett, *Atlanta and Environs: A Chronicle of Its People and Events* (Athens: University of Georgia Press, 1969), 511–512.
2. Ibid.
3. Lowell D. Black and Sara H. Black, *An Officer and a Gentleman: The Military Career of Lieutenant Henry O. Flipper* (Dayton, OH: The Lora Company, 1985), 17.
4. Ibid. 4.
5. Ibid., 5, quoting *Race Mixture: Studies in Intermarriage and Race Mixture* by Edward Byron Reuter (New York, 1931).
6. David Herbert Donald, *Lincoln* (New York: Simon and Schuster, 1995), 206.
7. Henry Ossian Flipper, *The Colored Cadet at West Point: Autobiography of Lieut. Henry Ossian Flipper* (New York: Homer Lee, 1878), 11.
8. Ibid., 18–19.
9. Flipper, *The Colored Cadet*, 27.
10. Ibid., 28.
11. Ibid., 30–31.
12. Ibid., 35.
13. Ibid., 36–37.
14. Ibid., 37.

Chapter 2

1. Flipper, *The Colored Cadet*, 38.
2. Ibid., 44–45.
3. Ibid., 61–62.
4. Ibid., 46–47.
5. Ibid., 47.
6. Ibid., 47–48.
7. Ibid., 166.
8. Ibid., 171.
9. Ibid., 151–152.
10. Ibid., 150.
11. Ibid., 123–124.
12. Ibid., 173–174.

13. Ibid., 178.
14. Ibid., 170.
15. Ibid., 138.
16. Ibid., 164–165.
17. Ibid., 289.
18. Ibid., 134.
19. Ibid., 160–161.
20. John F. Marszalek, *Assault at West Point: The Court-Martial of Johnson Whittaker* (New York: Collier, 1972), 22.
21. Ibid., 23.
22. Ibid., 185.
23. Ibid., 240.
24. Ibid., 167.
25. Ibid., 169.
26. Ibid., 192, 194–195.
27. Ibid., 198.
28. "West Point Military Academy. The Annual Examination — A Large Graduating Class — A Colored Cadet-the Board of Examiners — An Entertainment in the Evening — Amateur Minstrels," *New York Times*, June 3, 1877, p. 1, col. 6.
29. Flipper, *The Colored Cadet*, 249.
30. Ibid., 249–250.
31. Ibid., 146.
32. Ibid., 150–151.
33. Ibid., 153.
34. Ibid., 137.
35. Ibid., 179–180.
36. Ibid., 181.
37. Ibid., 185.

Chapter 3

1. Flipper, *The Colored Cadet*, 258.
2. Ibid., 262.
3. Ibid., 264.
4. Ibid., 266.
5. Ibid., 267.
6. Jane Eppinga, *Henry Ossian Flipper: West Point's First Black Graduate* (Plano, TX: Republic of Texas Press, 1996), 51.

7. *Charleston (SC) News and Carrier,* October 19, 1877.
8. Flipper, *The Colored Cadet,* 277.
9. Ibid., 275–276.
10. Ibid., 177.
11. William H. Leckie, *The Buffalo Soldiers: A Narrative of the Negro Cavalry in the West* (Norman: University of Oklahoma Press, 1967; 1987), 14–15, 97–98.
12. William A. Dobak and Thomas D. Phillips, *The Black Regulars, 1866–1898* (Norman: University of Oklahoma Press, 2001), 113.
13. Ibid., 106.
14. Ibid., 112.
15. Ibid., 280.
16. Ibid., 206.
17. Henry O. Flipper, *Negro Frontiersman: The Western Memoirs of Henry O. Flipper,* ed. Theodore D. Harris (El Paso: Texas Western Press, 1963), 3.
18. Ibid., 3.
19. Ibid., 4.
20. Ibid., 7.
21. Ibid., 11.
22. Ibid., 14.

Chapter 4

1. Ibid., 106
2. Ibid., 17
3. Ibid., 17
4. Paul H. Carlson, *"Pecos Bill": A Military Biography of William R. Shafter* (College Station: Texas A&M University Press, 1989), 109.
5. *Indianapolis Leader,* September 18, 1880, p. 1, col. 4.
6. *Indianapolis Leader,* August 14, 1880.
7. Flipper, *Negro Frontiersman,* 19.
8. Ibid., 19.
9. Carlson, xi.
10. Ibid., 29.
11. Ibid., 41.
12. Ibid., xi.
13. Ibid., xii.
14. Ibid., xi-xii.
15. Ibid., 73.
16. Ibid., 72.
17. "Records Relating to the Army Career of Henry Ossian Flipper," United States National Archives, microfilm publication T-1027.

18. B. Johnson, 18.
19. "Records Relating to the Army Career of Henry Ossian Flipper"; B. Johnson, 20.
20. "Records Relating to the Army Career of Henry Ossian Flipper."
21. B. Johnson, 24; "Correction Board," Case Summary, 7–17.
22. "Records Relating to the Army Career of Henry Ossian Flipper"; B. Johnson, 25.
23. B. Johnson, 25.

Chapter 5

1. "Records Relating to the Army Career of Henry Ossian Flipper," United States National Archives, microfilm publication T-1027.
2. Barry C. Johnson, *Flipper's Dismissal: The Ruin of Lt. Henry O. Flipper, U.S.A., First Coloured Graduate of West Point* (London: Privately printed, 1980), 40.
3. Ibid., 38.
4. B. Johnson, 38.
5. Charles M. Robinson III, "Don't Ruin a Good Story with the Facts: An Analysis of Henry Flipper's Account of His Court-Martial in *Black Frontiersman,*" *Southwest History Quarterly* (July 2007).
6. *New York Herald,* August 17, 1881.
7. *New York Times,* August 25, 1881, p. 1, col. 3.
8. *Chicago Tribune,* August 19, 1881.
9. *Atlanta Constitution,* August 25, 1881, p. 2, col. 2.
10. *Atlanta Constitution,* September 1, 1881, p. 2, col. 2.
11. *Army Navy Journal,* August 27, 1881, p. 71.
12. *Chicago Tribune,* September 1, 1881.
13. *The Nation* 33, no. 844 (September 1, 1881): 164.
14. *Chicago Tribune,* September 2, 1881.
15. Ibid.
16. *St. Louis Daily Globe-Democrat,* September 5, 1881.
17. *San Antonio Express,* September 7, 1881, p. 1.
18. *The Nation* 33, no. 845 (September 8, 1881): 184.
19. *New York Times,* September 2, 1881.
20. *Army Navy Journal,* October 1, 1881, p. 183, 184.

Chapter 6

1. Robinson, "Don't Ruin a Good Story."
2. Flipper, *Negro Frontiersman,* 40.
3. *Atlanta Constitution,* October 5, 1881 p. 1, cols. 3 & 4.
4. *The Nation* 33, no. 849 (October 6, 1881): 269.
5. *Army Navy Journal,* October 15, 1881, p. 234, 235.
6. *New York Times,* October 30, 1881.
7. *St. Louis Daily Globe-Democrat,* November 1, 1881.
8. "Records Relating to the Army Career of Henry Ossian Flipper."

Chapter 7

1. Quotes from Flipper's trial come from "Records Relating to the Army Career of Henry Ossian Flipper," United States National Archives, microfilm publication T-1027.
2. *The Nation* 33, no. 855 (November 17, 1881): 385.
3. Robinson, *The Court-Martial of Lieutenant Henry Flipper,* 76.
4. Ibid., 65.

Chapter 8

1. B. Johnson, 121.
2. *St. Louis Daily Globe Democrat,* December 14, 1881, p. 2.
3. Robinson, 96.
4. Robinson, 97.
5. B. Johnson, 120.
6. Ibid., 82.
7. "Records Relating to the Army Career of Henry Ossian Flipper," United States National Archives, microfilm publication T-1027.
8. Marszalek, 246.
9. "Records Relating to the Army Career of Henry Ossian Flipper," United States National Archives, microfilm publication T-1027.
10. *The Nation* 34, no. 873 (March 16, 1882): 220.
11. *New York Times,* May 27, 1882.
12. B. Johnson, 87.
13. Ibid., 87–88.

14. *New York Times,* June 16, 1882.
15. Robinson, 115.

Chapter 9

1. Eugene O. Porter, *Lord Beresford and Lady Flo,* Southwestern Studies Monograph No. 25 (El Paso: Texas Western College Press, 1970), 9–10.
2. *St. Louis Republican,* November 3, 1883, p. 3.
3. *St. Louis Republican,* November 5, 1883, p. 4, col. 2.
4. Flipper, *Negro Frontiersman,* 22.
5. Flipper, *Western Memoirs,* 22.
6. Ibid., 25.
7. Flipper, *Negro Frontiersman,* 26.
8. Ibid., 27.
9. Ibid., 27–28.
10. Ibid., 31.
11. Eppinga, *Henry Ossian Flipper,* 168–169.
12. Ezra J. Warner, "A Black Man in the Long Gray Line," *American History Illustrated* 4, no. 9 (January, 1970).
13. Flipper, *Negro Frontiersman,* 33.
14. Ibid., 34.
15. Ibid.
16. Ibid., 35.
17. Ibid., 42.
18. Ibid., 37.
19. Ibid., 37–38.
20. Ibid., 38.
21. Ibid., 39.
22. B. Johnson, 93.
23. Ibid., 94.
24. Ibid., 96.
25. Ibid., 95.
26. Ibid., 96.
27. Ibid., 99.
28. Ibid., 101.
29. Ibid., 102.

Chapter 10

1. Flipper, *Negro Frontiersman,* 45.
2. Ibid., 46.
3. Enrique Krauze, *Mexico, Biography of Power: A History of Modern Mexico, 1810–1996,* trans. Hank Heifetz (New York: Harper-Collins, 1997), 219.
4. Krauze, 158–159.

5. A copy of this letter is housed at the Fort Davis Historic Site Archive, Fort Davis, Texas.

6. Flipper, *Negro Frontiersman*, 11, 187.

7. Ibid., 7.

8. Theodore D. Harris, ed., *Black Frontiersman: The Memoirs of Henry O. Flipper* (Fort Worth: Texas Christian University Press, 1997), 98.

9. Ibid., 217.

10. Ibid., 108.

11. Ibid.

12. Ibid., 110–111.

13. Ibid., 115.

Chapter 11

1. John Egerton, *Speak Now Against the Day: The Generation Before the Civil Rights Movement in the South* (New York: Alfred A. Knopf, 1994), 38.

2. Ibid., 38.

3. Ibid., 40.

4. Taylor Branch, *Parting the Waters: America in the King Years, 1954–63* (New York: Simon and Schuster, 1988), 36.

5. Ibid., 3.

6. Ibid.

7. Harris, ed., *Black Frontiersman*, 119–120.

8. Ibid., 122.

9. Daniel Yergin, *The Prize: The Epic Quest for Oil, Money & Power* (New York: Touchstone, 1991), 212.

10. Herman B. Weisner, *The Politics of Justice: A.B. Fall and the Teapot Dome Scandal, A New Perspective* (Albuquerque, New Mexico: Creative Designs, 1988), 82.

11. Ibid., 213.

12. Ibid.

13. Ibid., 214.

14. A copy of this letter is housed at the Fort Davis Historic Site Archive, Fort Davis, Texas.

15. Eugene P. Trani and David L. Wilson, *The Presidency of Warren G. Harding* (Lawrence: University Press of Kansas, 1977), 71.

Chapter 12

1. Yergin, *The Prize*, 233.

2. Ibid.

3. Ibid., 213–216.

4. Eppinga, *Henry Ossian Flipper*, 205.

5. Harris, ed., *Black Frontiersman*, 98.

6. Yergin, 216.

7. Branch, *Parting the Waters*, 251.

Chapter 13

1. Harris, ed., *Black Frontiersman*, 126.

2. Ibid., 146.

3. Ibid., 135.

4. Ibid., 147.

5. Ibid., 146.

6. Ibid., 133.

7. Ibid., 146.

8. Ibid., 128.

9. Ibid., 130.

10. Ibid., 132.

11. Ibid., 136.

12. Ibid., 148–149.

13. Ibid., 129.

14. Ibid., 135.

15. Ibid., 147.

16. Ibid., 153.

17. Ibid., 154.

18. Ibid.

19. Ibid., 133–134.

20. Ibid., 148–149.

21. Ibid., 149–150.

22. Ibid., 150.

23. Ibid.

24. Ibid., 151–152.

25. Ibid., 141.

26. Ibid., 143.

27. Ibid., 129–130.

28. Ibid., 157.

Chapter 14

1. Jim Specht, "Clinton Issues Pardon '117 Years Overdue,'" February 20, 1999, n.p.

2. John Hanchette, "Flipper's Long-awaited Pardon More Than a Century in Coming," *El Paso Times*, February 21, 1999.

Bibliography

Altshuler, Constance Wynn. *Cavalry Yellow & Infantry Blue: Army Officers in Arizona Between 1851 and 1886.* Tucson: Arizona Historical Society, 1991.

_____. *Chains of Command: Arizona and the Army, 1856–1875.* Tucson: Arizona Historical Society, 1981.

Ambrose, Stephen E. *Duty, Honor, Country: A History of West Point.* Baltimore: Johns Hopkins Press, 1966.

Andrew, George L. "West Point and the Colored Cadets." *The International Review* (November 1880).

Army Navy Journal (August 27, 1881): 71; (October 1, 1881): 183; (October 15, 1881): 234–235.

Athearn, Robert C. *William Tecumseh Sherman and the Settlement of the West.* Norman: University of Oklahoma Press, 1956.

Atkinson, Rick. *The Long Gray Line.* Boston: Houghton Mifflin, 1989.

Atlanta Constitution, August 25, 1881, p. 2, col. 2; September 1, 1881, p. 2, col. 2; September 3, 1881, p. 2, col. 2; October 5, 1881, p. 1, cols. 3 & 4.

"Atlanta University Alumni Lose William Baxter Matthews and Henry Ossian Flipper." *Atlanta University Bulletin* (July 1940).

Ayers, Edward. *The Promise of a New South: Life after Reconstruction.* New York: Oxford University Press, 1992.

Bacote, Clarence Albert. *The Story of Atlanta University: A Century of Service, 1865–1965.* Atlanta: Atlanta University, 1965.

Ballew, Coco. "Film Moves Viewers, Makers. Docudrama Premiere Draws Crowd." *El Paso Times*, January 30, 1996.

Baumler, Mark F., and Richard V.N. Ahlstrom. "The Garfield Monument:

An 1886 Memorial of the Buffalo Soldiers in Arizona." *Cochise County Quarterly* 18, no. 1 (Spring 1988).

Beck, Warren A. *New Mexico: A History of Four Centuries.* Norman: University of Oklahoma Press, 1962.

Billington, Monroe Lee. *New Mexico's Buffalo Soldiers, 1866–1900.* Niwot: University of Colorado Press, 1991.

Black, Lowell D., and Sara H. Black. *An Officer and a Gentleman: The Military Career of Lieutenant Henry O. Flipper.* Dayton: The Lora Company, 1985.

"Black Gets Military Funeral." February 12, 1978. Article on file at El Paso Public Library.

Braddy, Haldeen. *Cock of the Walk: The Legend of Pancho Villa.* Albuquerque: University of New Mexico Press, 1955.

Bradford, Ned, ed. *Battles and Leaders of the Civil War.* New York: Appleton-Century-Crofts, 1956.

Bradfute, Richard Wells. *The Court of Private Land Claims: The Adjudication of Spanish and Mexican Land Grant Titles, 1891–1904.* Albuquerque: University of New Mexico Press, 1975.

Branch, Taylor. *Parting the Waters: America in the King Years, 1954–63.* New York: Simon and Schuster, 1988.

Brown, D. Alexander. *Grierson's Raid.* Urbana: University of Illinois Press, 1954.

Brown, Wesley A. "Eleven Men of West Point." *The Negro History Bulletin* 19 (April 1956).

Carhart, Thomas M. "African American West Pointers during the Nineteenth Century." PhD diss., Princeton University, 1998.

Carlson, Paul H. *"Pecos Bill": A Military*

Biography of William R. Shafter. College Station: Texas A&M University Press, 1989.

Carroll, John M., ed. *The Black Military Experience in the American West.* New York: Liveright, 1971.

Cashin, Hershel V., et al. *Under Fire with the Tenth Cavalry.* Chicago: American Publishing House, n.d.

Charleston (SC) News and Carrier, October 19, 1877.

Chicago Tribune, August 19, 1881; September 1, 2, and 5, 1881; December 9, 1881.

Coerver, Don M., and Linda B. Hall. *Texas and the Mexican Revolution: A Study in State and National Border Policy, 1910–1920.* San Antonio: Trinity University Press, 1984.

Cornish, Dudley Taylor. *The Sable Arm: Negro Troops in the Union Army, 1861–1865.* New York: W.W. Norton, 1966.

Cusic, Don. *Cowboys and the Wild West: An A-Z Guide from the Chisholm Trail to the Silver Screen.* New York: Facts on File, 1994.

Davis, Margaret Leslie. *Dark Side of Fortune: Triumph and Scandal in the Life of Oil Tycoon Edward L. Doheny.* Berkeley: University of California Press, 1998.

DeHart, William Chetwood. *Observations on Military Law and the Constitution and Practice of Courts-Martial, with a Summary of the Law of Evidence, as Applicable to Military Trials; Adapted to the Laws, Regulations and Customs of the Army and Navy of the U.S.* New York: D. Appleton, 1869.

Dinges, Bruce J. "Court-Martial of Lieutenant Henry O. Flipper: An Example of Black-White Relationships in the Army, 1881." *The American West* (January 1972).

_____. "The Court-Martial of Lt. Henry O. Flipper." *The American West* 9, no. 1 (January 1972).

_____. "The Irrepressible Captain Armes: Politics and Justice in the Indian-Fighting Army." *Journal of the West* (April 1993).

Dobak, William A., and Thomas D. Phillips. *The Black Regulars, 1866–1898.* Norman: University of Oklahoma Press, 2001.

"Dr. Joseph S. Flipper, Bishop of the African M.E. Church 36 Years, Is Dead." *New York Times,* October 12, 1944, p. 27.

Donald, David Herbert. *Lincoln.* New York: Simon and Schuster, 1995.

DuBois, W.E.B. *Black Reconstruction: An Essay toward a History of the Part which Black Folk Played in the Attempt to Reconcile Democracy in America, 1860–1880.* New York: Russell & Russell, 1956.

Ebony. Ebony, Pictorial History of Black America: Reconstruction to Supreme Court Decision 1954. Nashville: Johnson, 1971.

Egerton, John. *Speak Now against the Day: The Generation before the Civil Rights Movement in the South.* New York: Alfred E. Knopf, 1994.

Egleston, C. Gerald. "The Black in Blue: Court-Martial of Lt. Henry O. Flipper, the First Negro Graduate of West Point." Master's thesis, Morehead State University, 1977.

El Paso Herald, "Henry O. Flipper, 84, First Negro Graduate of West Point," May 10, 1940, p. 11.

_____, "Indian Miller Asserts Flipper Did Not Disprove Truth," June 12, 1919, p. 6.

_____, "Lieut Flipper Picked Up a Literary Curiosity in Chihuahua," August 16, 1895, p. 4.

_____, "New Georgia Post Office Named in Flipper's Honor," April 29, 1999.

"El Pasoan Attempting to Exonerate Soldier." *El Paso Times,* September 22, 1975.

Eppinga, Jane. *Henry Ossian Flipper: West Point's First Black Graduate.* Plano, TX: Republic of Texas Press, 1996.

Everett, Robinson O. *Military Justice in the Armed Forces of the United States.* CT: Greenwood Press, 1956.

Feron, James. "1st Black to Get a Diploma Cited by West Point." *New York Times,* May 4, 1977.

"First Black West Pointer Reburied with Honors." *El Paso Times*, February 21, 1978.

"First Negro Graduate of West Point Dies at 84." *Washington Tribune*, May 11, 1940.

Flipper, Henry Ossian. *The Colored Cadet at West Point: The Autobiography of Lieut. Henry Ossian Flipper.* New York: Homer Lee, 1878.

_____. "Early History of El Paso." *Old Santa Fe* (July 1914).

_____. *Negro Frontiersman: The Western Memoirs of Henry O. Flipper.* Edited by Theodore D. Harris. El Paso: Texas Western Press, 1963.

Flipper, Henry O., trans. *Law Governing Hydrocarbons and Other Combustible Minerals of the Republic of Venezuela.* New York: Evening Post Job Printing Office, 1922.

_____. *Mining Laws of the United States and Mexico and the Law of Federal Property Tax on Mines with Regulation Thereunder and Other Laws Relating Thereto.* Nogales, Arizona Territory: P. Aguire Press, 1892.

"Flipper, Formerly of the United States Army, New Chief Clerk in a Laundry, and Full of Business. His Case to be Brought before Congress at the Coming Session. Efforts of His Friends to Have Him Reinstated — He Tells His Own Story." *St. Louis Republican*, November 3, 1883.

Flynn, Ken. "Flipper: A Desert Outpost Set the Scene for a Black Military Hero's Story." March 24, 1983. Article on file at El Paso Public Library.

Foner, Eric. *Reconstruction: America's Unfinished Revolution, 1863–1877.* New York: Harper & Row, 1988.

Foote, Shelby. *The Civil War: A Narrative.* Vol. 3, *Red River to Appomattox.* New York: Random House, 1974.

Ganoe, William A. *The History of the United States Army.* New York: D. Appleton, 1924.

Garrett, Franklin M. *Atlanta and Environs: A Chronicle of Its People and Events.* 2 volume set. Athens: University of Georgia Press, 1969.

Glass, Major E.N. *History of the Tenth Cavalry.* Tucson: Acme Printing, 1921.

Gledhill, Renee Hope. "Henry O. Flipper: Black Man in Blue, 1856–1882." Master's thesis, University of North Carolina, 1970.

Greene, Robert Ewell. *Black Defenders of America, 1775–1973.* Chicago: Johnson Publishing, 1974.

Griess, Thoma E. *Atlas for the American Civil War.* West Point Military History Series. Wayne, NJ: Avery Publishing, 1986.

Gruening, Martha. "Houston, an N.A.A.C.P. Investigation." *The Oasis* (November 1917).

Hail, Marshall. "TWC Book Gives Rare View of Southwest Life." *El Paso Herald Post,* April 10, 1963.

Haley, J. Evetts. *Fort Concho and the Texas Frontier.* San Angelo, TX: San Angelo Standard-Times, 1952.

Hall, Linda B., and Don M. Coerver. *Revolution on the Border.* Albuquerque: University of New Mexico Press, 1988.

Harris, Theodore D. "Henry Ossian Flipper, African American Western Pioneer." *The Human Tradition in the American West.* Vol.10, *Human Tradition in America.* Edited by Benson Tong and Regan A. Lutz. Wilmington, DE: SR Books, 2002.

_____, ed. *Black Frontiersman: The Memoirs of Henry O. Flipper.* Fort Worth: Texas Christian University Press, 1997.

Harris, Theodore Delano. "Henry Ossian Flipper: The First Negro Graduate of West Point." PhD diss., University of Minnesota, 1971.

Hayes, Gayle. "Honor Restored after 96 Years." *Thomasville (GA) Times-Enterprise,* February 13, 1978.

Haynes, Robert V. *A Night of Violence: The Houston Riot of 1917.* Baton Rouge: Louisiana State University Press, 1976.

Herr, John K., and Edward S. Wallace. *The Story of the United States Cavalry, 1775–1942.* Boston: Little, Brown, 1953.

Higginson, Thomas Wentworth. *Army Life in a Black Regiment*. East Lansing: Michigan State University Press, 1960.

Hilton, David. "Henry Flipper: America's First Black Officer." *Texas Historian* (September, 1989).

Hoehling, A.A. *Last Train from Atlanta*. New York and London: Thomas Yoseloff, 1958.

Hopkins, Sam. "Lt. Flipper's Unmarked Grave Unearthed for Honorable Burial." *Atlanta Journal and Constitution*, February 11, 1978.

"In the Matter of the Court-Martial of Henry Ossian Flipper, Second Lieutenant, Tenth Cavalry, U.S. Army, before the Committee on Military Affairs, United States Senate, Sixty-Seventh Congress, First Session, Petition for Redress of Grievances," Senate Bill 2455, 1921.

Indianapolis Leader, August 14, 1880; September 18, 1880, p. 1, col. 4.

Ives, Rollin Augustus. *A Treatise on Military Law and the Jurisdiction, Constitution, and Procedure of Military Courts, with a Summary of the Rules of Evidence as Applicable to Such Courts* [1881]. New York: D. Van Nostrand, 1979.

Jackson, Darryl W., Jeffrey H. Smith, and Edward H. Sisson. "The Fight for Lt. Flipper: The Lawyers' Perspective of the Nation's First Posthumous Presidential Pardon." March 7, 2002. Report on file at Fort Davis Historic Site Archive, Fort Davis, Texas.

Jet. "West Point Celebrates Flipper's Graduation: Black Victim of Racial Injustice 100 years," May 26, 1977.

Johnson, Barry C. *Flipper's Dismissal: The Ruin of Lt. Henry O. Flipper, U.S.A., First Coloured Graduate of West Point*. London: Privately printed, 1980.

Johnson, William Weber. *Heroic Mexico*. Garden City, NY: Doubleday, 1968.

Katz, William Loren. *The Black West*. New York: Doubleday, 1971.

Krauze, Enrique. *Mexico: Biography of Power: A History of Modern Mexico, 1810–*

1996. Translated by Hank Heifetz. New York: HarperCollins, 1997.

Lane, Jack C., ed. *Chasing Geronimo: The Journal of Leonard Wood, May–September 1886*. Albuquerque: University of New Mexico Press, 1970.

Leckie, William H. *The Buffalo Soldiers: A Narrative of the Negro Cavalry in the West*. Norman: University of Oklahoma Press, 1967.

_____, and Shirley A. *Unlikely Warriors: General Benjamin H. Grierson and His Family*. Norman: University of Oklahoma Press, 1984.

Litwack, Leon F. *Trouble in Mind: Black Southerners in the Age of Jim Crow*. New York: Alfred A. Knopf, 1998.

Logan, Rayford W., and Michael R. Winston. *Dictionary of American Negro Biography*. New York: W.W. Norton, 1982.

Maraniss, David. "Due Recognition and Reward." *Washington Post Magazine* (January 20, 1991).

Marszalek, John F. *Assault at West Point: The Court-Martial of Johnson Whittaker*. New York: Collier, 1972.

Mattison, Ray H. "Early Spanish and Mexican Settlements in Arizona." *New Mexico Historical Review* 21, no. 4.

McBeth, B.S. *Juan Vicente Gomez and the Oil Companies of Venezuela, 1908–1936*. Cambridge: Cambridge University Press, 1988.

McClung, Paul. "First Black West Point Graduate Due New Honor." *(Lawton, OK) Sunday Constitution*, October 23, 1977.

_____. "Flipper's Ditch to Be Honored in Thursday Ceremony." *Fort Sill (OK) Cannoneer*, October 27, 1977.

McConnell, H.H. *Five Years a Cavalryman*. Jacksboro, TX: J.N. Rogers, 1889.

McGaw, William. "Flipper, a Hero in Georgia, Nearly Found Mexican Grave." *El Paso Journal*, February 22, 1978.

_____. "Henry Flipper Had Deep 'Roots' in El Paso Southwest Country." *El Paso Journal* (March 2, 1977).

McPherson, James M. *Battle Cry of Freedom:*

The Civil War Era. New York: Oxford University Press, 1988

McRae, Marcia. "Army Gives the Best Gift." *Valdosta Daily Times,* December 26, 1976.

Meier, August. *Negro Thought in America, 1880–1915.* Ann Arbor: University of Michigan Press, 1968.

_____, and David Lewis. "History of the Negro Upper Class in Atlanta, Georgia." *Journal of Negro Education* (Spring 1959).

Meyer, Michael C. "Albert Bacon Fall's Mexican Papers: A Preliminary Investigation." *New Mexico Historical Review* 40 (April 1965).

Middagh, John. *Frontier Newspaper: The El Paso Times.* El Paso: El Paso Times, 1958.

The Nation. 33, no. 844 (September 1, 1881): 164.

_____. 33, no. 845 (September 8, 1881): 184.

_____. 33, no. 849 (October 6, 1881): 269.

_____. 33, no. 855 (November 17, 1881): 385.

_____. 34, no. 872 (March 16, 1882): 220.

_____. "Lieutenant Flipper's Defence," October 6, 1881.

_____. "The Plot against Lieutenant Flipper," September 29, 1881.

New York Herald, August 17, 1881. Article on file at Fort Davis Historic Site Archive, Fort Davis, Texas.

New York Times, August 25, 1881, p. 1, col. 3; September 2, 1881; October 30, 1881; May 27, 1882; June 16, 1882. Articles on file at Fort Davis Historic Site Archive, Fort Davis, Texas.

New York Tribune, August 24, 1881. Article on file at Fort Davis Historic Site Archive, Fort Davis, Texas.

Nye, Colonel W.S. *Carbine & Lance: The Story of Old Fort Sill.* Norman: University of Oklahoma Press, 1969.

Oswald, James M. "History of Fort Elliott." *Panhandle-Plains Historical Review* 22 (1959).

Oxford Dictionary of Quotations. 2nd ed. London: Oxford University Press, 1966.

Perez, Daniel. "Clinton to Pardon West Point's 1st Black Graduate Today." *El Paso Times,* February 19, 1999.

"Petition for Pardon for Second Lieutenant Henry Ossian Flipper, 10th Cavalry, United States Army." From Law Firm of Arnold & Porter, Washington, D.C. October 21, 1997.

Pfeifer, Kathryn Browne. *Henry O. Flipper.* New York: Twenty-First Century Books, 1993.

Phillips, Thomas D. "The Black Regulars: Negro Soldiers in the United States Army, 1866–1891." PhD diss., University of Wisconsin, 1970.

Porter, Eugene O. *Lord Beresford and Lady Flo.* Southwestern Studies Monograph No. 25. El Paso: Texas Western College Press, 1970.

Quarles, Benjamin. *The Negro and the Civil War.* Boston: Little, Brown, 1953.

Ratcliffe, Robert. "Lt. Flipper Is Claimed by Death." File copy of obituary at Atlanta-Clark University.

"Records Relating to the Army Career of Henry Ossian Flipper." United States National Archives. Microfilm publication T-1027.

Reeves, Alexis Scott. "Ceremonies to Honor Flipper." *Atlanta Constitution,* March 21, 1977.

Renteria, Ramon. "KCOS Film Pops into Elite Market." *El Paso Times,* January 17, 1996.

Reynolds, Matthew G., and Henry O. Flipper, trans. *Spanish and Mexican Land Laws: New Spain and New Mexico.* St. Louis, MO: Buston & Skinner Stationery, 1895.

Rickey, Don, Jr. *Forty Miles a Day on Beans and Hay: The Enlisted Soldier Fighting the Indian Wars.* Norman: University of Oklahoma Press, 1963.

Rieber, Dick. "Lt. Flipper Was a Man of 'Firsts.'" *Thomasville (GA) Times-Enterprise,* February 13, 1978.

Robinson, Charles M., III. "The Court-Martial of Lt. Henry Flipper." *True West* (June 1989).

_____. "Don't Ruin a Good Story with the Facts: An Analysis of Henry Flipper's Account of His Court-Martial in *Black Frontiersman.*" *Southwest Historical Quarterly* (July 2007).

Roeder, Wilfried E. *Antepasados: Surveyors in History.* Albuquerque: New Mexico Professional Surveyors, 1995.

Rogers, William Warren. *Ante-Bellum Thomas County, 1825–1861.* Tallahassee: Florida State University Studies (39), 1963.

_____. *Thomas County during the Civil War.* Tallahassee: Florida State University Studies (41), 1964.

_____. *Thomas County, 1865–1900.* Tallahassee: Florida State University Press, 1973.

Russell, James M. *Atlanta, 1847–1890: City Building in the Old South and the New.* Baton Rouge and London: Louisiana State University Press, 1988.

St. Louis Daily Globe-Democrat, September 5, 1881; November 1, 1881; December 14, 1881, p. 2.

St. Louis Republican, November 3, 1883, p. 3; November 5, 1883, p. 4, col. 2.

St. Louis Republican, "A Letter from the Late Lieutenant in the U.S. Army. He Corrects a Few Trivial Errors in a Recent Interview and Reviews His Own Record in an Interesting Manner," November 19, 1883.

Sampson, Bill. "Flipper's Ditch Gains Historic Niche." *Tulsa Tribune,* November 2, 1977.

San Antonio Express, September 7 and 15, 1881.

Scobee, Barry. "Army Drums Out Lt. Flipper after Episode at Ft. Davis." Article on file at Fort Davis Historic Site Archive, Fort Davis, Texas.

_____. *Old Fort Davis.* San Antonio: Naylor, 1947.

"Second Lieut. Henry Ossian Flipper." Adverse Report, To accompany H.R. 3598, Report No. 2981, House of Representatives, 56th Congress, 2nd Session, 1900.

Senate Bill 2455. A Bill: To enable the President to Restore Second Lieutenant Henry Ossian Flipper to grade, rank, and status in the United States Army. August 22, 1921.

Shannon, Margaret. "Another Chance for Henry Flipper." *Atlanta Journal and Constitution Magazine* (December 7, 1975).

Siegel, Fred. "Artisans and Immigrants in the Politics of Late Antebellum Georgia." *Civil War History* 27 (1981).

Sonnichsen, C.L. *Colonel Greene and the Copper Skyrocket.* Tucson: University of Arizona Press, 1974.

_____. *Tularosa: Last of the Frontier West.* Albuquerque: University of New Mexico Press, 1960.

Specht, Jim. "Clinton Issues Pardon '117 Years Overdue.'" February 20, 1999. n.p. Article on file at El Paso Public Library.

Taylor, John J. "Does Anyone Care? Henry O. Flipper and the United States Army." Master's thesis, U.S. Army Command and General Staff College, 1995.

Thompson, Erwin N. "The Negro Soldiers on the Frontier: A Fort Davis Case Study." *Journal of the West* 7, no. 2 (April 1968).

Thrapp, Dan L. *Encyclopedia of Frontier Biography.* Glendale, CA: A.H. Clark, 1988.

Tipton, Will M., and Henry O. Flipper. *Official Report on the Condition of the Archives or Records of the Titles to Land Grants in Arizona.* n.p. n.d. Report on file at Fort Davis Historic Site Archive, Fort Davis, Texas.

Trani, Eugene P., and David L. Wilson. *The Presidency of Warren G. Harding.* Lawrence; University Press of Kansas, 1977.

Unrau, William E. *Tending the Talking Wire: A Buck Soldier's View of Indian Country, 1863–1866.* Salt Lake City: University of Utah Press.

Utley, Robert M. *Fort Davis National Historic Site, Texas.* Washington D.C.: National Park Service Historical Handbook Series No. 38 (1965).

_____. *Frontier Regulars: The United States Army and the Indian, 1866–1891.* Lincoln: University of Nebraska Press, 1973.

Wagoner, J. *Early Arizona: Prehistory to the Civil War.* Tucson: University of Arizona Press, 1985.

Wakin, Edward. *Black Fighting Men in U.S. History.* New York: Lothrop, Lee & Shepard, 1971.

Ward, Geoffrey C. *The Civil War: An Illustrated History.* New York: Alfred A. Knopf, 1990.

Warner, Ezra J. "A Black Man in the Long Gray Line." *American History Illustrated* 4, no. 9 (January 1970).

Warren, David M. "Black West Point Graduate." *Dawn* (September 13, 1975).

Watts, Geneva Roberts. "The Court-Martial: A Career Biography of Henry O. Flipper." Master's thesis, Sanoma State College, 1970.

Weisner, Herman B. *The Politics of Justice: A.B. Fall and the Teapot Dome Scandal, A New Perspective.* Albuquerque, NM: Creative Designs, 1988.

West Point Military Academy. "The Annual Examination — A Large Graduating Class — A Colored Cadet-the Board of Examiners — An Entertainment in the Evening — Amateur Minstrels." *New York Times*, June 3, 1877, p. 1, col. 6.

Wien, Gary A. "The Military Career of Henry O. Flipper, First Black Graduate of West Point." Master's thesis, University of Toledo, 1970.

Wilson, Steve. "A Black Lieutenant in the Ranks." *American History Illustrated* (December 1983).

Wintz, Cary D., ed. *African American Political Thought, 1890–1930: Washington, DuBois, Garvey, and Randolph.* Armonk, NY: M.E. Sharpe, 1996.

Woodward, Arthur, ed. *On the Bloody Trail of Geronimo.* Tucson: Westernlore Press, 1986.

Wooster, Robert. *Fort Davis: Outpost on the Texas Frontier.* Fred Rider Cotton Popular History Series No. 8. Austin: Texas State Historical Association, 1994.

Yergin, Daniel. *The Prize: The Epic Quest for Oil, Money & Power.* New York: Touchstone, 1991.

Zanetell, Myrna. Book Review. *The Court-Martial of Lieutenant Henry Flipper* by Charles M. Robinson III. *El Paso Scene* (April 1999).

Index

Numbers in **bold italics** indicate pages with photographs.